CASSANDRA DARKE

by the same author

Mrs Weber's Diary
True Love
Pick of Posy
Very Posy
Pure Posy
Mustn't Grumble
Gemma Bovery
Literary Life
Tamara Drewe
Mrs Weber's Omnibus
Literary Life Revisited

for children
Fred
Lulu and the Flying Babies
The Chocolate Wedding
Bouncing Buffalo
F-Freezing ABC
Lavender
Baker Cat

CASSANDRA DARKE

Posy Simmonds

JONATHAN CAPE
LONDON

2017

Evening Argus Friday 17 November 2017

Woman's body found in local woods was "homicide victim"

Surrey police believe the death of an unidentified woman, whose remains were found recently in woods near Wrysley, was the the result of homicide.

Following the discovery of the remains in thick undergrowth by a couple searching for their missing dog, forensic investigations recovered an entire female skeleton. The victim was about 1.5 metres tall with dyed red hair. The forensic odentologist report stated that she would have been aged between 20 and 30 years. Police believe she was killed elsewhere and dumped on the site

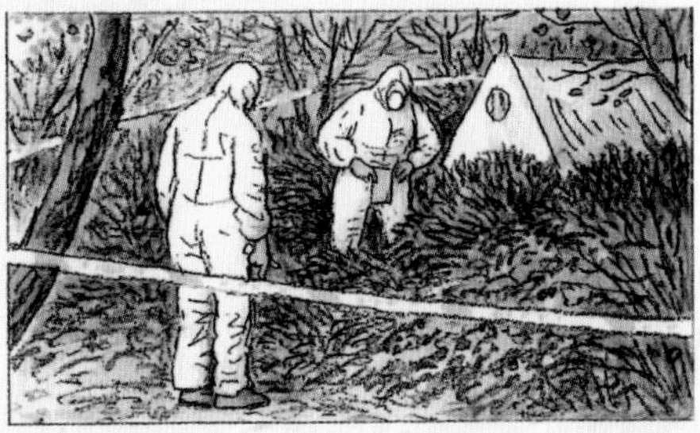

and estimate this would have occurred sometime between 9 months and one year ago.

Detectives said that identifying the young woman was crucial to th- opening of a murder investi-

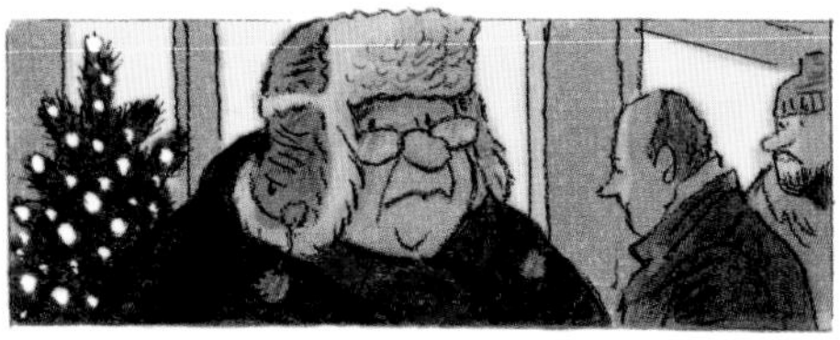

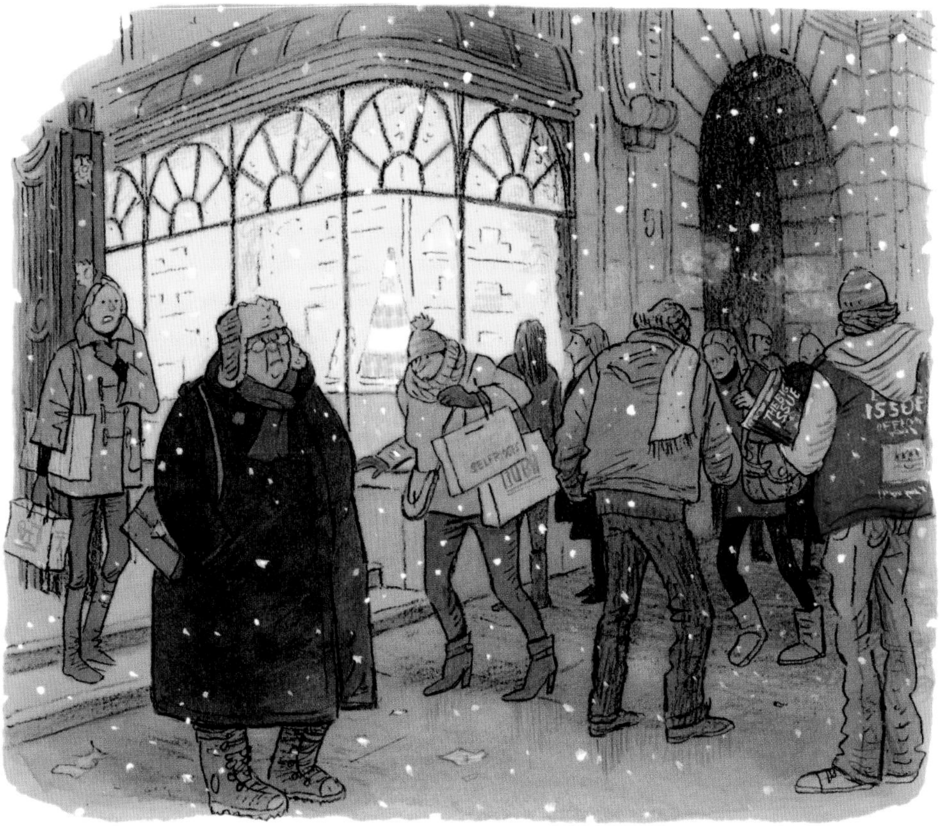

Last December – the 21st to be precise, and not so long before they came to arrest me – I remember buying macaroons in Burlington Arcade. I'd left Phoebe in charge of the gallery and had only meant to be out for the short time it took to walk to Piccadilly and back.
I polished off the macaroons in the street, each hit of chocolate and salted caramel lasting several seconds. Then I was on edge again. I knew very well that something was up, and sure enough, there was Jane McMullen waiting to cross the road. That day I had ignored all her calls and e-mails. Phoebe had been instructed to say that I was unavailable.

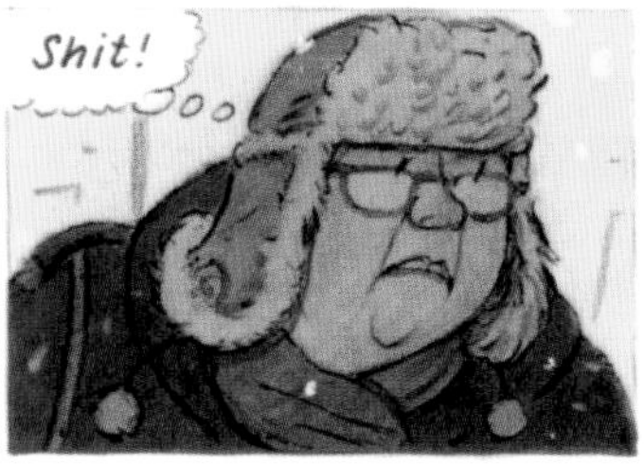
Shit!

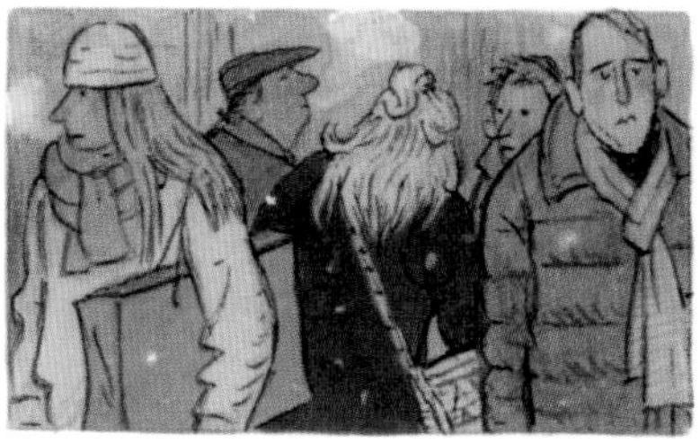

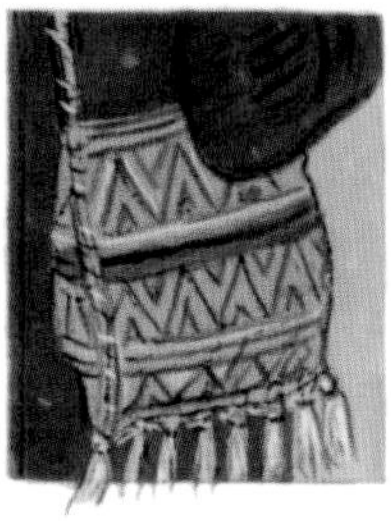

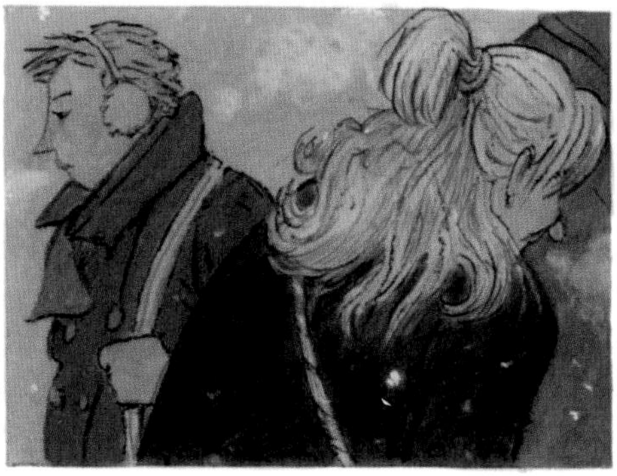

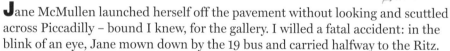

Jane McMullen launched herself off the pavement without looking and scuttled across Piccadilly – bound I knew, for the gallery. I willed a fatal accident: in the blink of an eye, Jane mown down by the 19 bus and carried halfway to the Ritz.

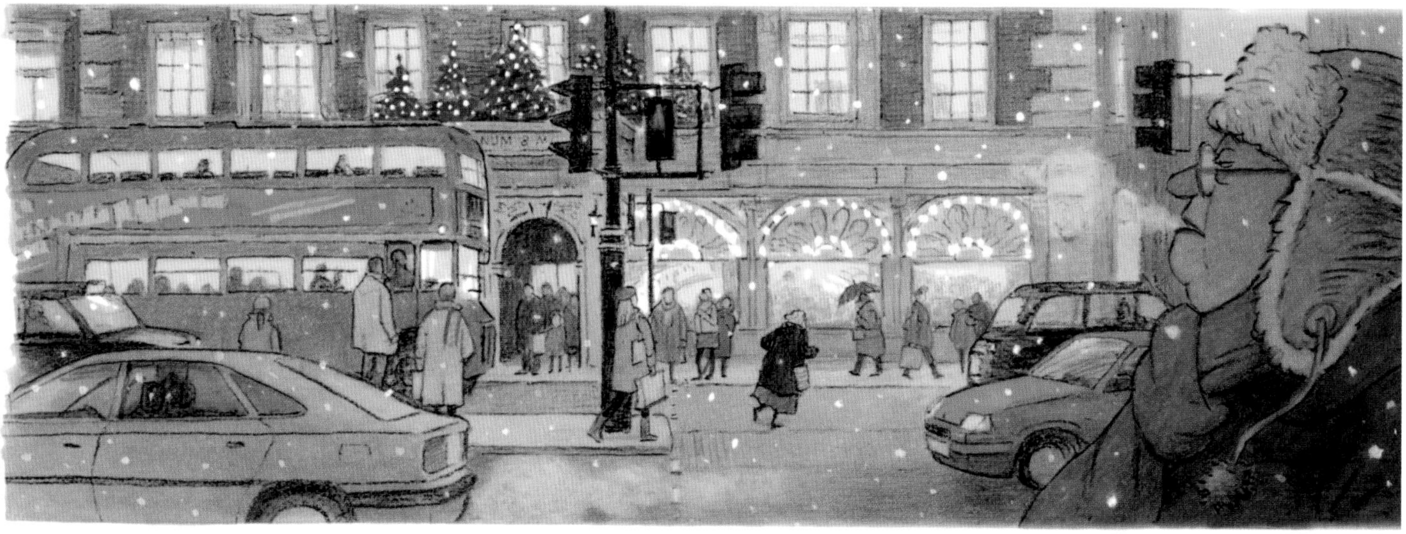

But Jane crossed the road unharmed and kept going in the direction of Brummell Yard. She is the widow of the sculptor Ken McMullen. I have known them both for years; my ex-husband Freddie Boult was Ken's long-term dealer.

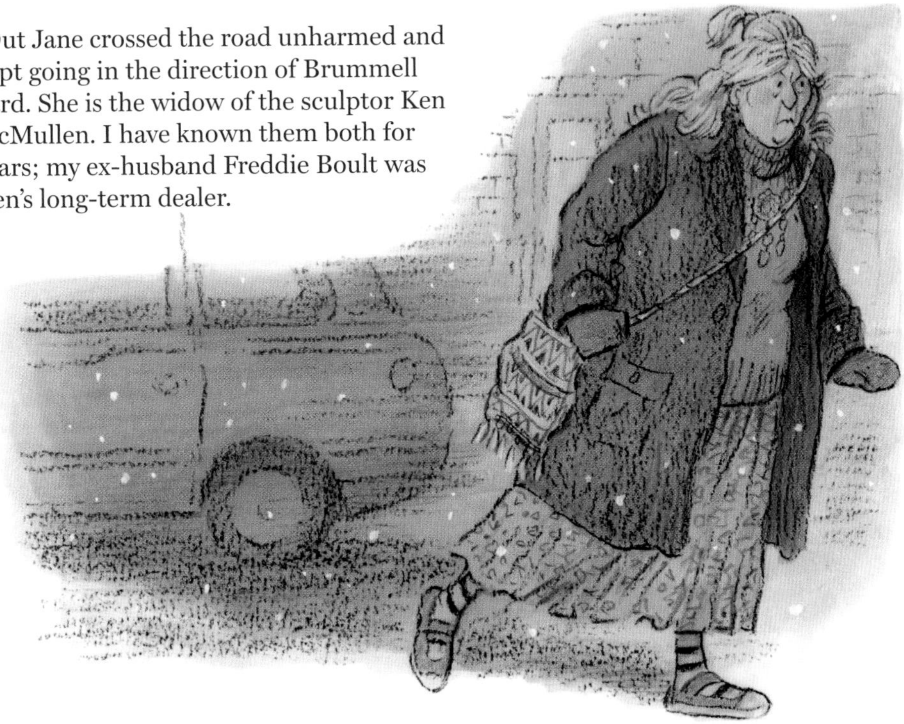

I panicked. Clearly Jane must have learned about the jiggery-pokery. I couldn't bear to face her. She is an innocent old sheep. A potter, maker of hulking tableware. And she is the steadfast keeper of her dead husband's flame. I just couldn't face her.

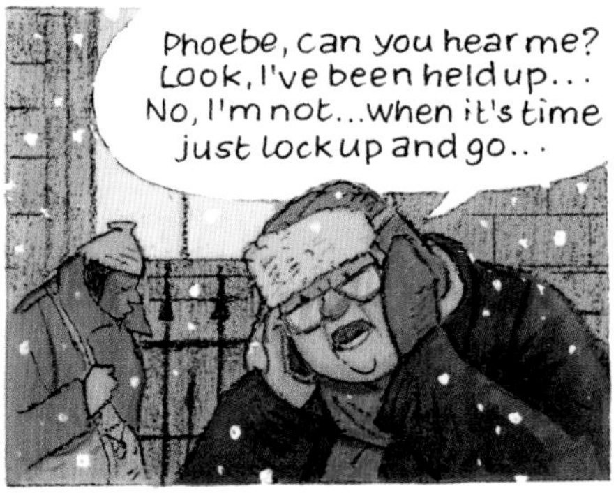
Phoebe, can you hear me? Look, I've been held up... No, I'm not... when it's time just lock up and go...

Usually, to kill time I might have gone to The Wolseley for eggs Benedict and some fruit scones but I needed air. I rang my driver to say that I would find my own way home and then wandered for hours through the crowds of imbecile Christmas shoppers.

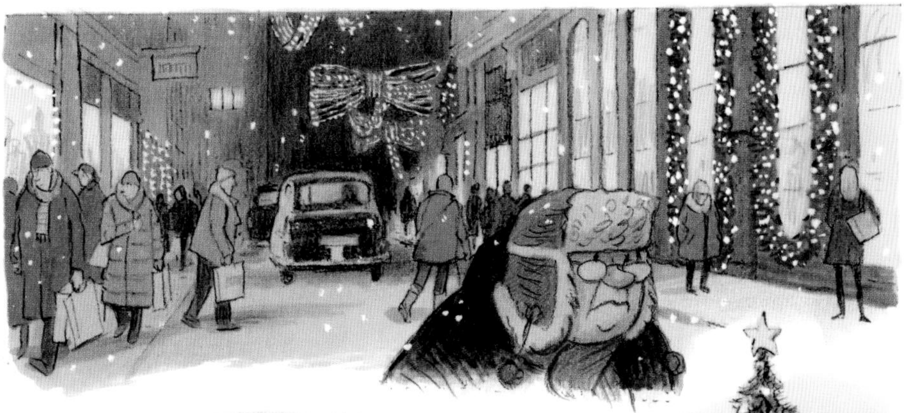

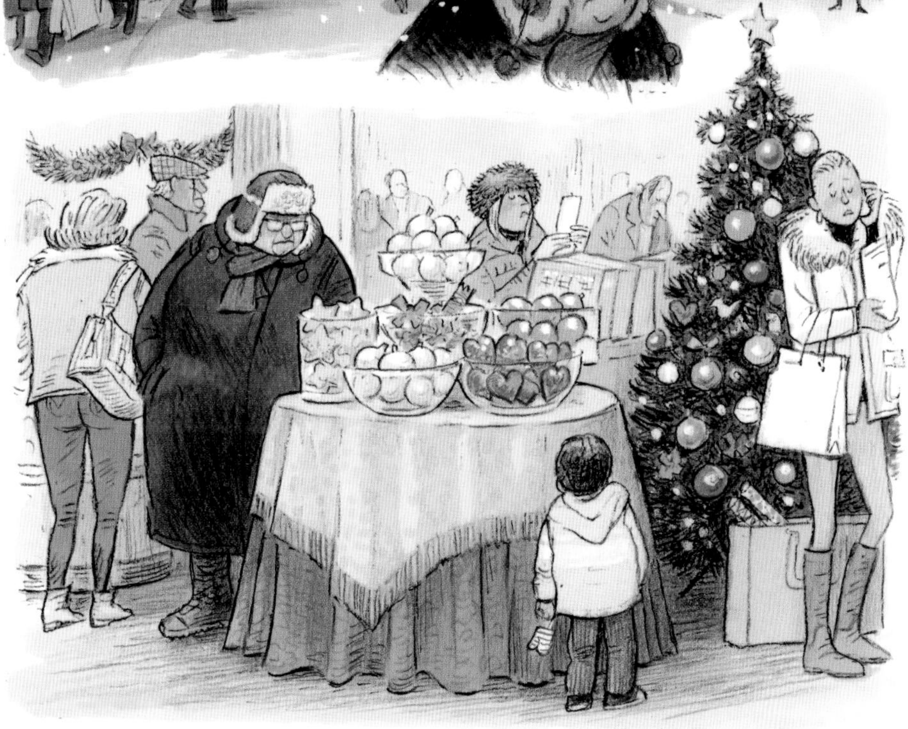

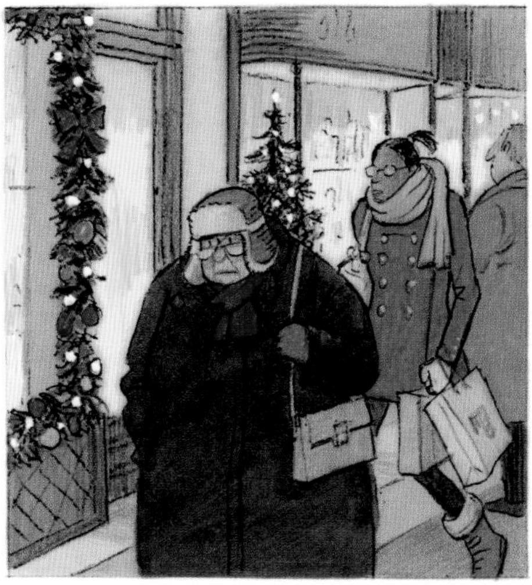

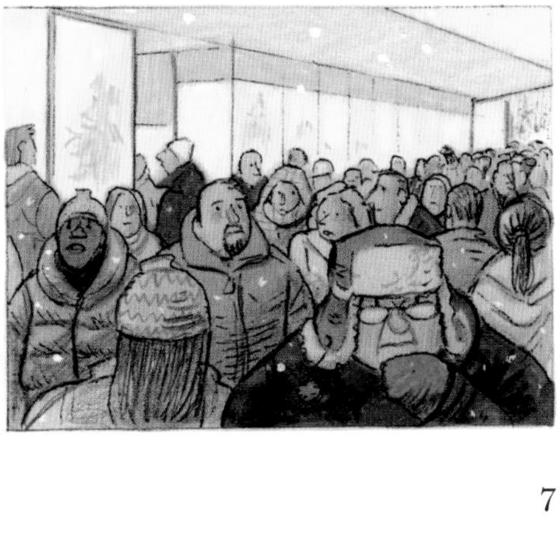

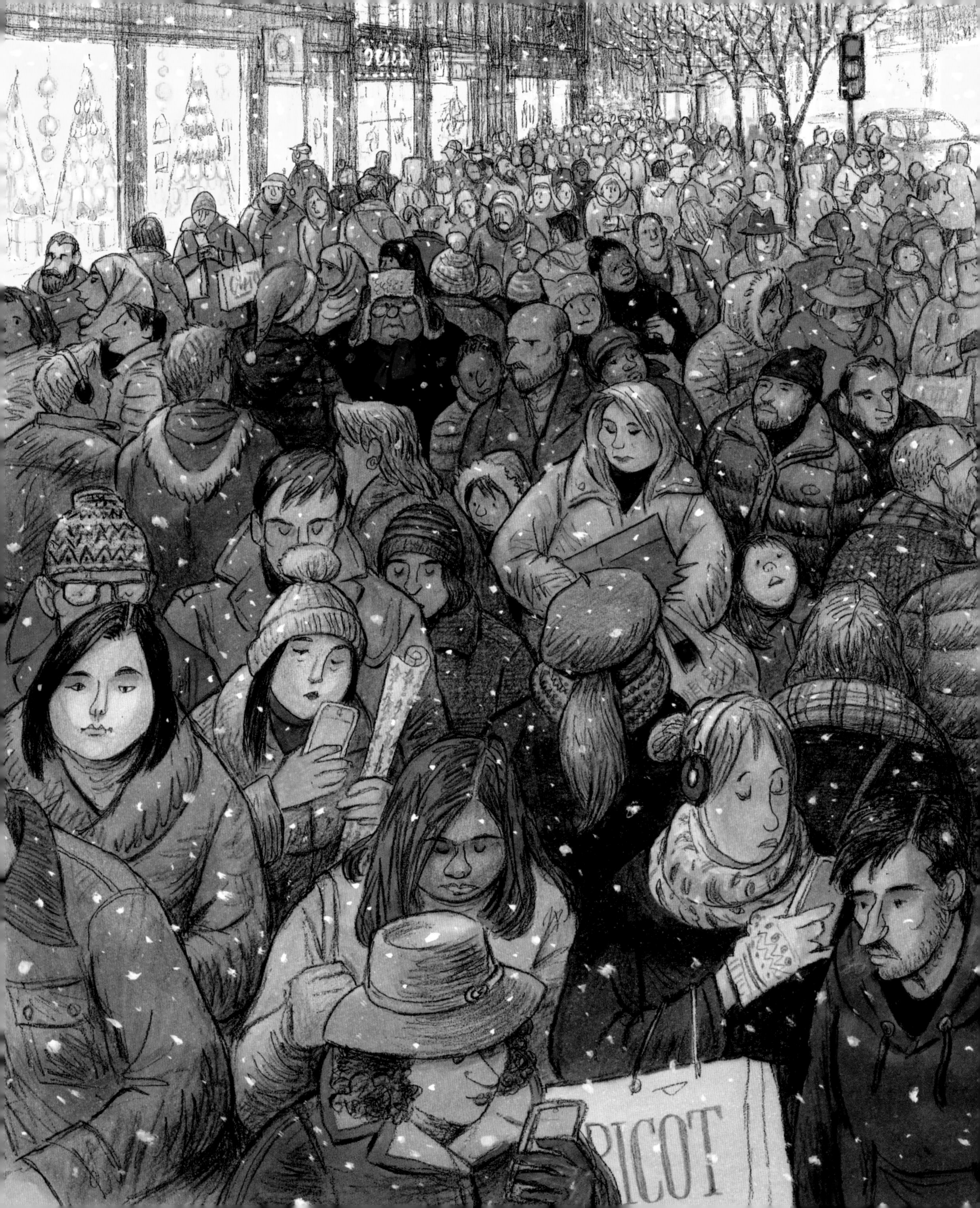

Jane was heading for my ex-husband's gallery, where I had been helping out for the last few years. In fact I had come full circle: during our marriage over 40 years ago, Freddie and I had run the gallery together. After the divorce (after Freddie ran off with my stepsister), he took over the shop and I began dealing from home. Mostly prints, which I've done ever since. And some writing on post-war British Sculpture.

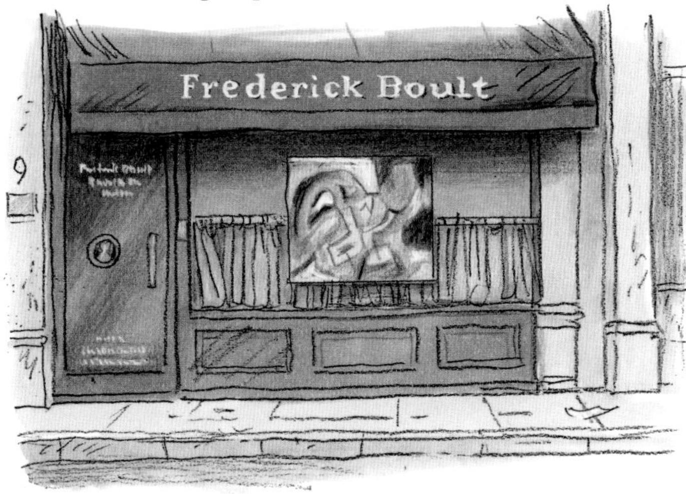
Frederick Boult
9

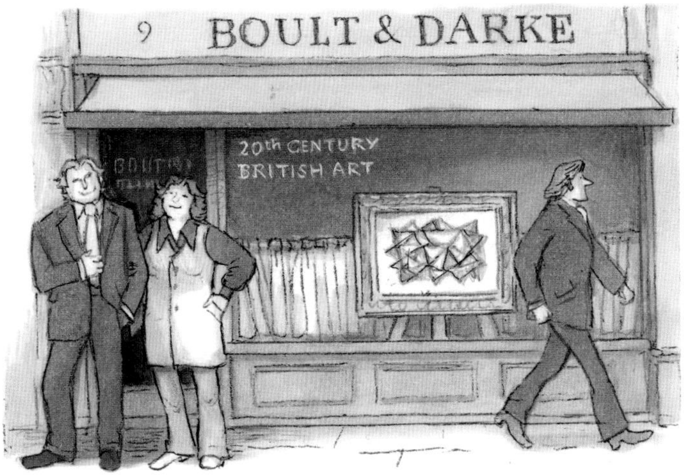
9 BOULT & DARKE
20th CENTURY BRITISH ART

Over the years, if we met, as we were bound to in the London art world, Freddie and I were always civil. No more than that. But in 2015 our paths crossed at an art fair and Freddie confided in me. He had just been diagnosed with Alzheimer's, his right-hand man at the gallery was leaving and he needed someone to hold the reins until the lease ran out. Or he became incapable, whichever came first.

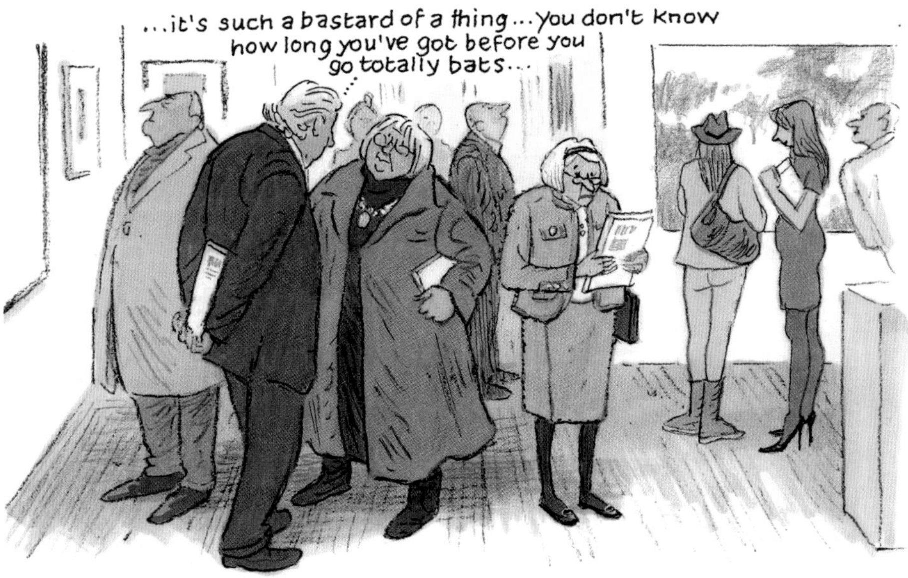
...it's such a bastard of a thing...you don't know how long you've got before you go totally bats...

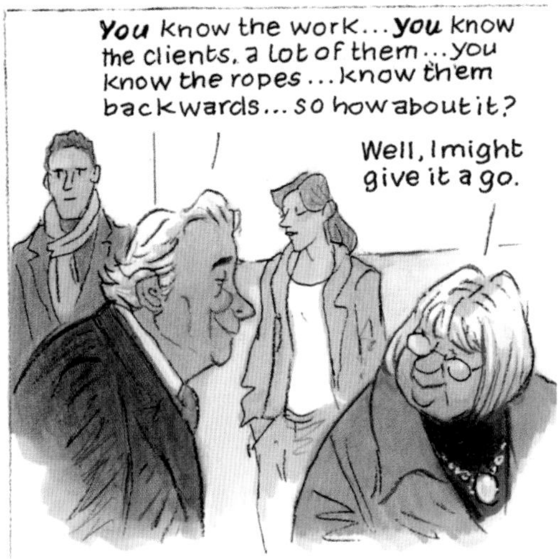
You know the work... you know the clients, a lot of them...you know the ropes...know them backwards...so how about it?
Well, I might give it a go.

Bit by bit, as Alzheimer's overtook him, Freddie stayed at his house in the country and came less and less to London, while I spent more and more time in the gallery.

As I walked the streets that evening, I remember feeling that at least Freddie was now too far gone and would never know what I'd done – all the things that I foresaw would be dragged up from the swamp.

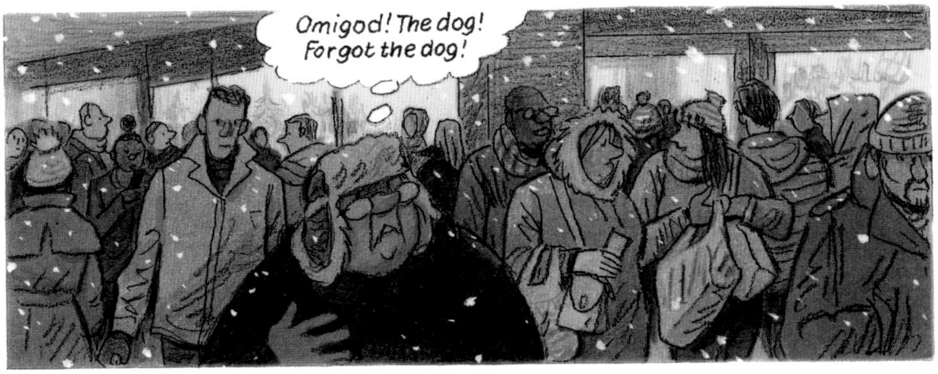
Omigod! The dog! Forgot the dog!

My dog was in the gallery. I retraced my steps, thinking that if Jane McMullen was still waiting for me, so be it. I would have to face her sometime. But in the event, only Phoebe was there.

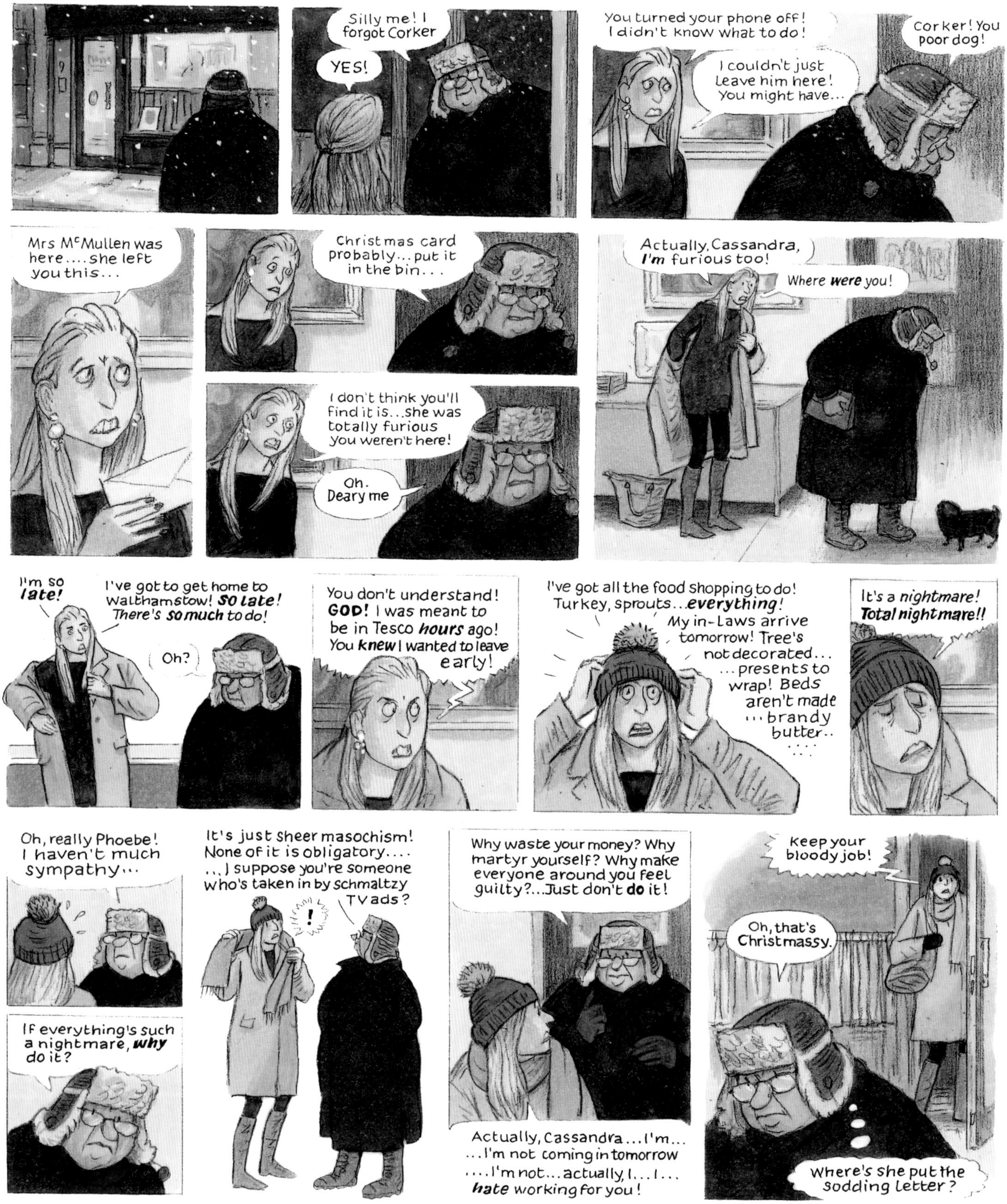
Silly me! I forgot Corker
YES!
You turned your phone off! I didn't know what to do!
I couldn't just leave him here! You might have...
Corker! You poor dog!
Mrs McMullen was here.... she left you this...
Christmas card probably... put it in the bin...
I don't think you'll find it is... she was totally furious you weren't here!
Oh. Deary me
Actually, Cassandra, I'm furious too!
Where were you!
I'm so late!
I've got to get home to Walthamstow! So late! There's so much to do!
Oh?
You don't understand! GOD! I was meant to be in Tesco hours ago! You knew I wanted to leave early!
I've got all the food shopping to do! Turkey, sprouts... everything!
My in-laws arrive tomorrow! Tree's not decorated... ... presents to wrap! Beds aren't made ... brandy butter.. ...
It's a nightmare! Total nightmare!!
Oh, really Phoebe! I haven't much sympathy...
If everything's such a nightmare, why do it?
It's just sheer masochism! None of it is obligatory.... ... I suppose you're someone who's taken in by schmaltzy TV ads?
!
Why waste your money? Why martyr yourself? Why make everyone around you feel guilty?... Just don't do it!
Actually, Cassandra... I'm... ... I'm not coming in tomorrow .... I'm not... actually, I... I... hate working for you!
Keep your bloody job!
Oh, that's Christmassy.
Where's she put the sodding letter?

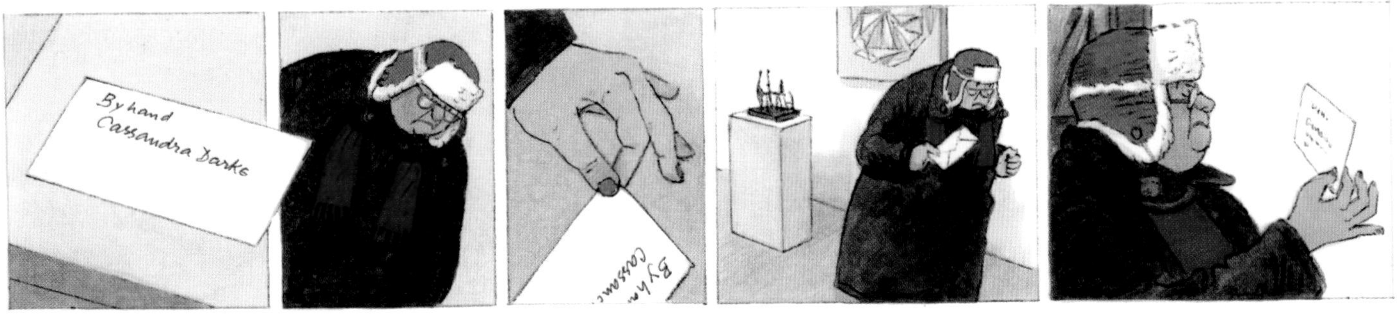

By hand
Cassandra Darke

I had seen Jane McMullen the evening before at a charity dinner. In fact, I'd told her off a bit – she has this habit of donating her husband's work to charity auctions …

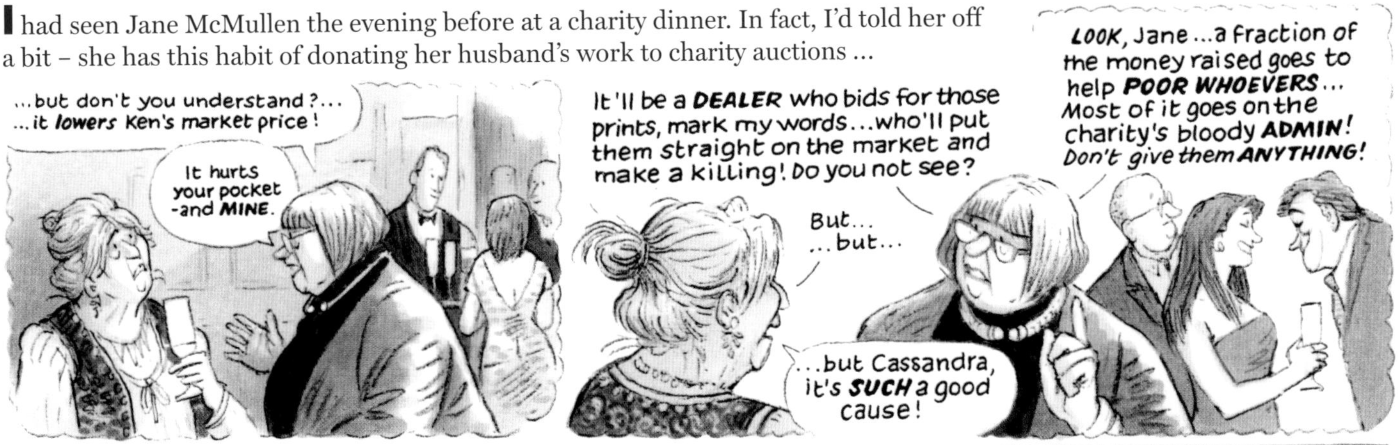

...but don't you understand?...
...it **lowers** Ken's market price!
It hurts your pocket -and **MINE**.
It'll be a **DEALER** who bids for those prints, mark my words...who'll put them straight on the market and make a killing! Do you not see?
But...
...but...
...but Cassandra, it's **SUCH** a good cause!
LOOK, Jane...a fraction of the money raised goes to help **POOR WHOEVERS**...
Most of it goes on the charity's bloody **ADMIN**!
Don't give them **ANYTHING**!

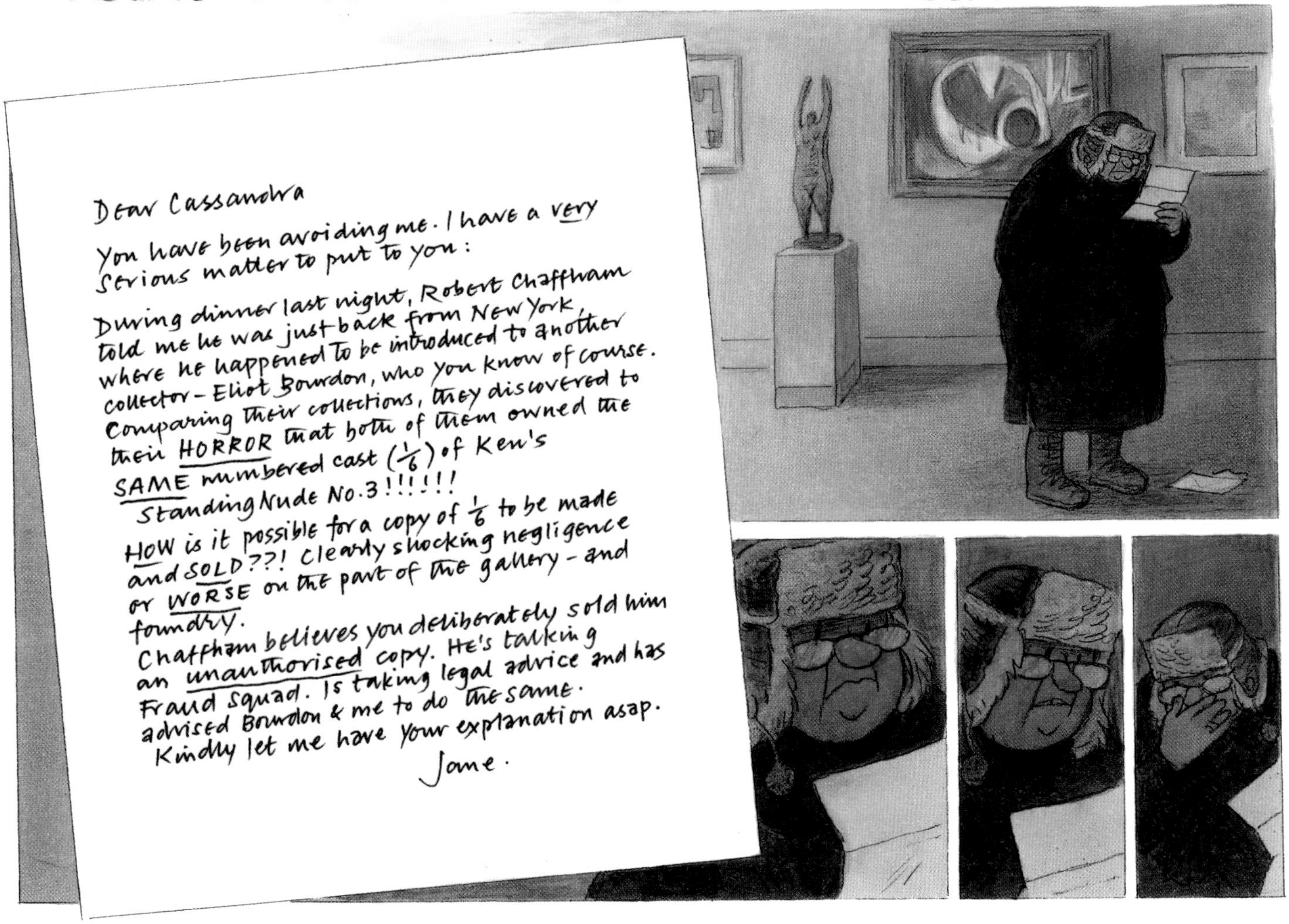

Dear Cassandra
You have been avoiding me. I have a very
serious matter to put to you:
During dinner last night, Robert Chaffham
told me he was just back from New York,
where he happened to be introduced to another
collector – Eliot Bowdon, who you know of course.
Comparing their collections, they discovered to
their HORROR that both of them owned the
SAME numbered cast (1/6) of Ken's
Standing Nude No.3!!!!!!
HOW is it possible for a copy of 1/6 to be made
and SOLD??! Clearly shocking negligence
or WORSE on the part of the gallery – and
foundry.
Chaffham believes you deliberately sold him
an unauthorised copy. He's talking
Fraud Squad. Is taking legal advice and has
advised Bowdon & me to do the same.
Kindly let me have your explanation asap.
Jane.

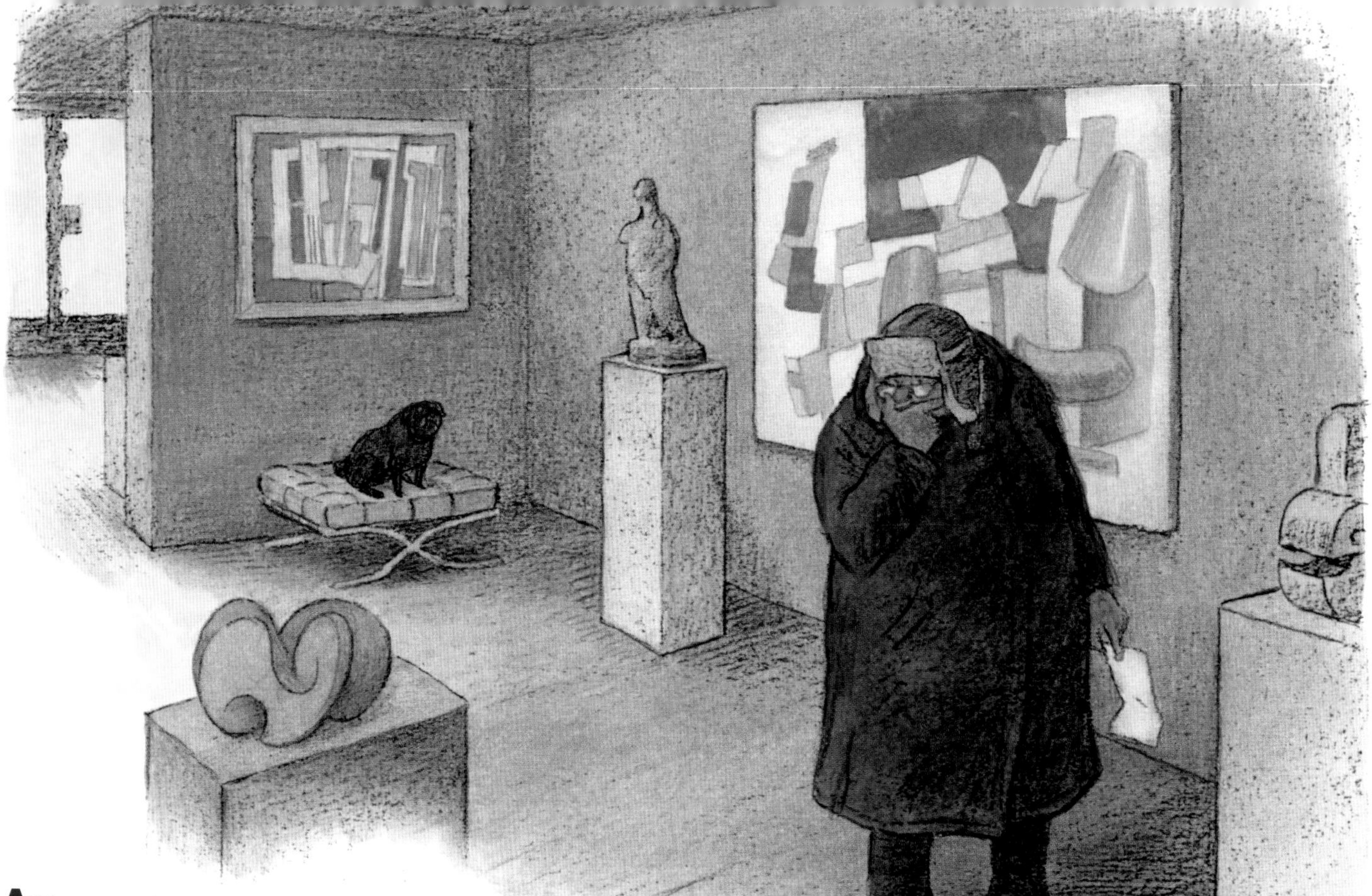

All became clear.
Why Robert and Kimberley Chaffham had cut me the evening before and why he spent dinner muttering in Jane McMullen's ear. I had been rumbled, as I'd foreseen, but even so I couldn't pretend it wasn't a shock. The fluke of Chaffham meeting Eliot Bourdon.*

*Bourdon is an old client of Freddie's, highly cultivated and a virtual recluse living in Minneapolis. His encounter with Chaffham must have repulsed him. Chaffham likes to swank and play Top Trumps with other collectors.

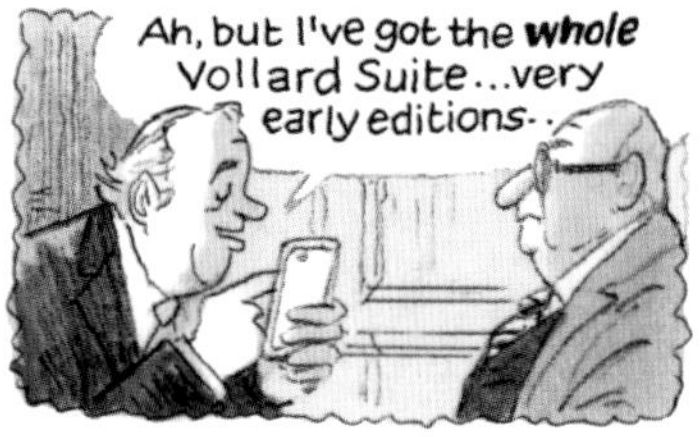
Ah, but I've got the **whole** Vollard Suite...very early editions..

I must have been aware of the risk of being found out, but until then my activity had hardly seemed criminal. More a way of giving certain clients what they asked for and what they deserved. Clients who pissed me off. Speculators, who had no interest whatsoever in the art they bought, except for its ability to hold its value. I spit on them, their ignorance, their vulgarity, their itchy palms. Anyway, the game was up. Assume the worst, I remember thinking (my usual motto).

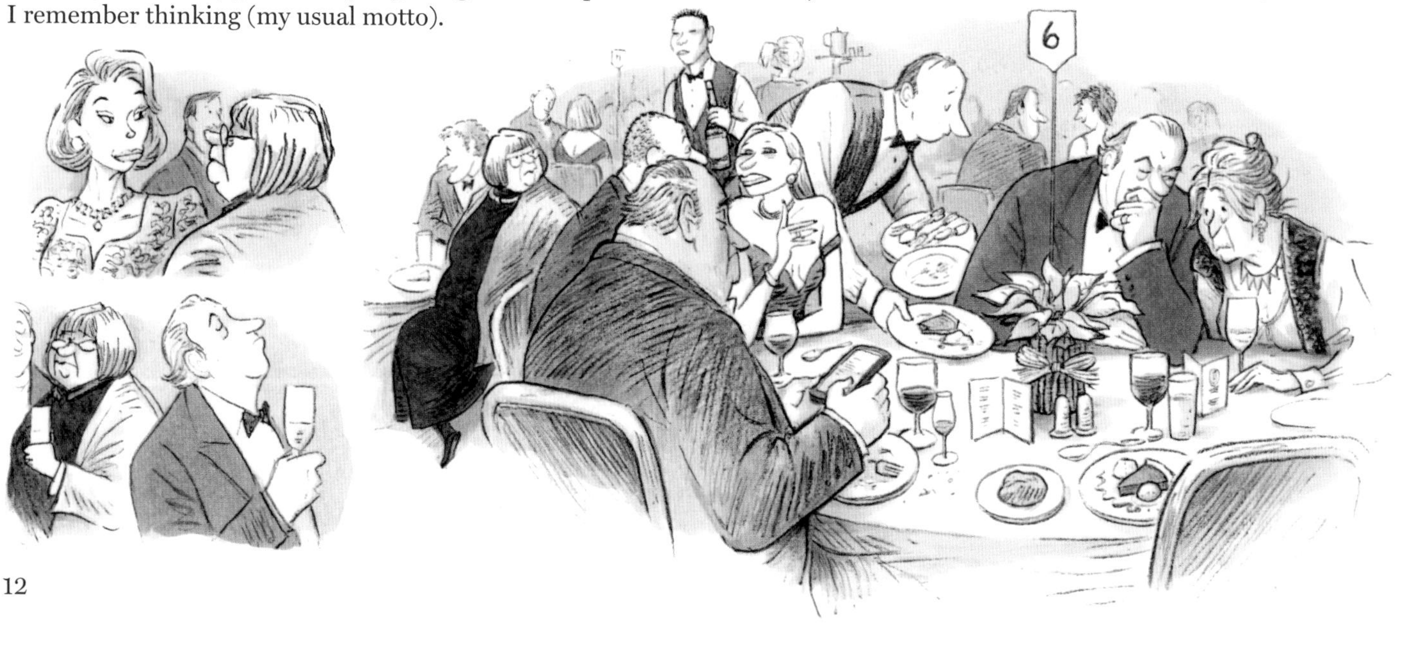
6

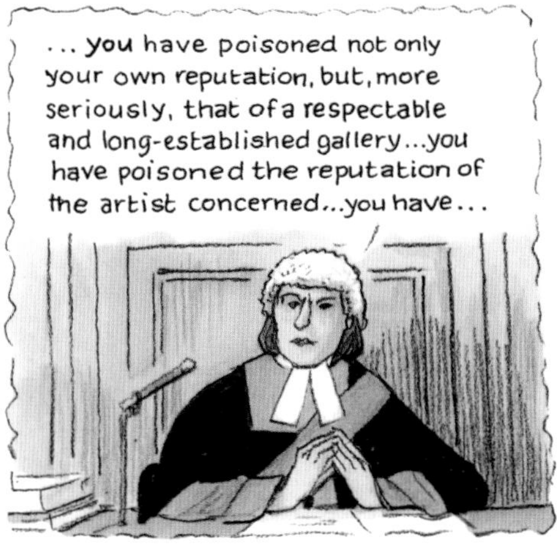
... you have poisoned not only your own reputation, but, more seriously, that of a respectable and long-established gallery ... you have poisoned the reputation of the artist concerned... you have ...

The very worst did not happen. I expected jail, had steeled myself for the horror of a shared cell. I had pressed my solicitor on the chances of being put in solitary, a prospect I could almost look forward to.

Things, however, were bad enough. My home was turned upside down, the computers taken away. People cut me in the street and abused me on e-mail. (I do not do social media.) There were tedious interviews, where I admitted everything, expressed regret, and offered nothing in mitigation. One of the fraud detectives made the asinine suggestion that my motive was revenge on my ex-husband for deserting me in 1980. One or two newspapers implied the same thing. The discovery that Freddie's wife is my stepsister led to their habitual policy of pitting woman against woman. There were photographs – Margot's taken years ago: Beauty and the Bitch. (The subtext of these pictures being: no husband could be blamed for desiring Margot. And no husband could be blamed for leaving me.)

I remember vividly every moment of the trial, even though my Day of Judgement was another routine Wednesday in court. In the scale of villainy my offence was paltry – there had been no weapons, no violence, no body. I underwent the due process of law with dignity. My name was now officially MUD and always would be, and I didn't much care. Any atonement, beyond the hours of community work, would be a waste of time.

No jail for West End art dealer found guilty of £400,000 fraud

Yasmin Gul

A West End art dealer was shown mercy by a judge, who did not jail her for a £400,000 art fraud. Cassandra Darke, 71, pleaded guilty at Southwark Crown Court to charges that she had sold four unauthorised copies of sculptures by the late Kenneth McMullen, RA. She admitted falsely telling prospective buyers that the works she was offering from the estate of Mr McMullen were legitimate and authenticated by the artist.

Sentencing Darke to a two-year suspended sentence and 200 hours community work, Circuit Judge Eleanor Dixon said she had thought long and hard about giving Darke a custodial sentence. Darke had created "a toxic miasma of untruth" and had committed four disgraceful acts over a period of two years and in doing so had undermined the art market, which depended on trust.

At the time of the offences Darke was working at the gallery of her ex-husband, Frederick Boult, in Brummell Court, St James's. She said in court that she had been acting as manager of the gallery, at her ex-husband's request, after his early diagnosis of dementia.

In a separate trial, foundry owner Antony Ricci, 68, pleaded guilty to having created new copies of the sculptures from the moulds that he had kept.

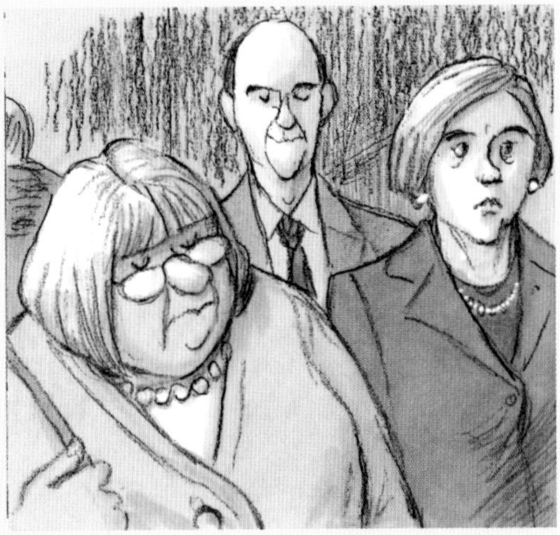

The accused, Cassandra Darke, left, on her way into court yesterday

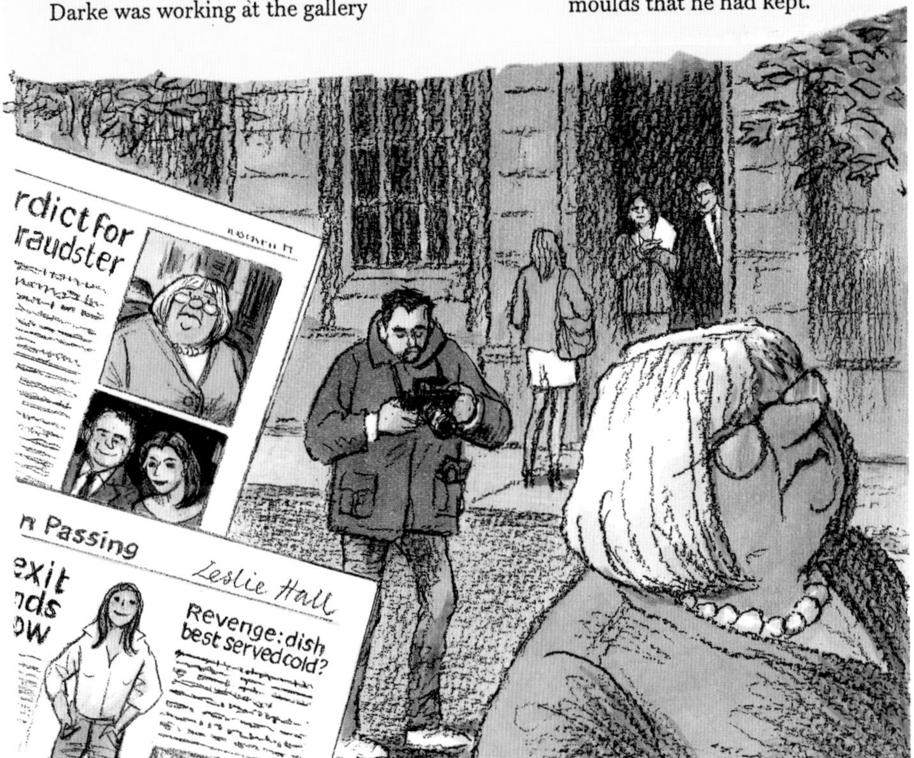
rdict for
raudster
n Passing
exit
nds
ow
Leslie Hall
Revenge: dish best served cold?

December 2017

Osmington Square, London SW3

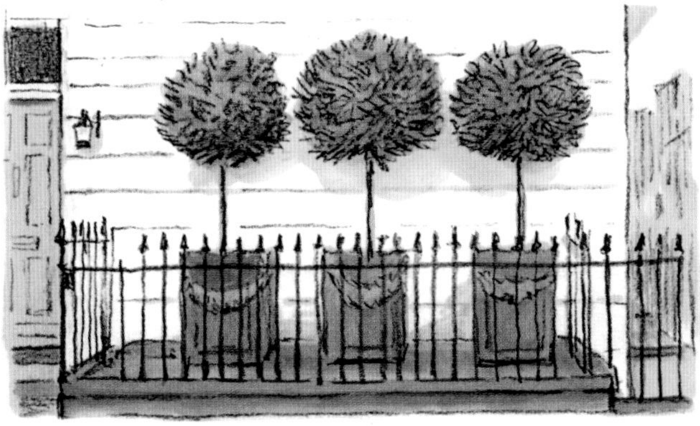

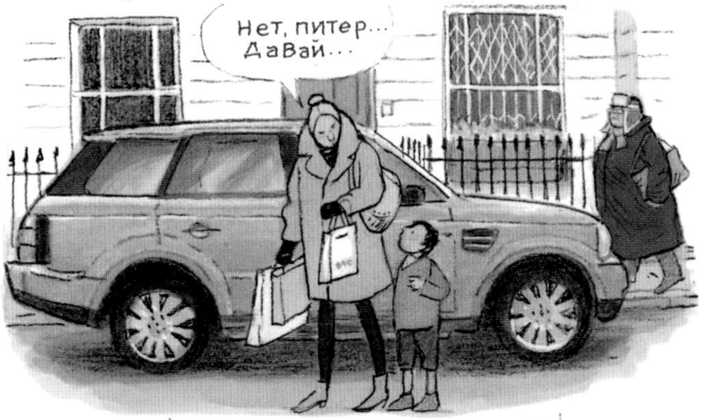
Нет, питер...
Давай...

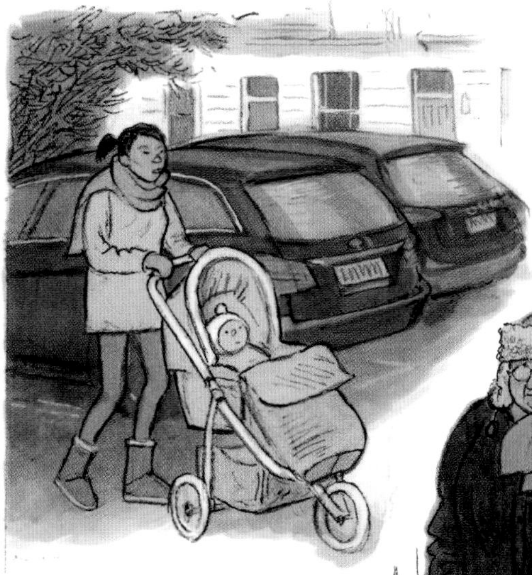

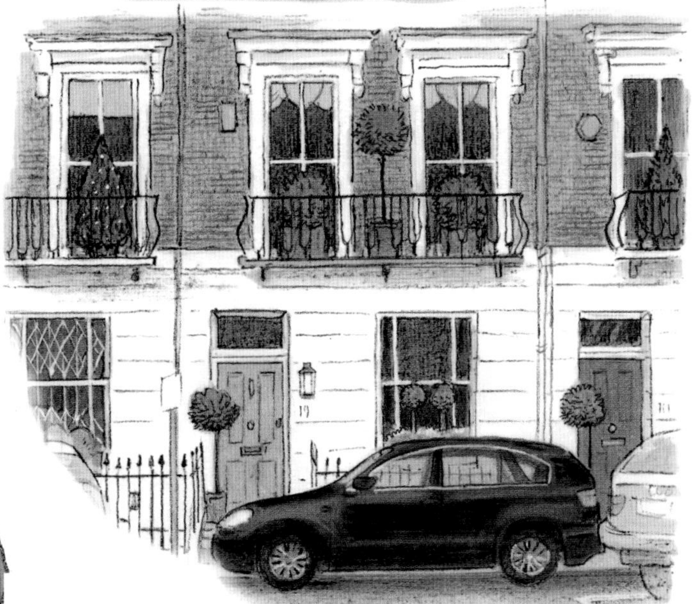

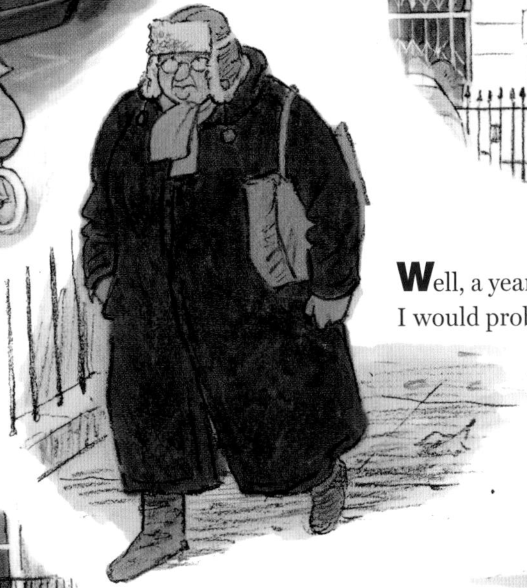

Well, a year's gone by. December again. If I wasn't so old and fat, I would probably have spent this morning with other offenders scrubbing out graffiti. But I was directed to a day centre, where I read aloud and wrote letters for the blind. Hardly onerous. Even so, I'm glad to get home.

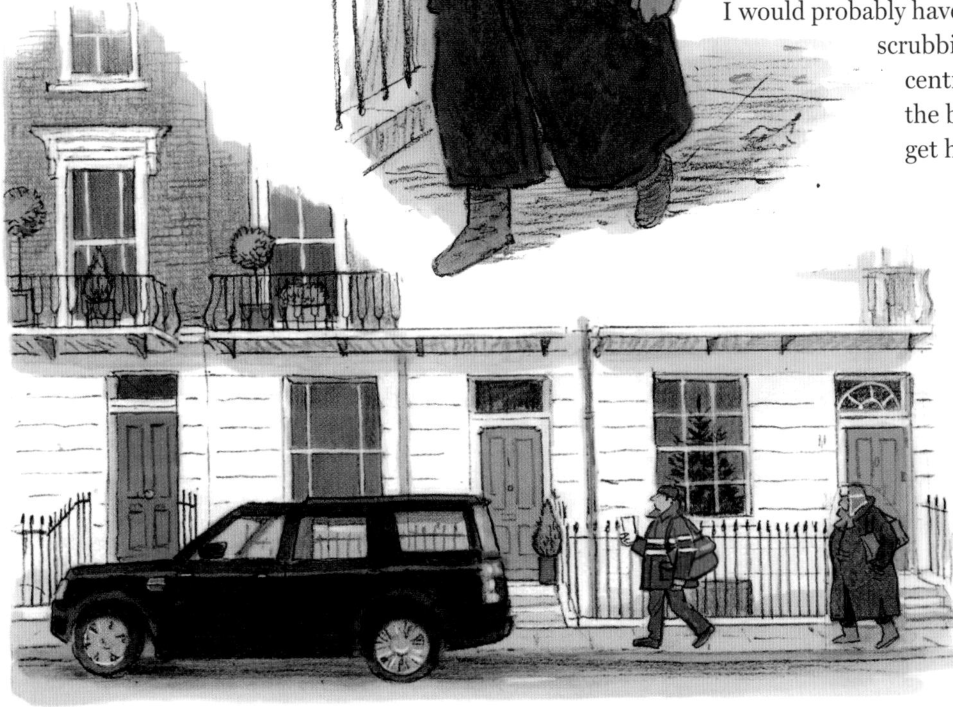

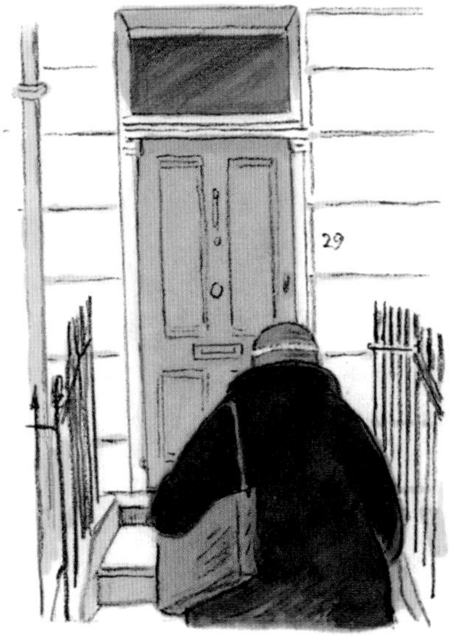

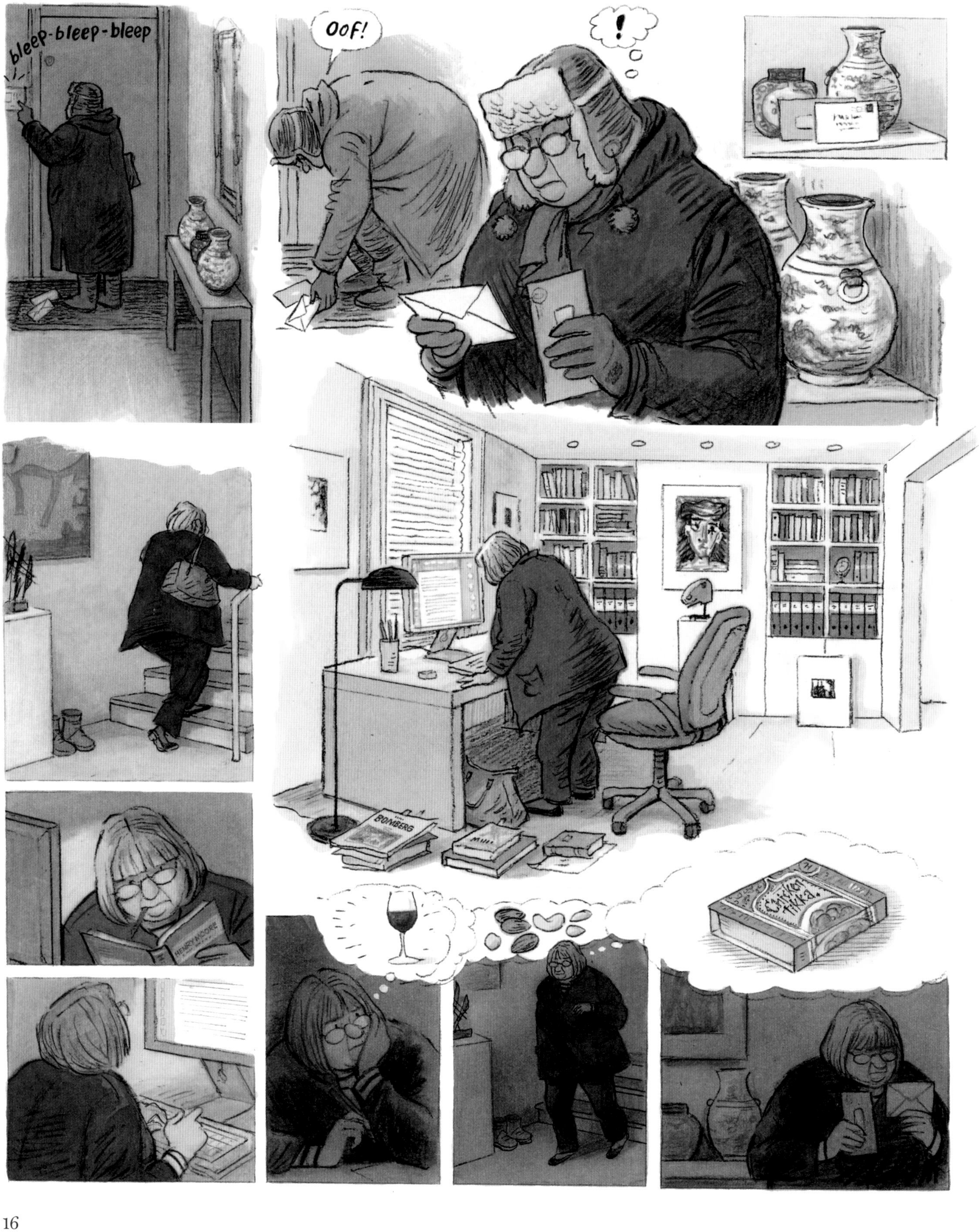
bleep-bleep-bleep
Oof!
!
BOMBERG
HENRY MOORE

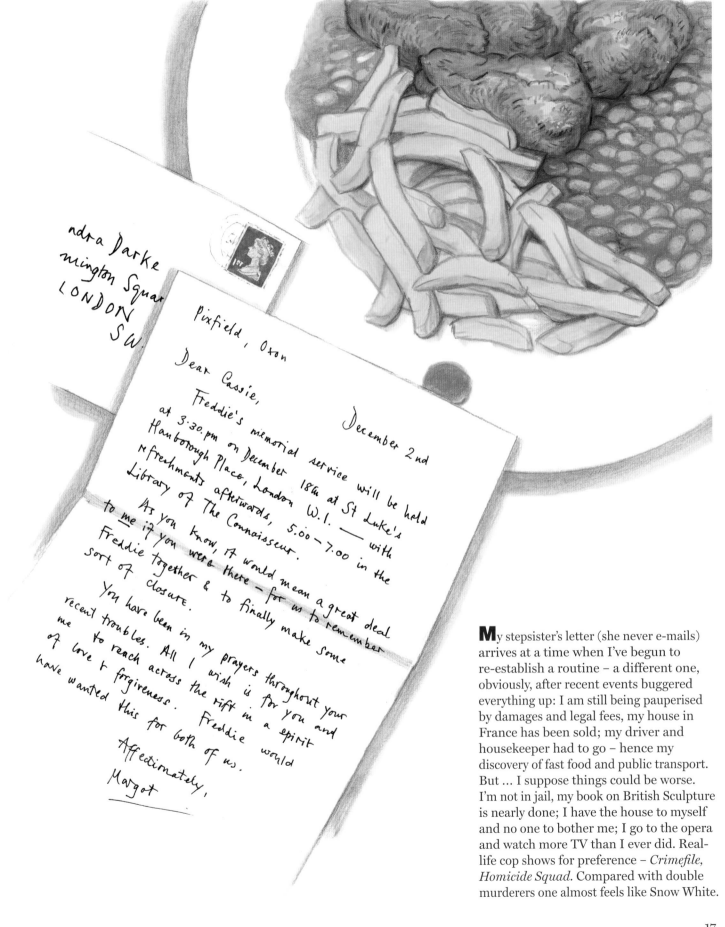

ndra Darke
mington Squar
LONDON
S.W.

1st

Pixfield, Oxon

December 2nd

Dear Cassie,

Freddie's memorial service will be held
at 3.30 pm on December 18th at St Luke's
Hanborough Place, London W.1. — with
refreshments afterwards, 5.00–7.00 in the
Library of The Connoisseur.

As you know, it would mean a great deal
to _me_ if you were there – for us to remember
Freddie together & to finally make some
sort of closure.

You have been in my prayers throughout your
recent troubles. All I wish is for you and
me to reach across the rift in a spirit
of love & forgiveness. Freddie would
have wanted this for both of us.

Affectionately,

Margot

My stepsister's letter (she never e-mails) arrives at a time when I've begun to re-establish a routine – a different one, obviously, after recent events buggered everything up: I am still being pauperised by damages and legal fees, my house in France has been sold; my driver and housekeeper had to go – hence my discovery of fast food and public transport. But … I suppose things could be worse. I'm not in jail, my book on British Sculpture is nearly done; I have the house to myself and no one to bother me; I go to the opera and watch more TV than I ever did. Real-life cop shows for preference – *Crimefile*, *Homicide Squad*. Compared with double murderers one almost feels like Snow White.

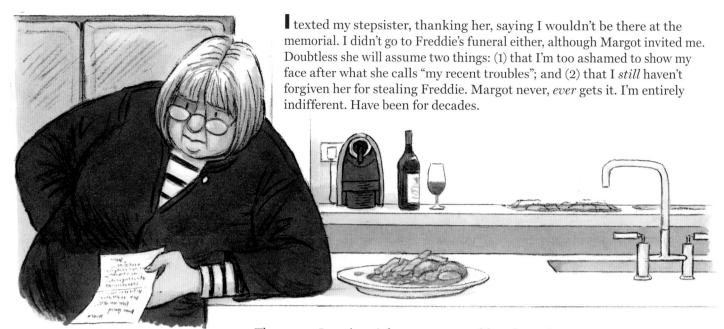

I texted my stepsister, thanking her, saying I wouldn't be there at the memorial. I didn't go to Freddie's funeral either, although Margot invited me. Doubtless she will assume two things: (1) that I'm too ashamed to show my face after what she calls "my recent troubles"; and (2) that I *still* haven't forgiven her for stealing Freddie. Margot never, *ever* gets it. I'm entirely indifferent. Have been for decades.

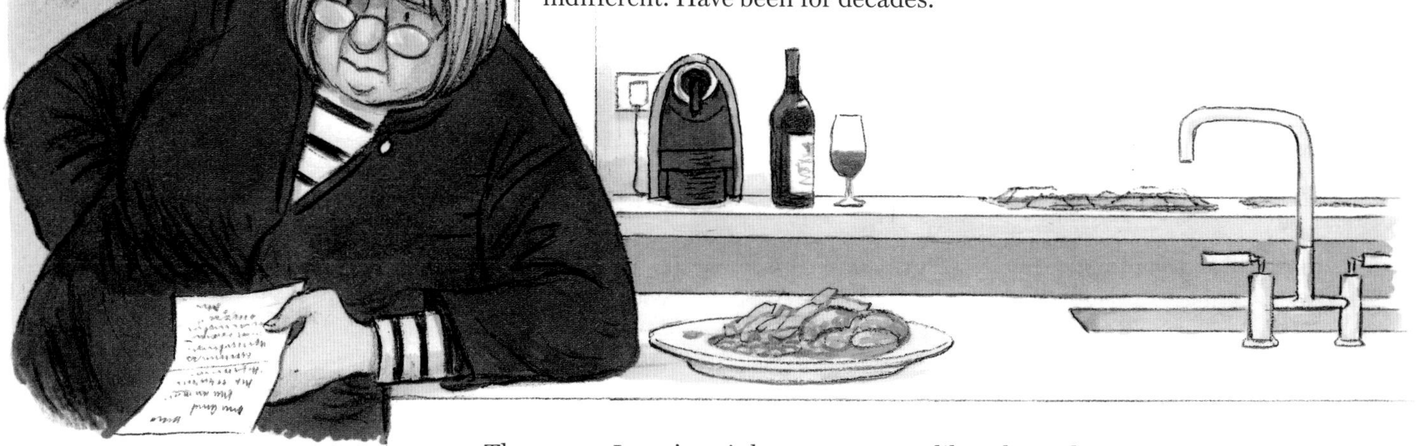

The reason I won't go is because Margot likes cheap drama.
Freddie's gallery closed, as it had been going to anyway (with its reputation in shreds, thanks to me). Margot has already accepted my apologies but I know that she'd like nothing better than to be seen in public forgiving me in some ghastly, hammy act of "closure". "Laying the Past to Rest" is what she'd call it ...

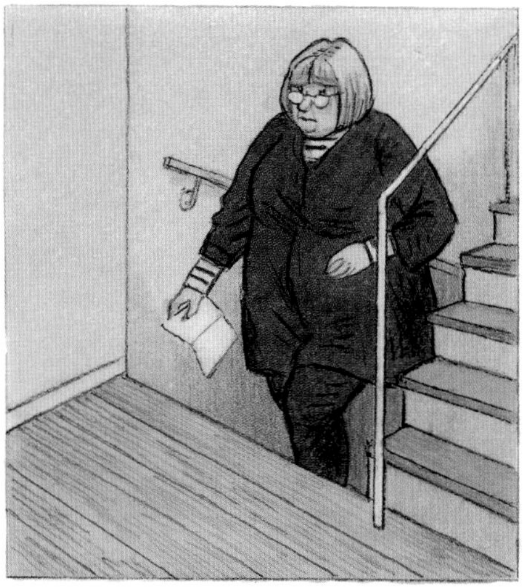

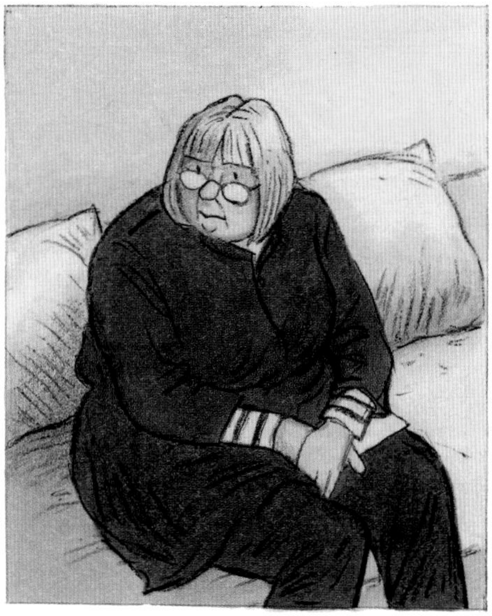

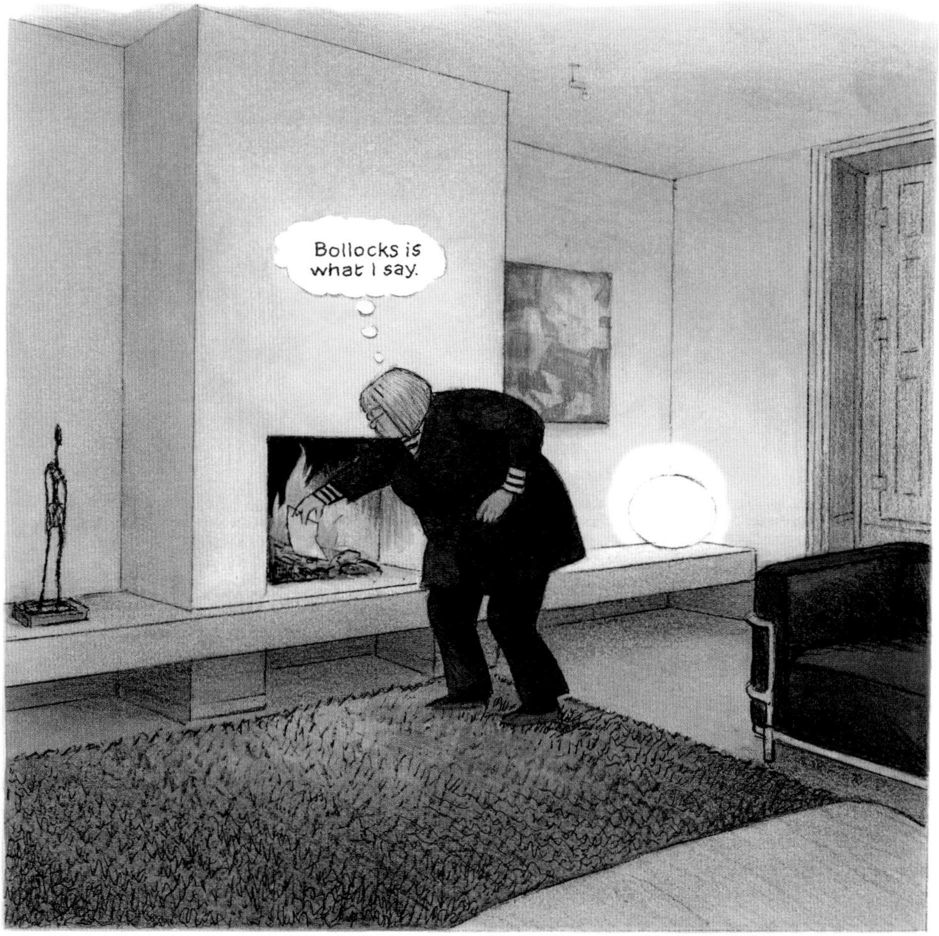
Bollocks is what I say.

But on December 18th there I am in a pine-scented minicab driven by a silent Afghan. (Coronet Cars is a discovery. The cheapest fares in town.)

Approaching Park Lane I begin to get cold feet. I dislike memorial services. In my experience people go to them for the drinks afterwards. And beforehand they sit there planning their own sendoffs and checking how old/ill/fat their contemporaries look. Not that my motive (curiosity) is any better.

The timing is perfect. They are already singing a hymn – "Bread of Heaven" – when I arrive at St Luke's, fortunately loud enough to drown the creaks and groans from the woodwork during my climb to the gallery.
By the time I reach the front I'm sweating. The church is overheated. There's a fug of dust and cooked overcoats.

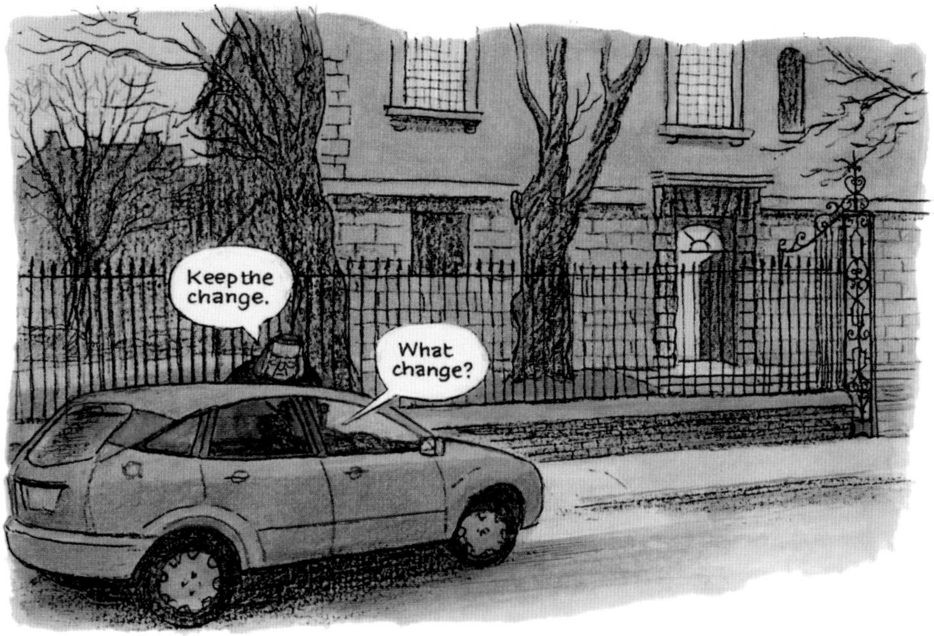
Keep the change.
What change?

And there they are, the relics of Freddie's past. Plus a rector, a canon, a choir and an organist. Margot's doing. Freddie would have been appalled. He was heathen, a talented blasphemer and a fount of dirty jokes.

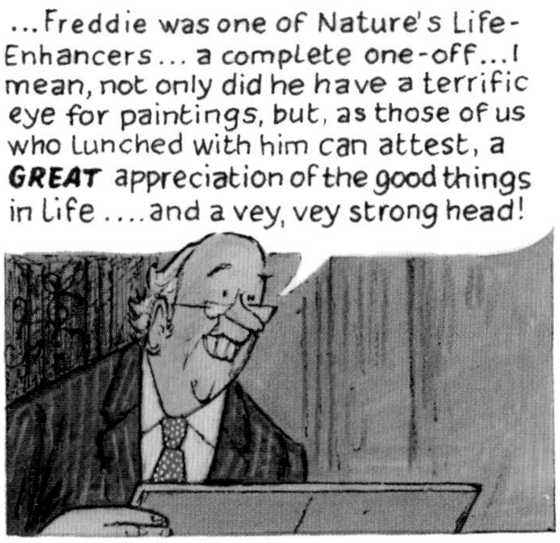
...Freddie was one of Nature's Life-Enhancers... a complete one-off...I mean, not only did he have a terrific eye for paintings, but, as those of us who lunched with him can attest, a GREAT appreciation of the good things in life....and a vey, vey strong head!

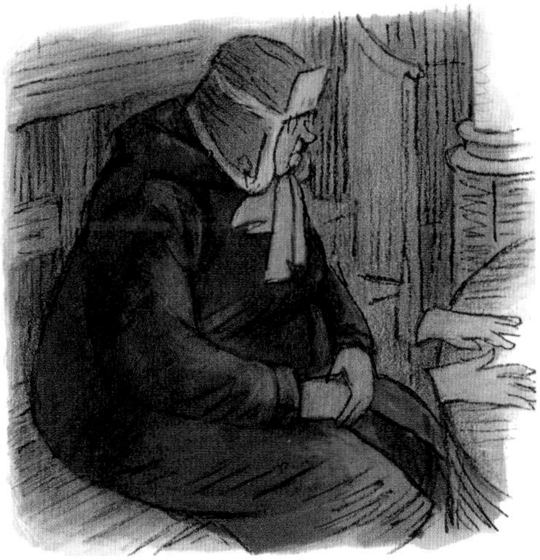

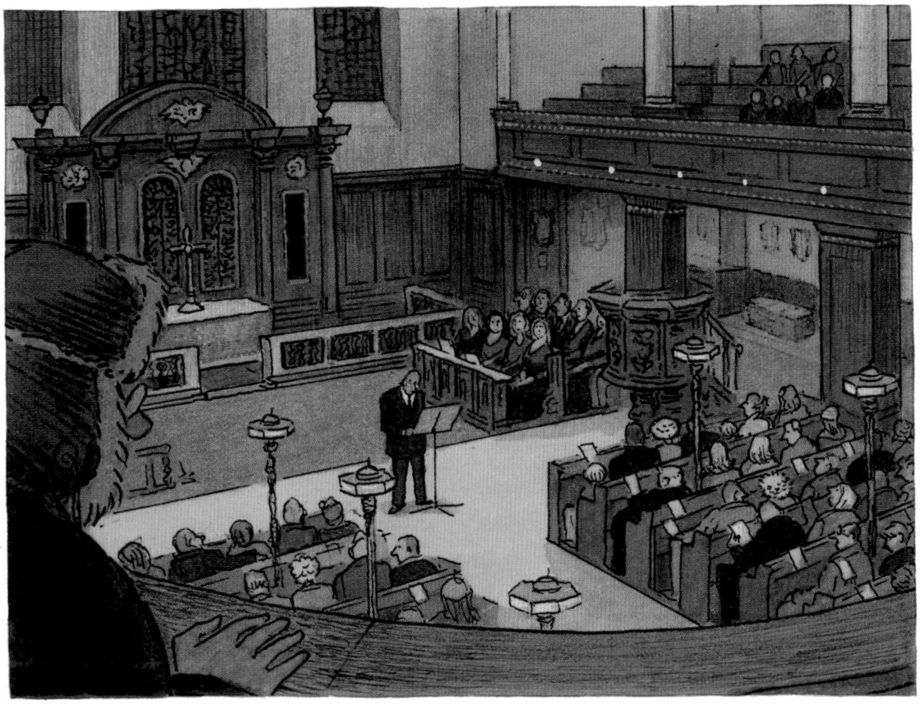

I count three pews of family, Margot at the front, flanked by her sons. Our half-brother Simon sits behind her, but tellingly no sign of her daughter Nicki. There are several dealers, one or two enemies, and dotted about other familiar faces: some old farts from Sotheby's, a couple of artists, Mrs Weiss, Lyn from the framers, Lady, Lady ... Thingummy.

A turnout of well over a hundred, much as I expected. Perhaps more women than men, some of whom, I dare say, Freddie must have rogered. Or tried to.

Directly below me are two familiar heads of hair, the rats' nest of Jane McMullen, the golden glue-do of Kimberley Chaffham. They and other injured parties sued my arse off. I settled out of court, selling my house in Brittany (at a loss) and various prints (which performed badly at auction). Perhaps it was fortunate that seven years ago, I was advised to donate my most valuable artworks (Picasso prints, Henry Moore, McMullen, etc) to a public gallery. The Partington Collection in Winchester accepted everything.

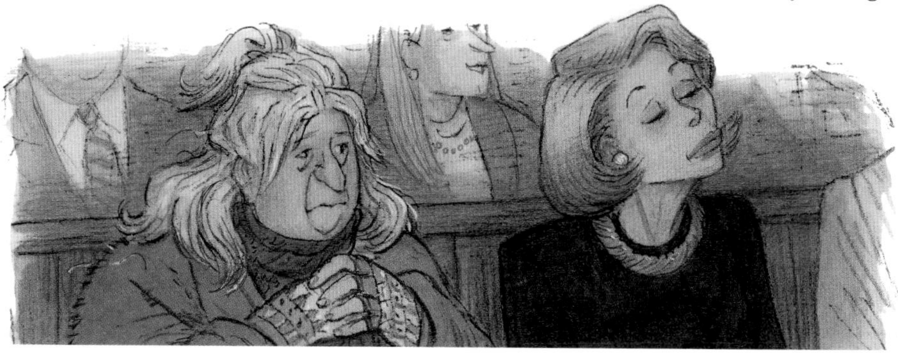

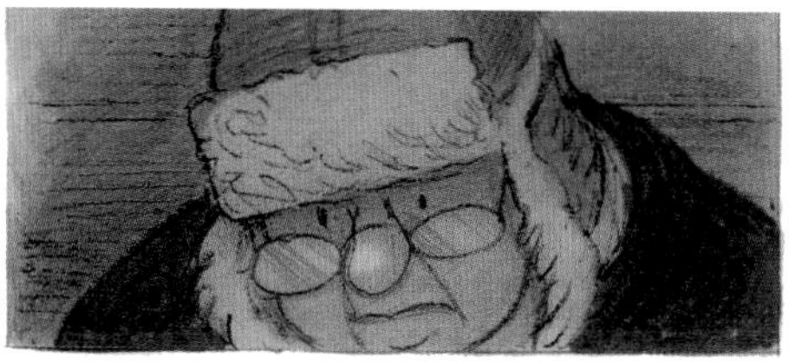

I am now pretty much penniless. Small wonder that I want to drop a hymn book on Mrs Chaffham's head. Or a hassock. But then people would spot me and I am well aware of how my presence would be interpreted. They'd think I was skulking up here, out of shame, befitting my pariah status. And I think of Freddie, who never skulked and who, in my place, would be down there in the congregation, braving the dirty looks. He was always landing himself in the shite, but never had trouble charming his way out. Angry husbands and ex-lovers forgave him. Up to a point. I once heard him say that it was all a matter of timing ...

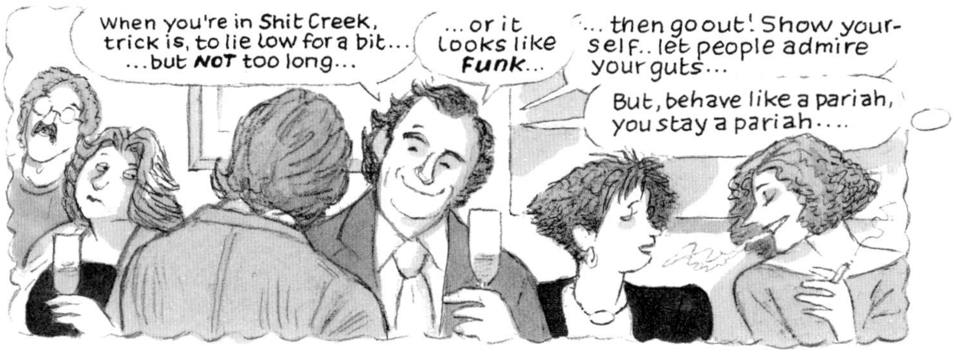
When you're in Shit Creek, trick is, to lie low for a bit... ...but NOT too long...
...or it looks like Funk...
...then go out! Show your-self.. let people admire your guts...
But, behave like a pariah, you stay a pariah....

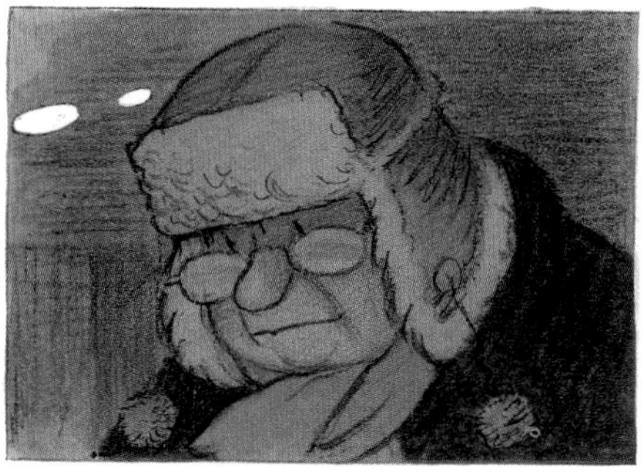

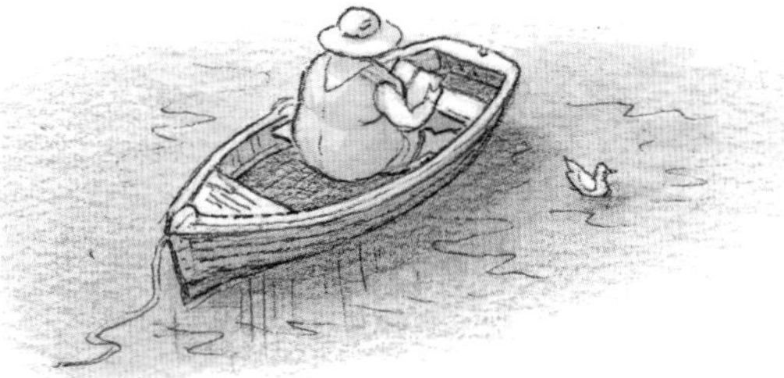

One would imagine drifting paddle-less to Shit Creek would be long and slow and one would certainly smell it coming. I didn't really, or only a faint whiff much too late ... And then I was over Shit Falls.

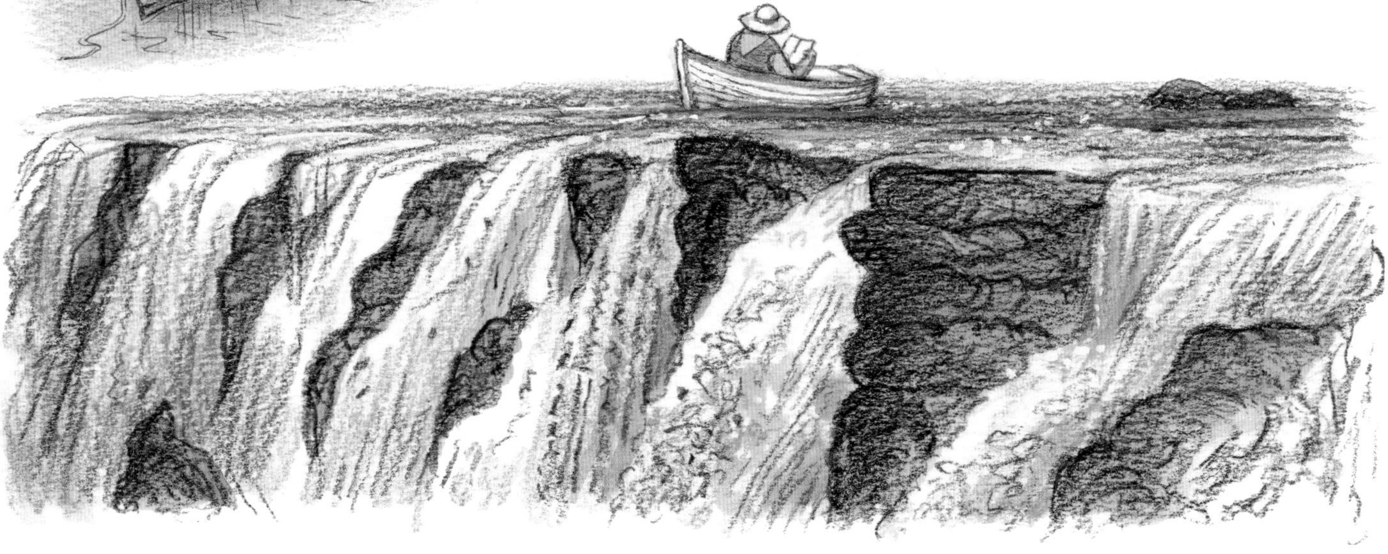

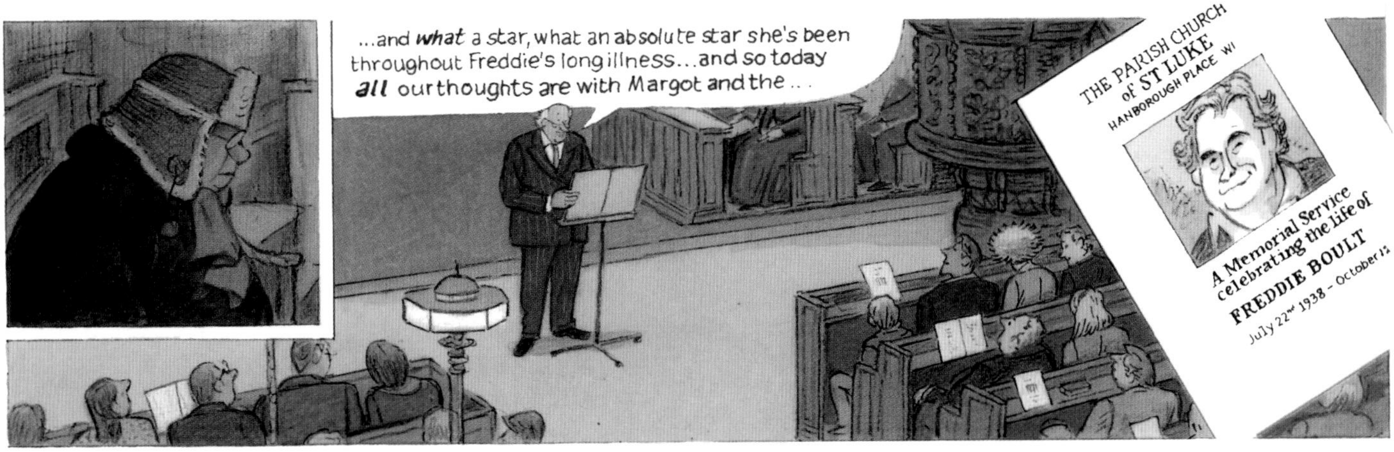
...and *what* a star, what an absolute star she's been throughout Freddie's long illness...and so today *all* our thoughts are with Margot and the ...
THE PARISH CHURCH of ST LUKE
HANBOROUGH PLACE W1
A Memorial Service celebrating the life of
FREDDIE BOULT
July 22nd 1938 - October

The paean to Margot rolls on. So many virtues! None of which I possess. If I'd been the widow today he'd be pushed to find a fitting cliché. "They broke the mould" (*thank God*); "Larger than life" (*obese*); "Blessed with a wonderful imagination" (*Liar. Utter crook*). I feel an unexpected pang, because not so long ago I would have thought myself at least principled. Of course, I've never pretended to be kind.

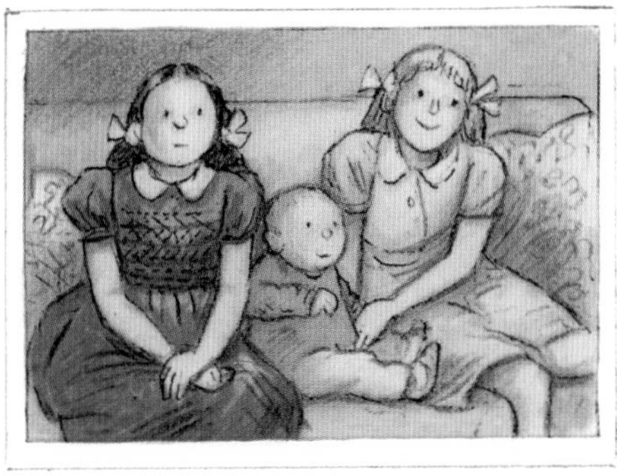

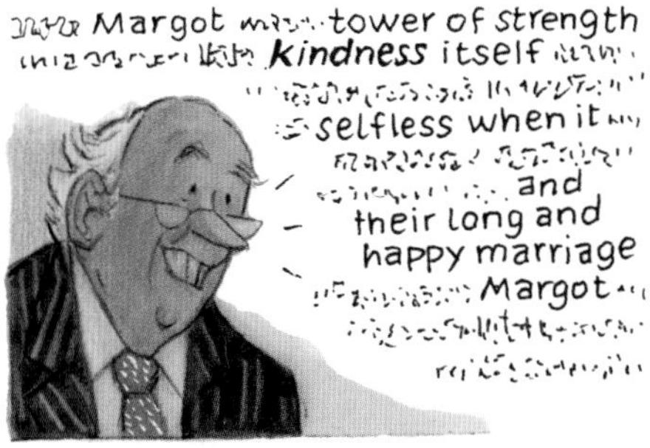
Margot
tower of strength
kindness itself
selfless when it
and
their long and happy marriage
Margot

Which Margot is. She spent her working life counselling people in their misery. She's a comforter and has been ever since we were children.
I remember her in the playground, always hugging some kid or other.

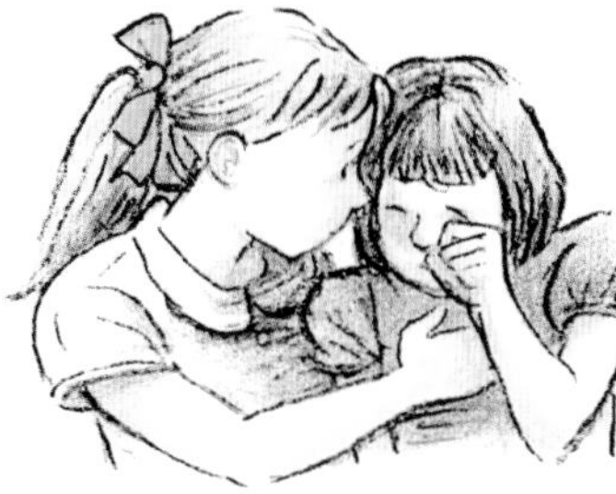

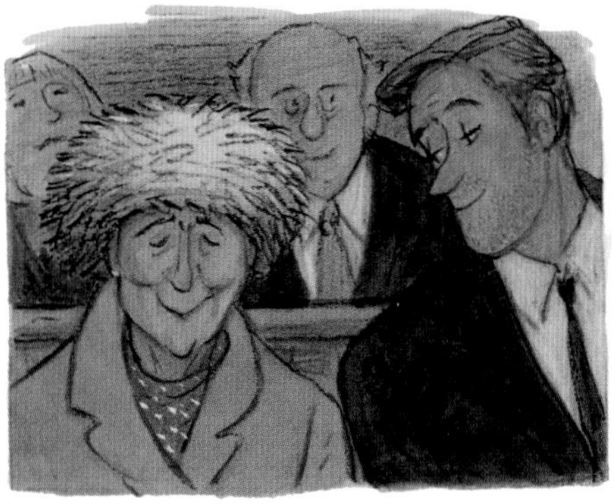

As a result, Margot was always catching nits. And passing them round the family. It was one of the few occasions when she joined me in the doghouse – my stepfather maintaining that long female hair attracted lice.

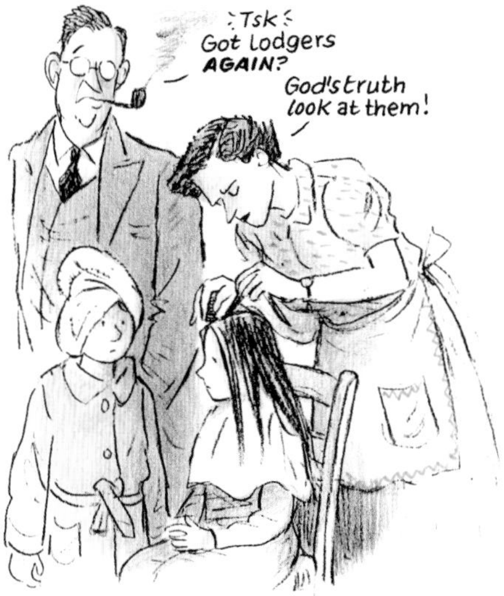
Tsk
Got lodgers *AGAIN?*
God'struth look at them!

Margot's sons dip their heads towards her. In the past weeks, I suppose, everyone in the family, except Nicki perhaps, will have felt bound to practise what she preached: lots of Group Hugs ... Nourishing Love ... and finding Positive Pathways for the Grieving Journey.

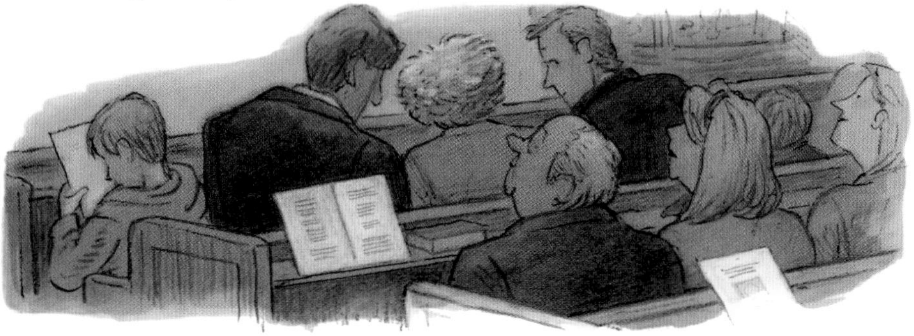

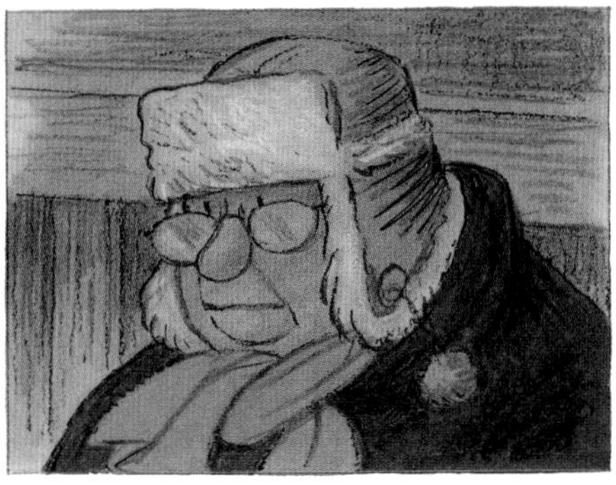

I am not unfeeling. I understand what Margot went through living with Freddie's creeping death – from his mild forgetfulness to the hallucinations, the false accusations of theft (which were quite correct in my case) and the violence. Too much for even Margot's saintly patience. I saw him at the care place once, parked in a wheelchair. Goggling. An image I try to forget.

At the lectern the eulogy winds down, Freddie and Margot's marriage now thoroughly burnished, loving, loyal and happy ever after. For 32 years. Freddie and I managed seven, and even if Margot hadn't lured him away we wouldn't have lasted much longer. She felt so bad about breaking us up, always suggesting we had counselling, she and I. These days it's just me, she thinks, who needs therapy.

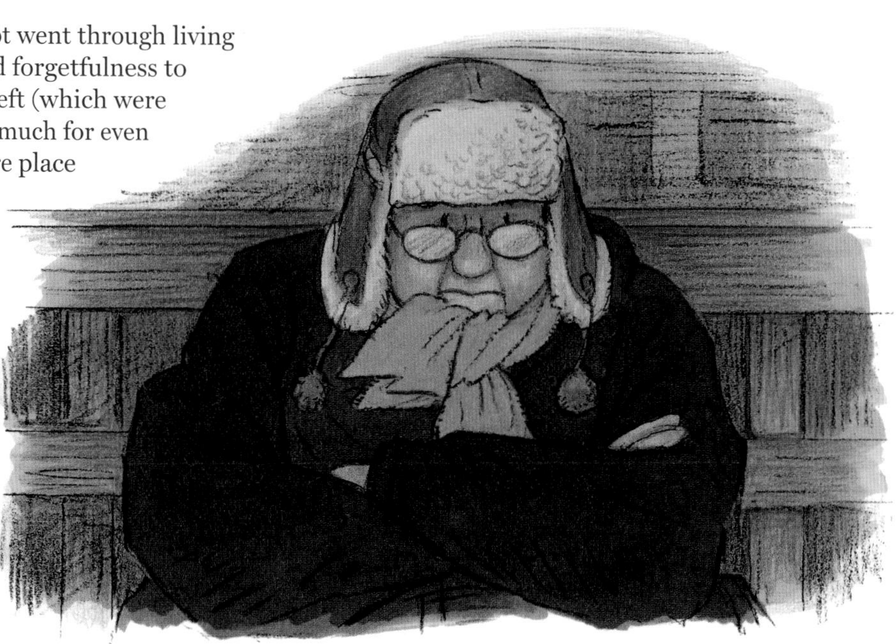

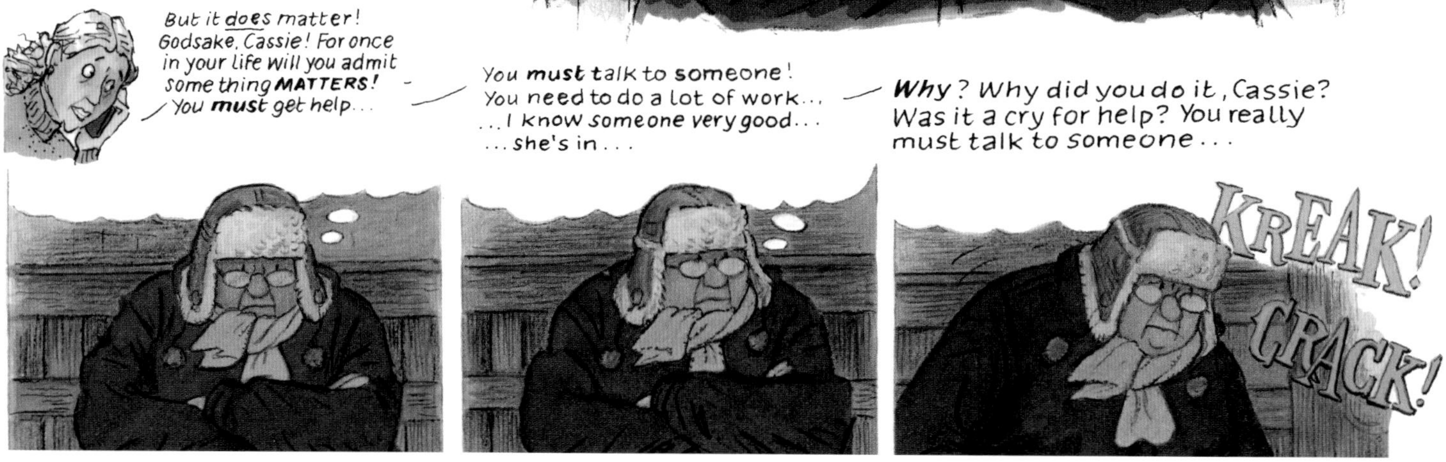

But it does matter! Godsake, Cassie! For once in your life will you admit something MATTERS! You must get help...
You must talk to someone! You need to do a lot of work... ...I know someone very good... ...she's in...
Why? Why did you do it, Cassie? Was it a cry for help? You really must talk to someone...
KREAK!
CRACK!

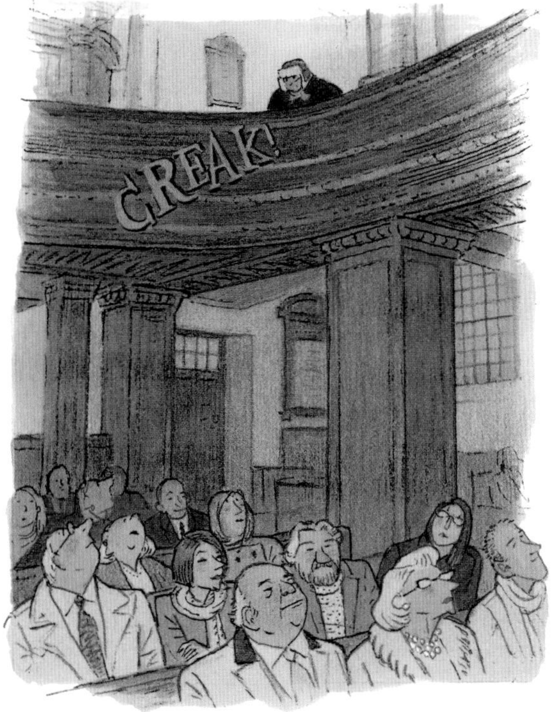

CREAK!

Time to go. A ripple of nudges goes along a pew and more faces look up. One of them is Nicki's. Nicki, treacherous little shit. But who has at least turned up to remember her father.

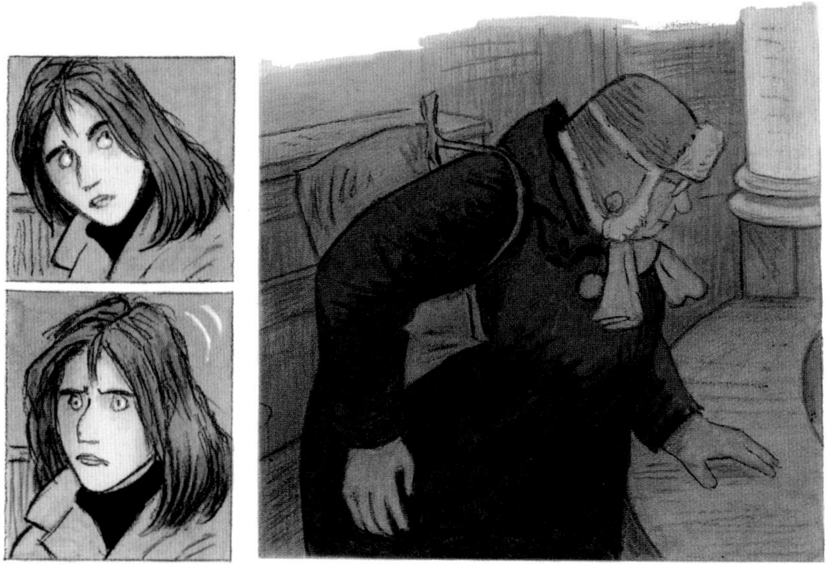

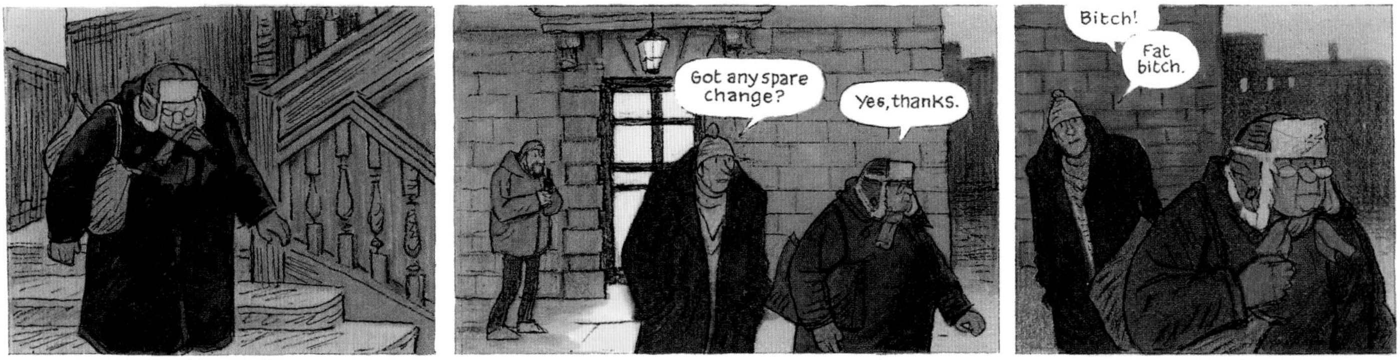
Got any spare change?
Yes, thanks.
Bitch!
Fat bitch.

One thing I didn't need reminding of in church was the risk of an awful lingering death like Freddie's. I am terrified of Alzheimer's – or anything else which leaves you half dead. Spoilt for choice, if it were a choice. While I am capable I plan to see myself out, to kick the bucket. And sooner rather than later given my age and size. I would rather be dead than rot in an "assisted living situation". And in any case I can't afford it without selling the house and I am NOT doing that.

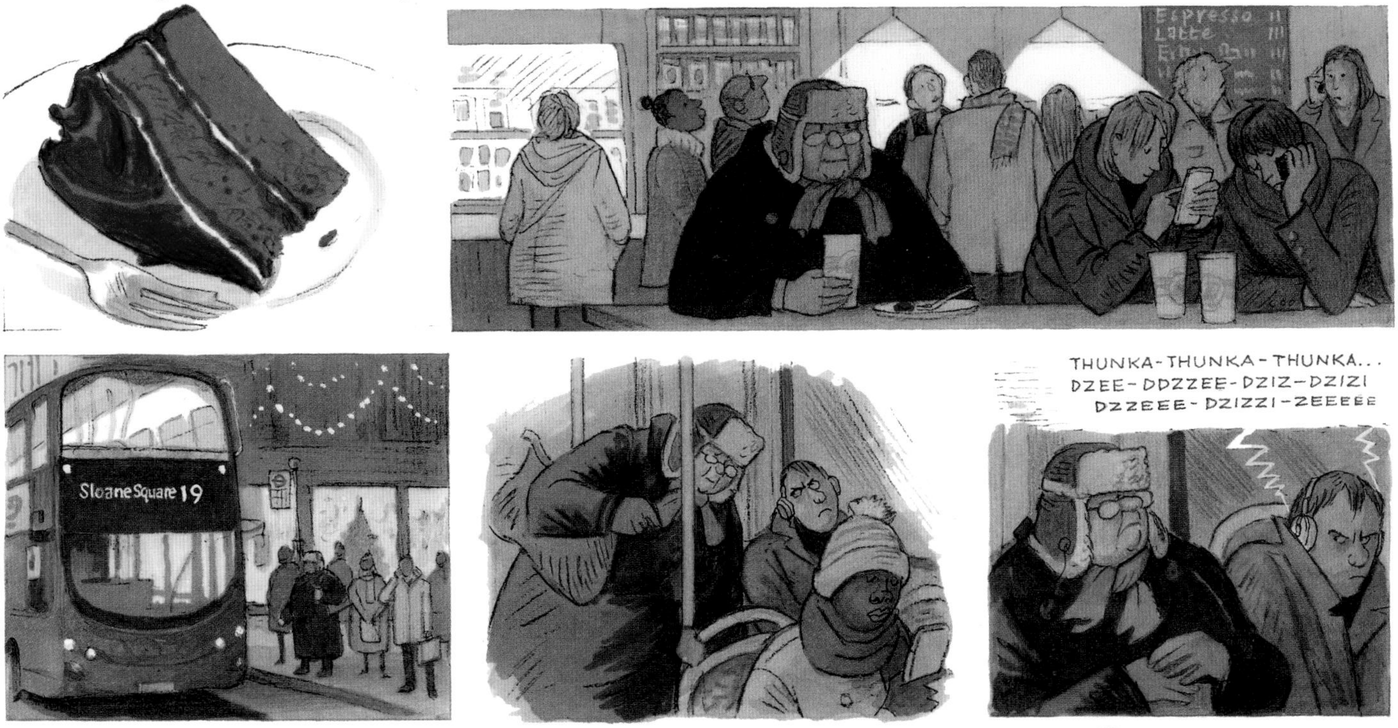
Sloane Square 19
THUNKA-THUNKA-THUNKA...
DZEE-DDZZEE-DZIZ-DZIZI
DZZEEE-DZIZZI-ZEEEEE

All the way to Sloane Square the horrors run through my head, of living with hoists, ramps and grab bars, of slow death in a locked ward, of Christmas after Christmas in the twilight home. Spare me that. I will see myself out, which means not leaving it too late.
Timing will be everything.
Croak while you can.

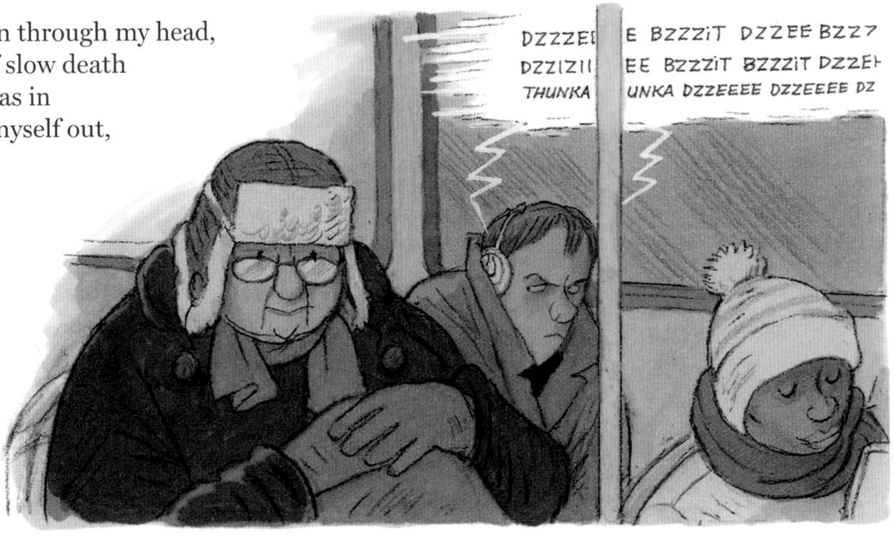
DZZZE E BZZZiT DZZEE BZZ
DZZIZI EE BZZZiT BZZZiT DZZE
THUNKA UNKA DZZEEEE DZZEEEE DZ

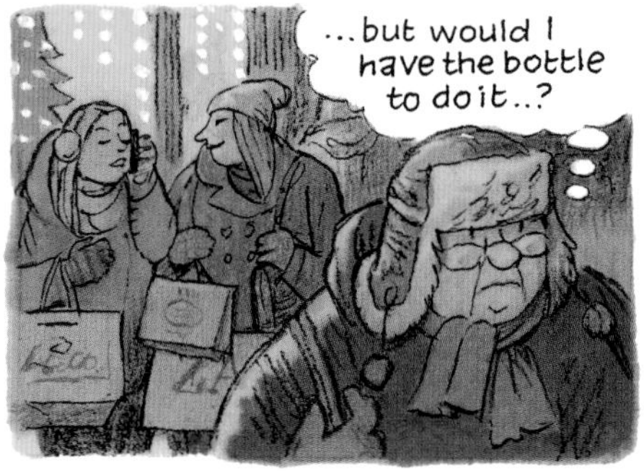
...but would I have the bottle to do it..?

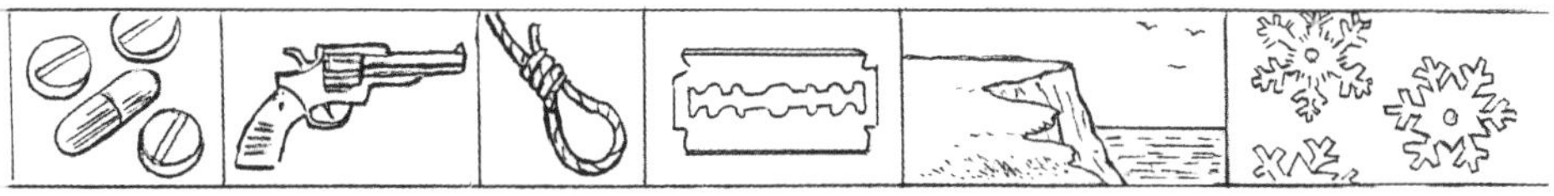

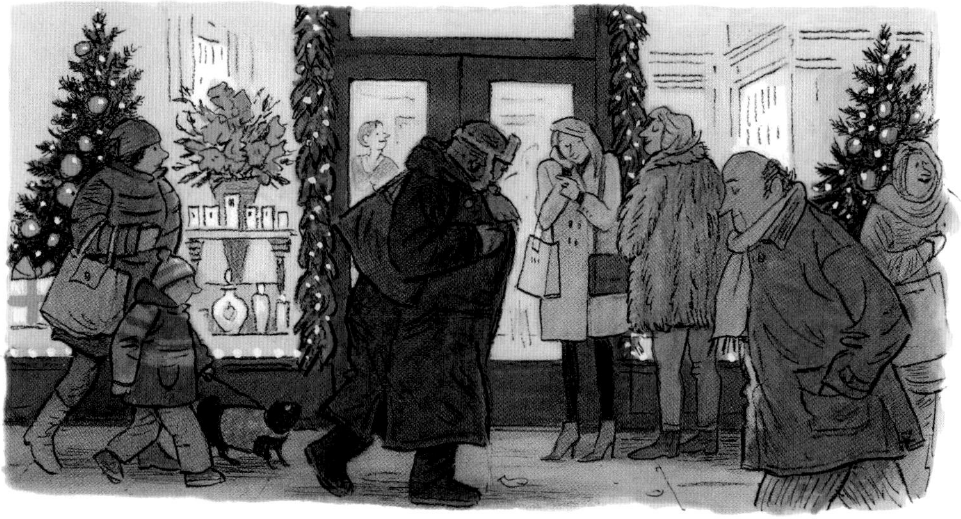

The Nazis did it with a revolver and 300mg of cyanide. Every method is grim. All things considered, I suppose hypothermia is best – a cold night, whisky, opera on the headphones, my garden the obvious place. The neighbours – Russians one side, Chinese the other – are rarely there, thank God. I dislike the garden, which is Zen-ish and a mistake. When I had a gardener the gravel was raked, but now it's a mess of weeds and algae and stinks of fox. There are four lumps of rock and, if push came to shove, come the frozen dawn, my body would make another. Then, very likely, builders would spot me. There's always scaffolding around here – people can't stop extending up, digging down. Gyms, cinemas, panic rooms.

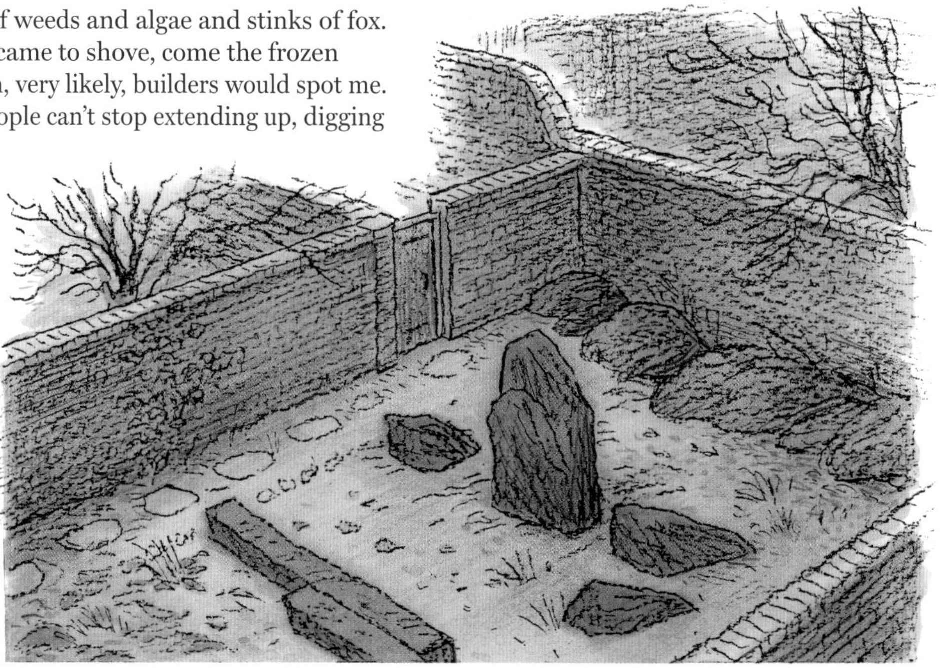

I haven't ignored the downside of freezing to death: the shivering, the confusion as major organs pack up; the urge to hide in a confined space ("terminal burrowing" it's called); the casting-off of clothes ("paradoxical undressing". Which, for me, would be the worst aspect, being found naked on dirty gravel. Hardly Zen.)

My ideal death would be soundless obliteration under deep, deep snow. Winter landscapes, in art and nature, have always appealed and I really wouldn't mind being another hump in a painting by Caspar David Friedrich. Of course, when the snow melted I'd end up spoiling someone's day ...

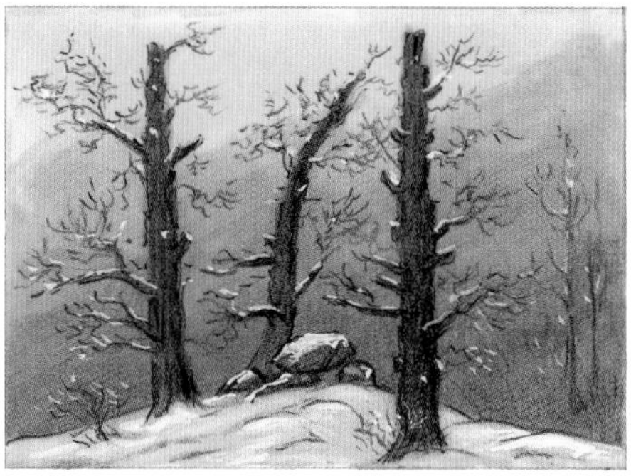

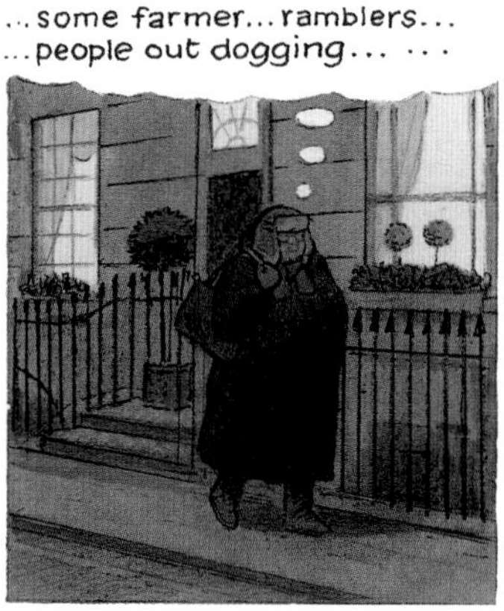
...some farmer...ramblers...
...people out dogging... ...

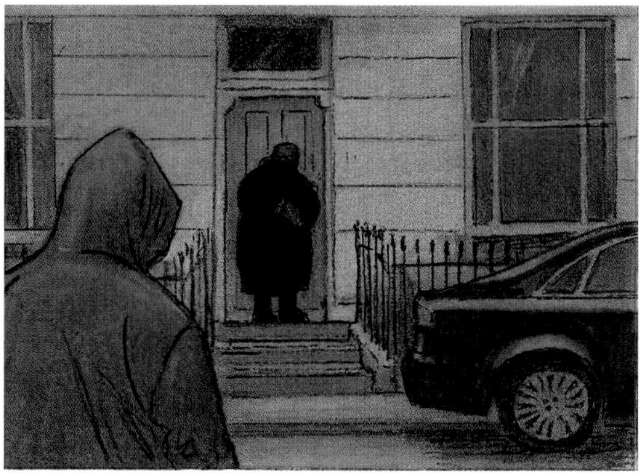

The alarm doesn't bleat.

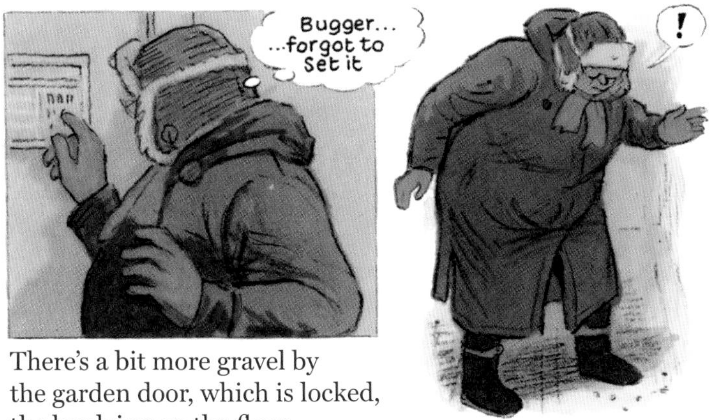
Bugger... ...forgot to set it
!

Then, as I trudge down the hall, something crunches underfoot.

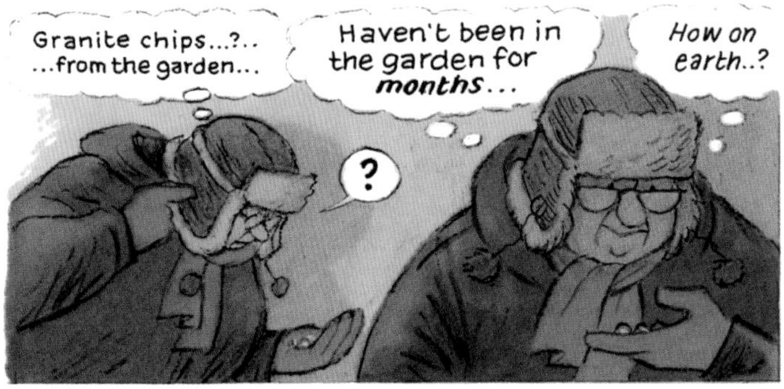
Granite chips...?.. ...from the garden...
Haven't been in the garden for *months*...
?
How on earth..?

There's a bit more gravel by the garden door, which is locked, the key lying on the floor.

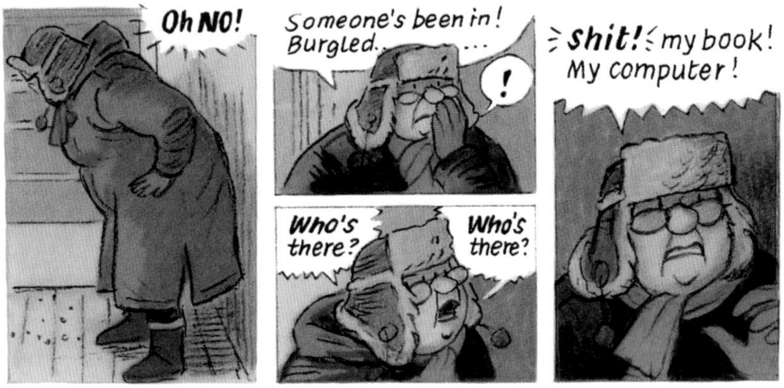
Oh NO!
Someone's been in! Burgled.. ...
!
Who's there?
Who's there?
shit! my book! My computer!

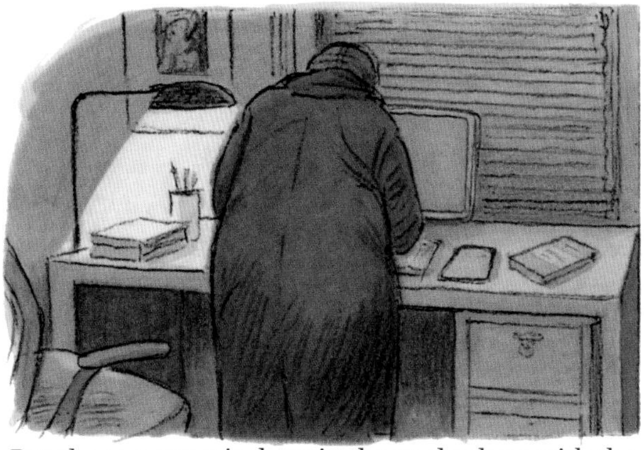

But the computer is there in the study along with the iPad, notebooks, everything.

I make my way through the house, snapping on the lights. As the cream of my art collection is in the gallery in Hampshire, there's nothing much worth stealing apart from a Patrick Heron, one or two prints and a couple of things which *look* right but I know to be fakes. All there anyway. Upstairs in the bedroom the Kang-xi porcelain is untouched. Nothing is disturbed or missing, even the pocketable stuff – my few bits and bobs of jewellery. I am unburgled, it seems.

There's an obvious explanation; no one comes in the house these days except the cleaner, Milena. Last week she must have gone in the garden for a smoke and brought the gravel in on her shoes – and I just haven't noticed. Or there is another more paranoid explanation.

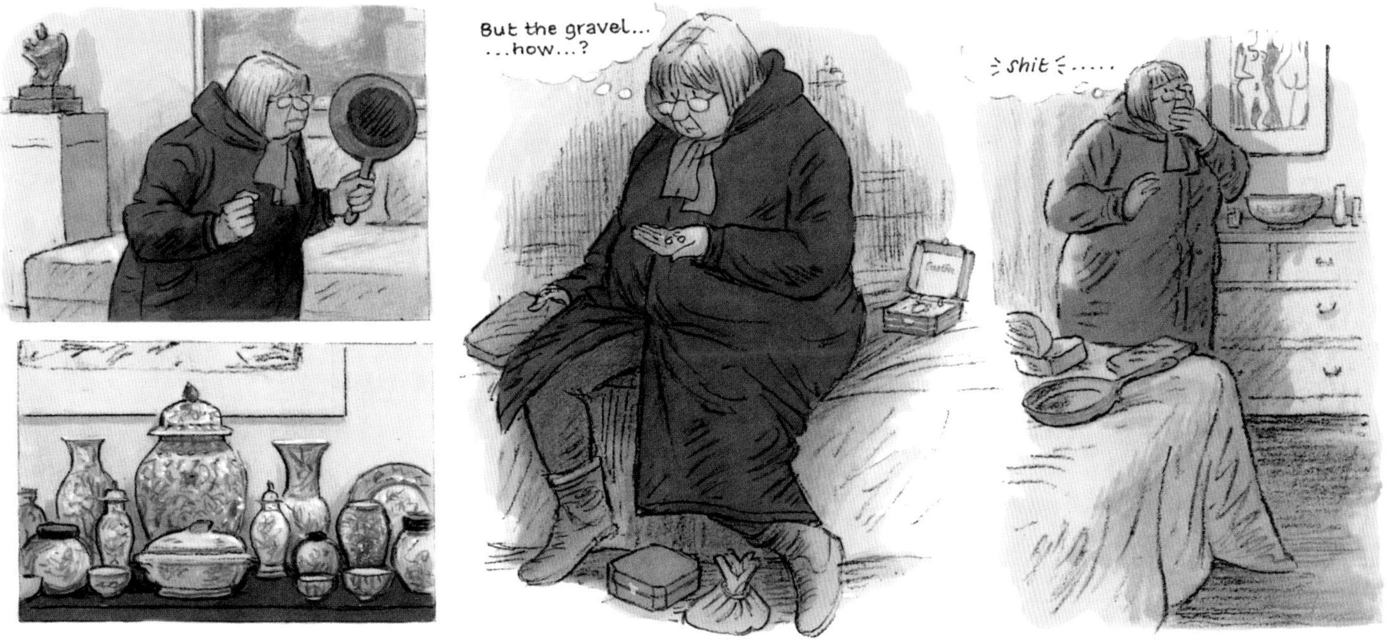
But the gravel... ...how...?
shit .....

Last year Freddie and Margot's daughter Nicki worked for me. I remember that she would also smoke in the garden and bring gravel in the house on her brothel creepers.

I realise this is a bit absurd, because after what happened later, Nicki has every reason to avoid me. But she did have keys and could have copied them; she knew at least one of my alarm codes. And she probably hates me. Good enough reason for checking the basement, where last year I stupidly let her stay.

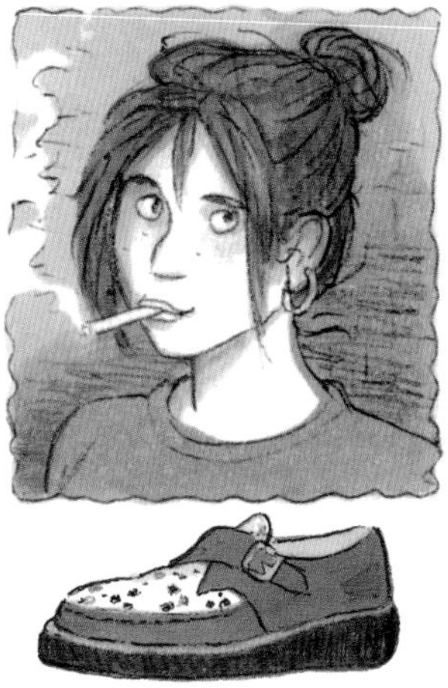

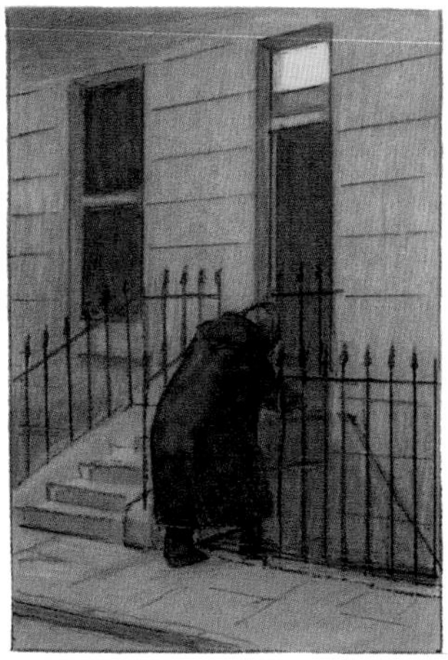

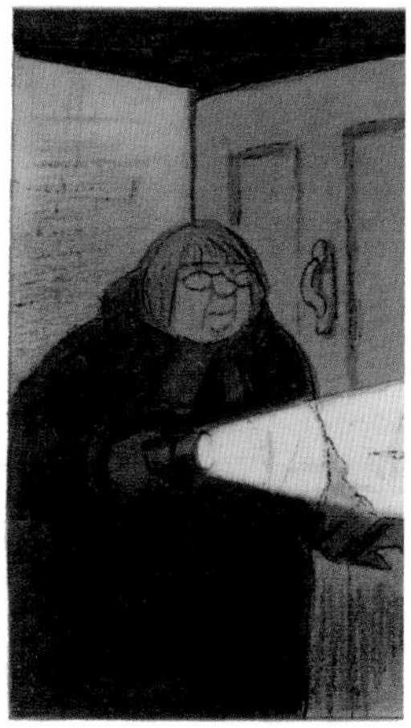

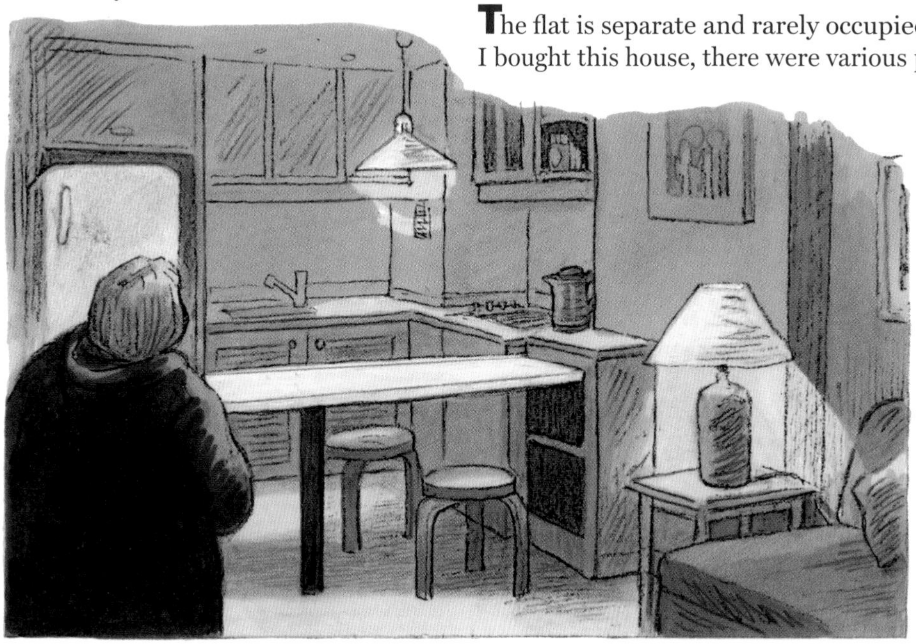

The flat is separate and rarely occupied. In the 1970s, when Freddie and I bought this house, there were various plans: it was where the nanny would live, supposing we had children; where children would doss as teenagers; it was for a lodger, if money was tight, and eventually for the staff who would look after us in old age. *Fat chance of affording that now.*

I haven't been down here since Nicki moved out, leaving it like a pigsty – Milena had to be paid extra to muck it out.

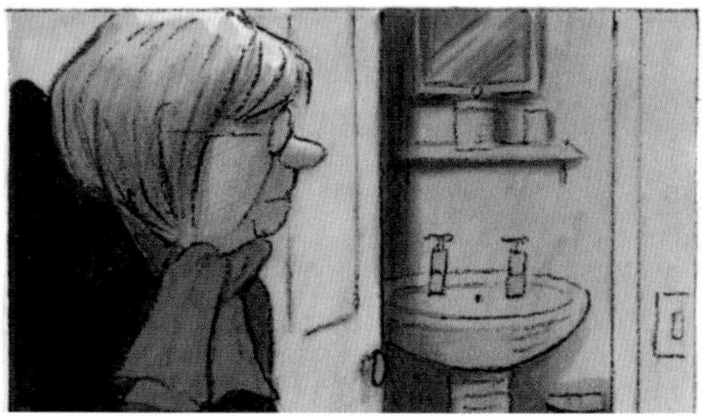

Everything is in order. There's no trace of Nicki, except for something glittering on the bathroom floor ...

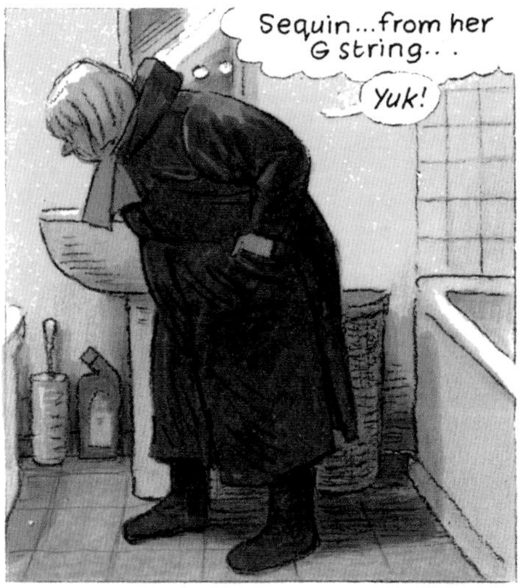
Sequin...from her G string...
Yuk!

... and a grubby towel in the bin.

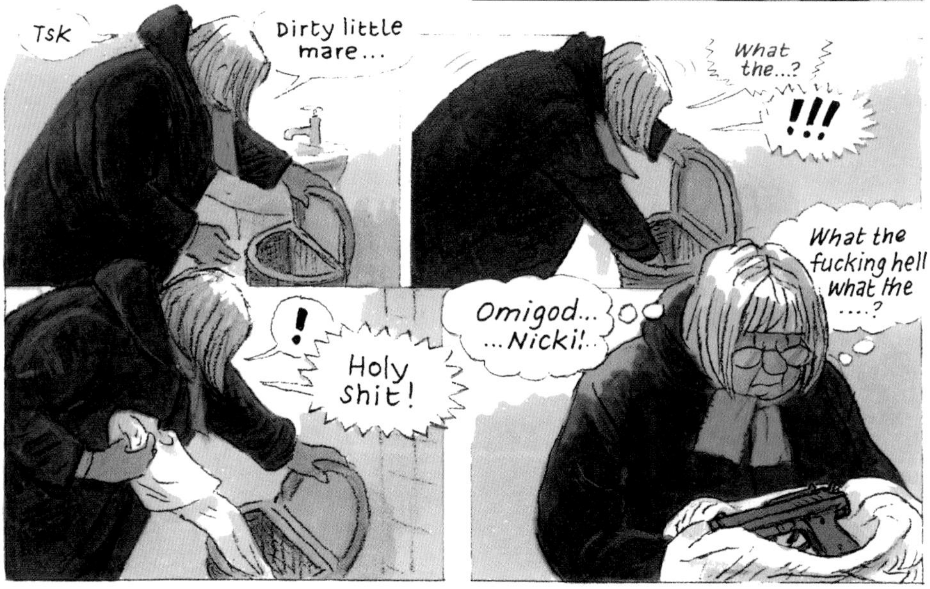
Tsk
Dirty little mare...
What the...?
!!!
!
Holy shit!
Omigod... ...Nicki!
What the fucking hell what the ....?

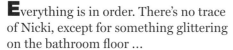

I saw two other things at the bottom of the bin: a magazine of bullets and a glove. Except I never saw them. I replaced the gun and shut the lid. I've been in enough trouble recently. I haven't seen a gun. I haven't seen anything at all.

I switched off the electrics, I locked up. Came in, ordered a burger …

… which I can barely eat.

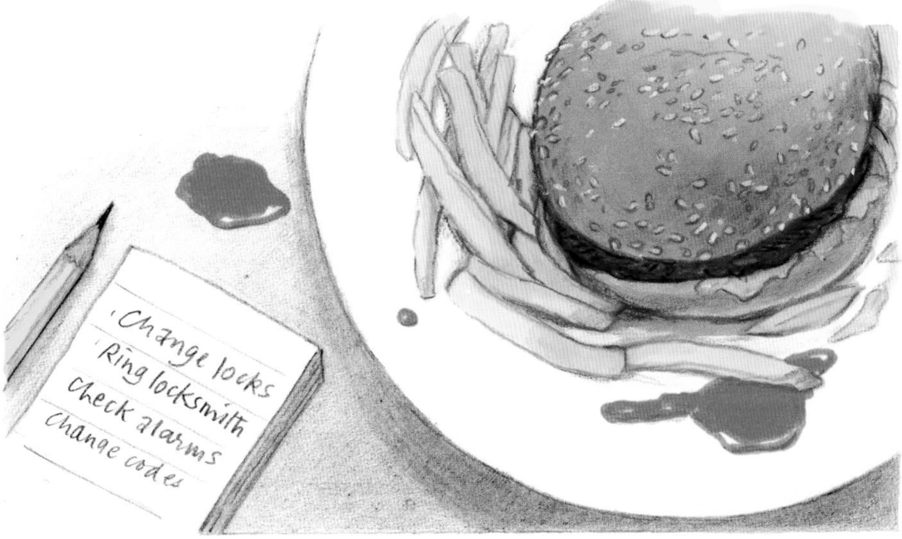
'Change locks
'Ring locksmith
Check alarms
Change codes

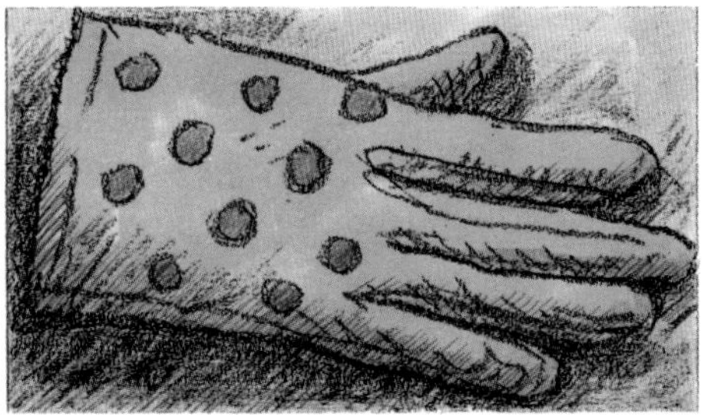

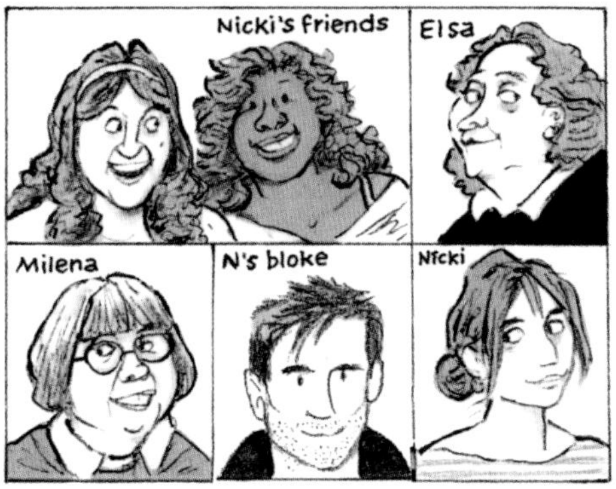
Nicki's friends
Elsa
Milena
N's bloke
Nicki

The gun seems to weigh down the house, weighs me down, as though I've swallowed it. The glove is a sort of lung pink, with raised spots like scabs. I watch enough police programmes on TV to know that gloves and guns are partners in crime. I imagine Nicki's pink wool finger on the trigger. *Am I, was I a target? Or someone else? How long had the things been in the bin?*

I sit for hours. Sometimes I'm rational, thinking of other people who've been in the basement. I eliminate Milena and Elsa, my ex-housekeeper, both grandmothers and devout Catholics – although I wonder if Milena found the gun when she cleaned and whether she left it where it was, like I did. And kept shtum, as I intend to.

I eliminate Nicki's girl friends, frightful gigglers. Which leaves Nicki's fellow, a sort of upper-class lizard who came round to fornicate. And Nicki herself. Towards the end of the bottle I have a good mind to stick the gun in Nicki's ribs, frighten the shit out of her for the way she leeched off my generosity, for her lies, and for generally buggering up my life. *But what to do? What to do?*

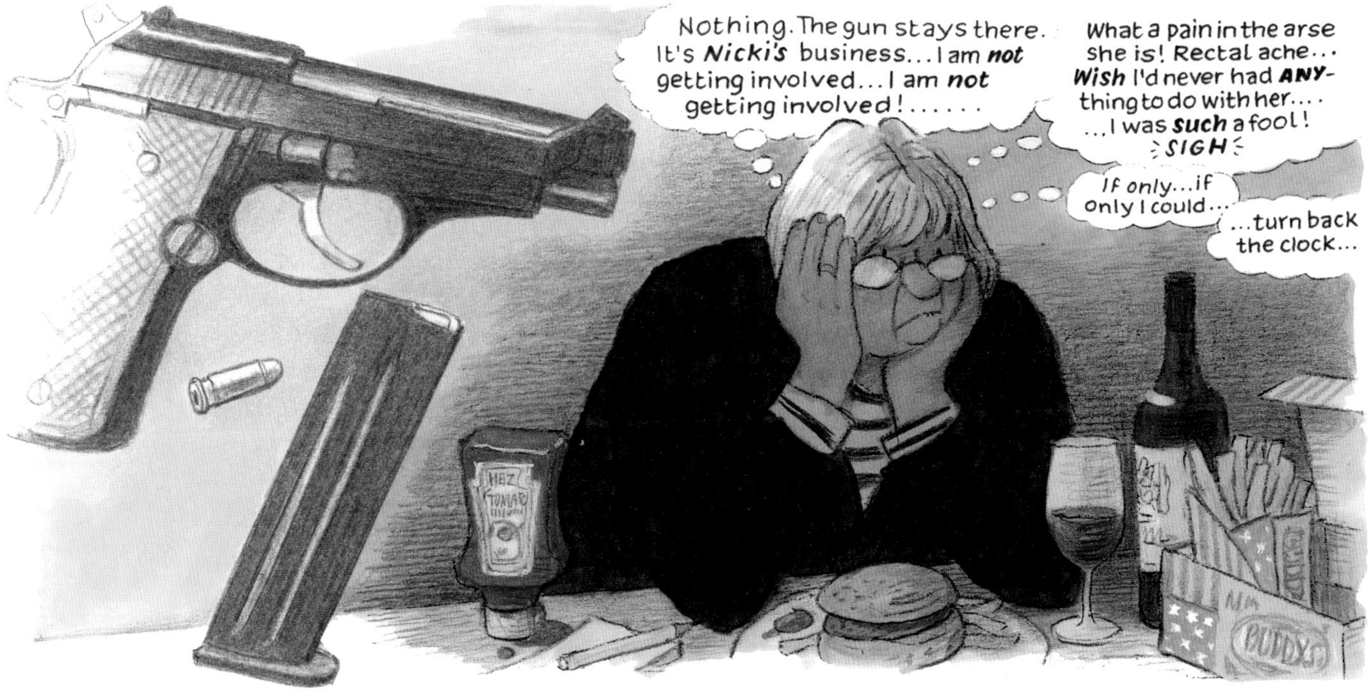
Nothing. The gun stays there. It's **Nicki's** business… I am **not** getting involved… I am **not** getting involved! ……
What a pain in the arse she is! Rectal ache… **Wish** I'd never had **ANY**-thing to do with her… …I was **such** a fool! **SIGH**
If only…if only I could…
…turn back the clock…

The Events of 2016

Nicki Boult came to see me out of the blue last September …

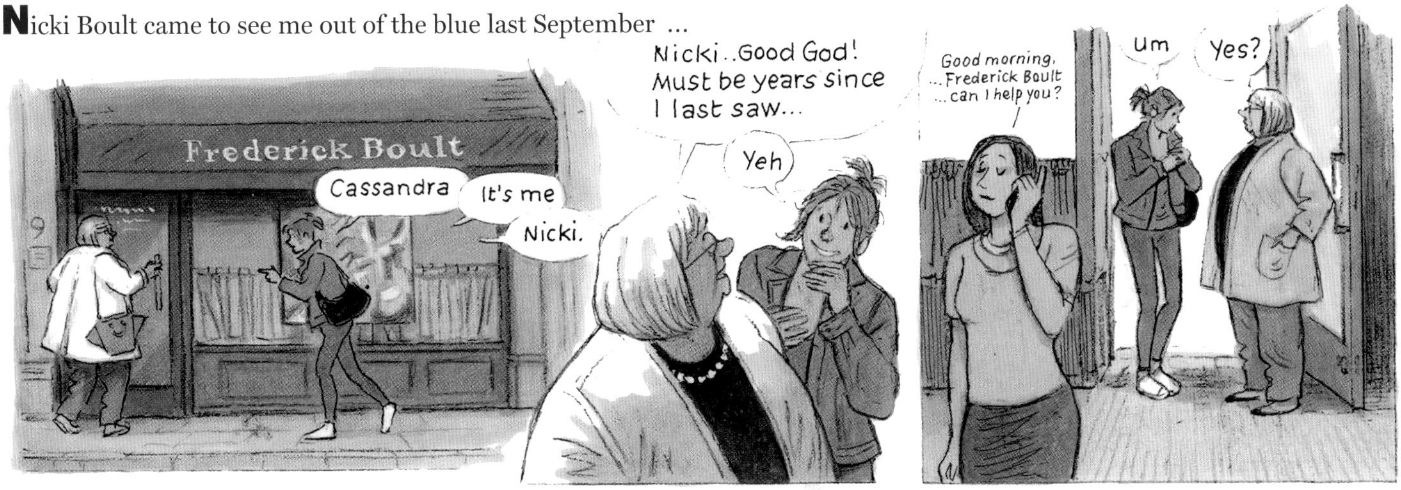

Frederick Boult
Cassandra
It's me
Nicki.
Nicki..Good God! Must be years since I last saw...
Yeh
Good morning, ...Frederick Boult ...can I help you?
Um
Yes?

Nicki came straight to the point and asked me if I would finance an art project of hers. She was completely broke, she said. A few years out of art college, she had lost her studio space in Deptford and her share of a flat; she was working nights in a bar and sleeping on friends' sofas. All this related quite cheerfully as if it was just a blip in an otherwise privileged life.

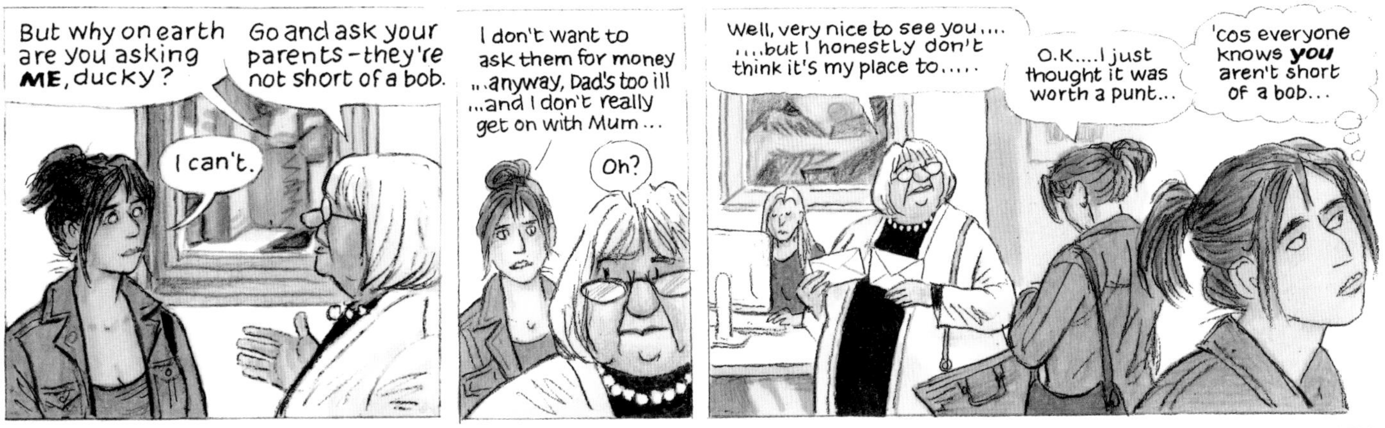

But why on earth are you asking **ME**, ducky?
Go and ask your parents – they're not short of a bob.
I can't.
I don't want to ask them for money ...anyway, Dad's too ill ...and I don't really get on with Mum...
Oh?
Well, very nice to see you.... ....but I honestly don't think it's my place to.....
O.K....I just thought it was worth a punt...
'cos everyone knows **you** aren't short of a bob...

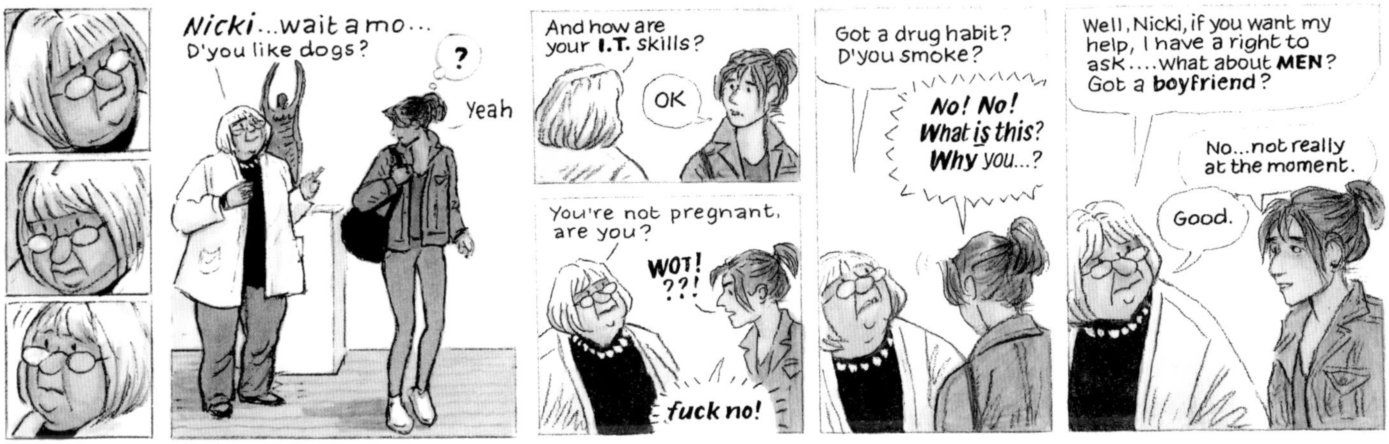

Nicki...wait a mo... D'you like dogs?
?
Yeah
And how are your **I.T.** skills?
OK
You're not pregnant, are you?
WOT! ??!
fuck no!
Got a drug habit? D'you smoke?
No! No! What is this? Why you...?
Well, Nicki, if you want my help, I have a right to ask....what about **MEN**? Got a **boyfriend**?
No...not really at the moment.
Good.

That was how I came to offer Nicki a very generous break – a roof over her head in my basement and a small loan. Naturally I didn't offer it to her on a plate (which is what young people seem to expect these days). I made certain conditions: There would be a trial period; Nicki would provide technical assistance – scanning, photoshopping images for my book, transcribing notes, and so on. And she would exercise my poor pug, who was alive then. (I had been paying a dog walker through the nose for this service.)

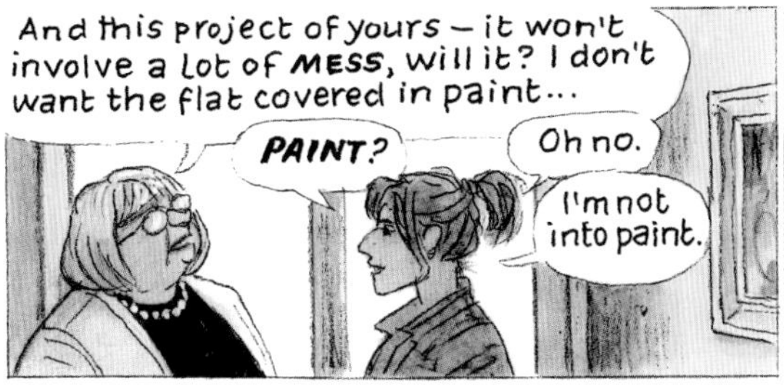

And this project of yours – it won't involve a lot of **MESS**, will it? I don't want the flat covered in paint...
PAINT?
Oh no.
I'm not into paint.

No, Nicki wasn't into paint. Her thing was "posing" – which seemed to involve being tiresome in art galleries, while a friend filmed her and posted the result online. As I shun social media, naturally I'd never heard of "Abused Nudes".

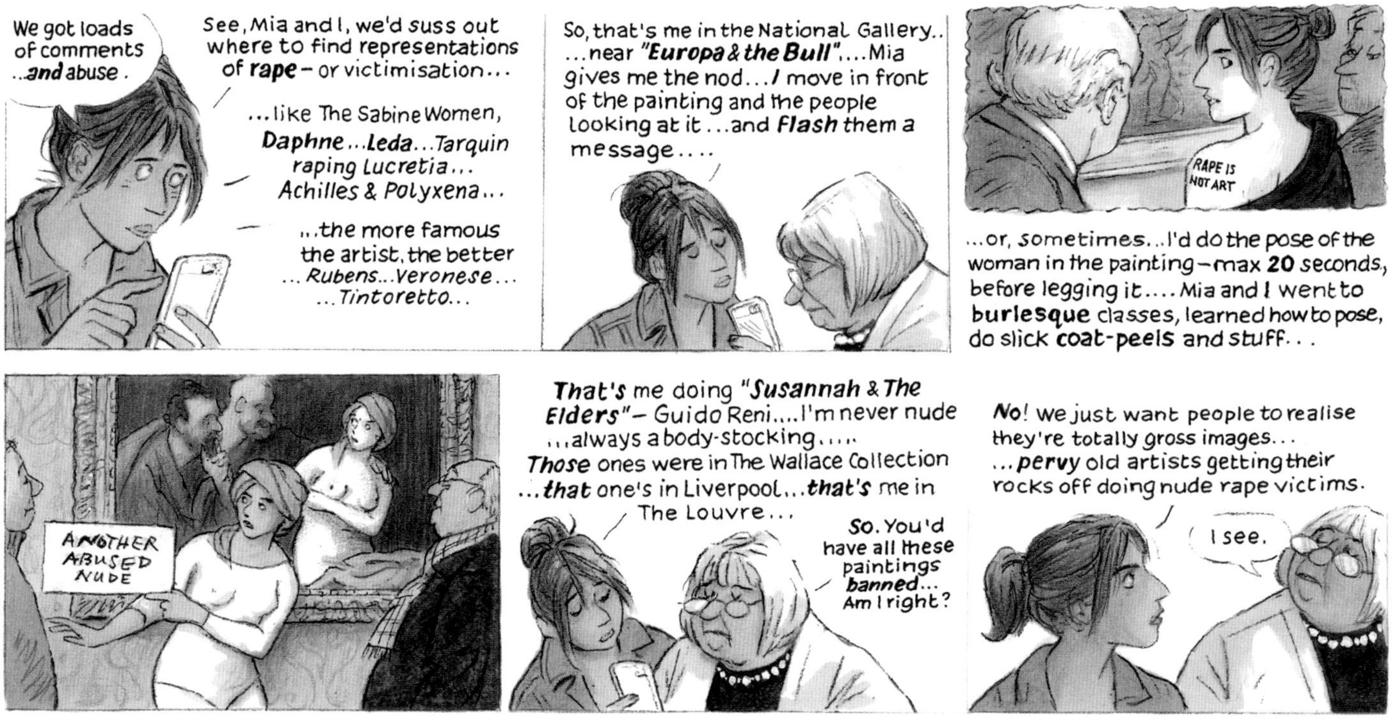
We got loads of comments ...**and** abuse.
See, Mia and I, we'd suss out where to find representations of **rape** – or victimisation...
...like The Sabine Women, **Daphne**...**Leda**...Tarquin raping Lucretia... Achilles & Polyxena...
...the more famous the artist, the better ... *Rubens*...*Veronese*... ...*Tintoretto*...
So, that's me in the National Gallery.. ...near "**Europa & the Bull**"....Mia gives me the nod... **I** move in front of the painting and the people looking at it...and **Flash** them a message....
RAPE IS NOT ART
...or, sometimes...I'd do the pose of the woman in the painting – max **20** seconds, before legging it.... Mia and **I** went to **burlesque** classes, learned how to pose, do slick **coat-peels** and stuff...
ANOTHER ABUSED NUDE
That's me doing "**Susannah & The Elders**" – Guido Reni....I'm never nude ...always a body-stocking.....
Those ones were in The Wallace Collection ...**that** one's in Liverpool...**that's** me in The Louvre...
So. You'd have all these paintings **banned**... Am I right?
No! we just want people to realise they're totally gross images... ...**pervy** old artists getting their rocks off doing nude rape victims.
I see.

"**A**nd you think people can't work that out for themselves?" I said. "How very patronising." Nicki said nothing and I saw that she was easily crushed. Anyway, she moved in downstairs and most days, came up and made herself useful. She was fine with the dog and OK on the computer – a spare Mac containing nothing personal, just drafts of my book. But she *was* a great interrupter, always asking about my art collection, the artists I have known ...

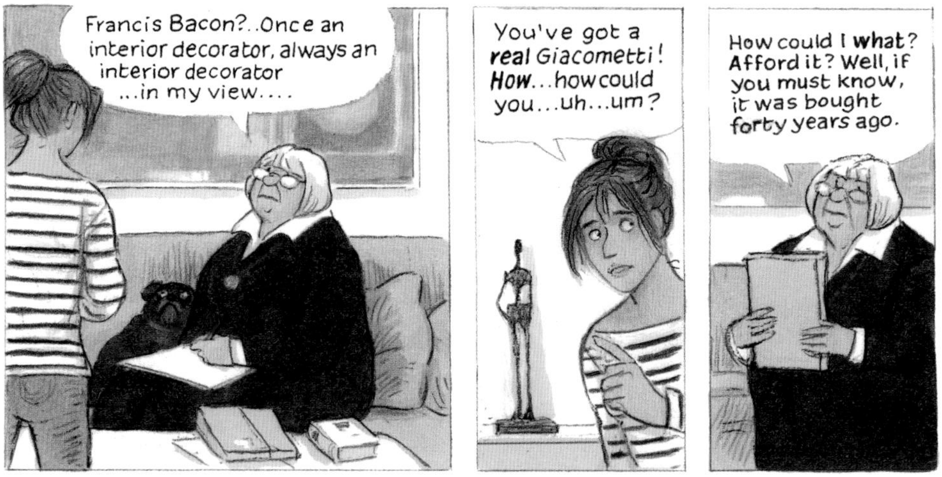
Francis Bacon?..Once an interior decorator, always an interior decorator ...in my view....
You've got a **real** *Giacometti*! **How**...how could you...uh...um?
How could I **what**? Afford it? Well, if you must know, it was bought forty years ago.

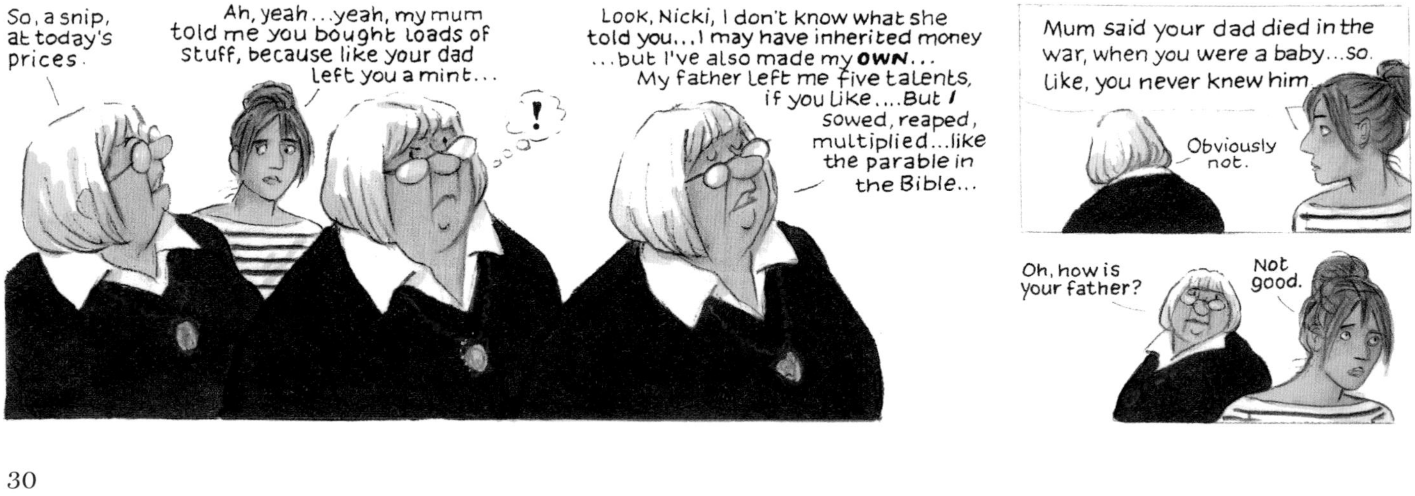
So, a snip, at today's prices.
Ah, yeah...yeah, my mum told me you bought loads of stuff, because like your dad left you a mint...
!
Look, Nicki, I don't know what she told you...I may have inherited money ...but I've also made my **OWN**... My father left me five talents, if you like....But **I** sowed, reaped, multiplied...like the parable in the Bible...
Mum said your dad died in the war, when you were a baby...so, like, you never knew him.
Obviously not.
Oh, how is your father?
Not good.

The advantage of Nicki was that she would do everything I couldn't ask my housekeeper or the girls in the gallery to do.

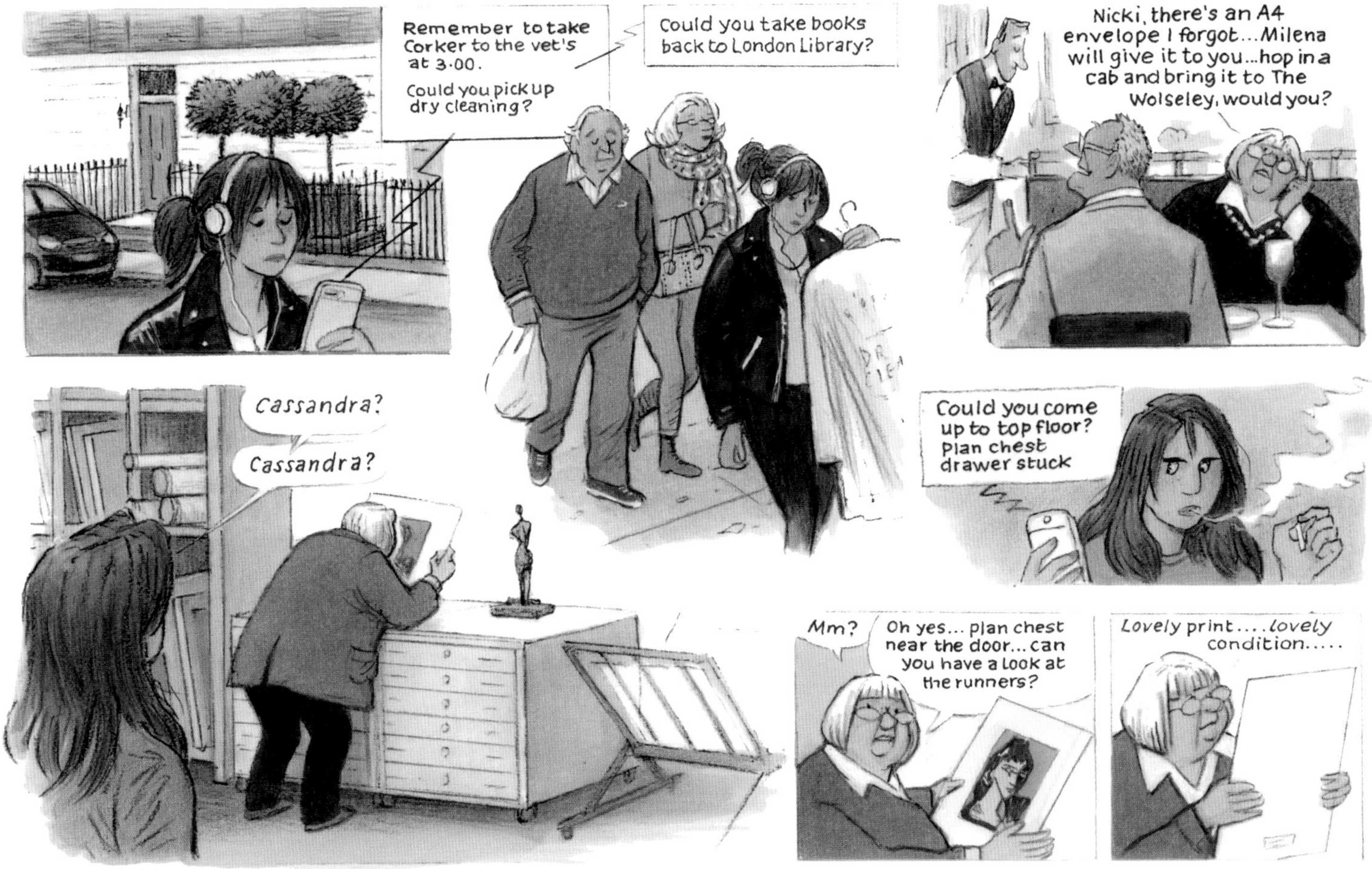

Remember to take Corker to the vet's at 3.00.
Could you pick up dry cleaning?
Could you take books back to London Library?
Nicki, there's an A4 envelope I forgot...Milena will give it to you...hop in a cab and bring it to The Wolseley, would you?
Cassandra?
Cassandra?
Could you come up to top floor? Plan chest drawer stuck
Mm?
Oh yes... plan chest near the door... can you have a look at the runners?
Lovely print.... lovely condition.....

I suppose I grew used to Nicki being around and trusted her to the extent of handing over petty cash and house keys when she ran errands. Otherwise I knew nothing about her life beyond the facts that she had a project to do and worked evenings in some bar. She did tell me that she found her mother difficult ("cut and run" was my advice). The main thing I noticed was her bloody phone. She was always fiddling with it or taking stupid photographs. She often sat gassing on the steps (in that attitude which always reminds me of Renaissance portrayals of Melancholia ... Dürer, or that woodcut by Virgilis Solis the Elder).

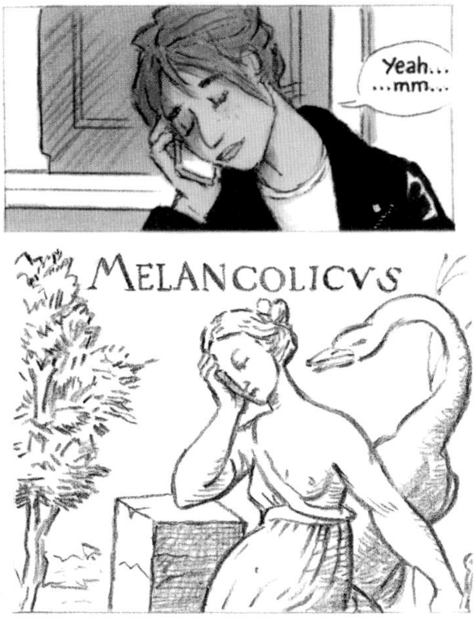

Yeah... ...mm...
MELANCOLICVS

I did notice when she dyed her hair pink. And once or twice I saw her arsing about in the square, but never thought to find out what she was doing.
My big mistake.

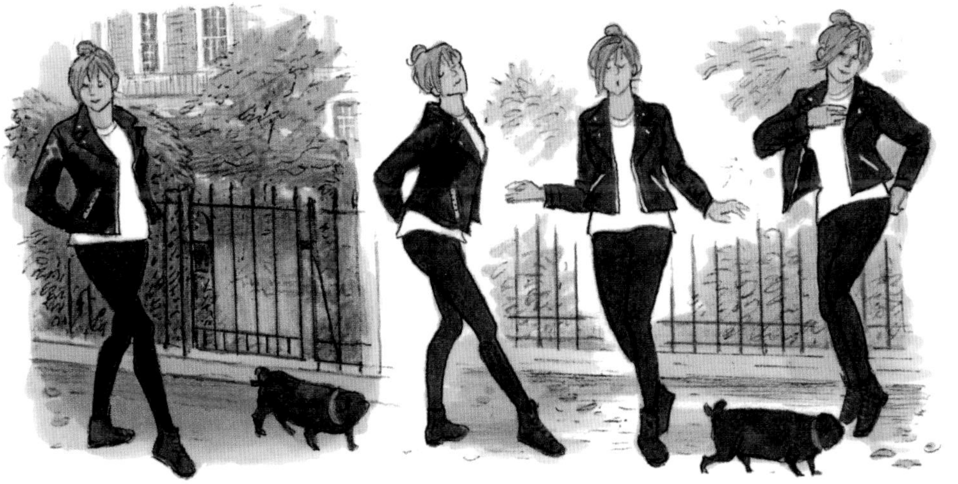

Nicki couldn't think how Cassandra was still alive, why she hadn't been stabbed or at least seriously duffed up. Most mornings, while waiting for the car, she would be out there snarling ...

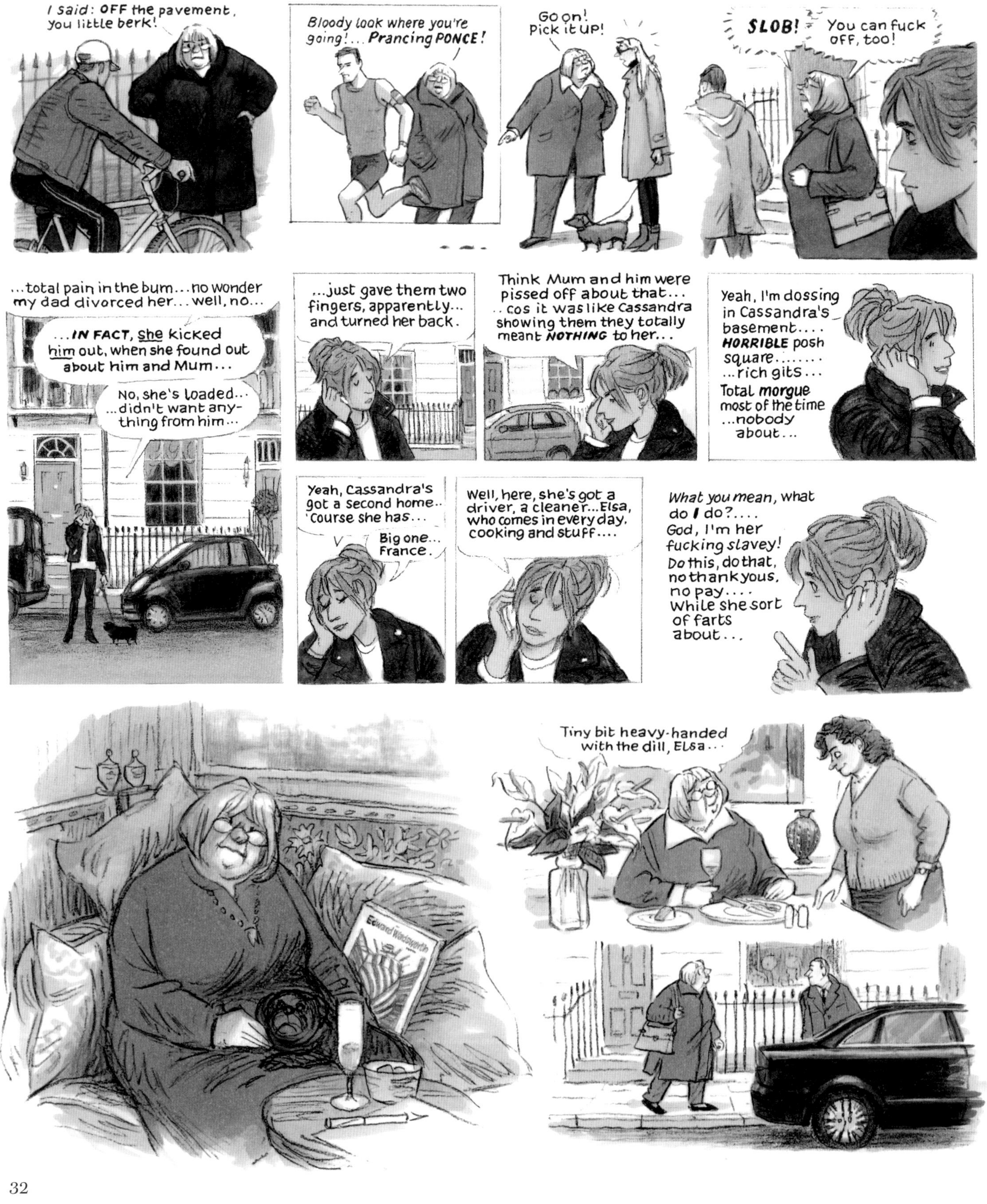

I said: OFF the pavement, you little berk!
Bloody look where you're going!... Prancing PONCE!
Go on! Pick it up!
SLOB!
You can fuck off, too!
...total pain in the bum... no wonder my dad divorced her... well, no...
...IN FACT, she kicked him out, when she found out about him and Mum...
No, she's loaded... ...didn't want anything from him...
...just gave them two fingers, apparently... and turned her back.
Think Mum and him were pissed off about that... ..cos it was like Cassandra showing them they totally meant NOTHING to her...
Yeah, I'm dossing in Cassandra's basement.... HORRIBLE posh square....... ...rich gits... Total morgue most of the time ...nobody about...
Yeah, Cassandra's got a second home.. 'Course she has...
Big one... France.
Well, here, she's got a driver, a cleaner...Elsa, who comes in every day, cooking and stuff....
What you mean, what do I do?.... God, I'm her fucking slavey! Do this, do that, no thank yous, no pay.... While she sort of farts about...
Edward Wadsworth
Tiny bit heavy-handed with the dill, Elsa...

The problem for Nicki was how to balance her distaste for the extreme ponciness of Cassandra's part of town with the benefits she enjoyed there – rent-free comfort, space, privacy, heating. It was easier to think of herself as a servant, a more privileged one, certainly, but not entirely unlike the Filipina maids she saw in Osmington Square. Nicki had barely touched her own work. Elsa had given her the remains of Cassandra's lunchtime bottle of Haut Brion, but it didn't help much. She felt blank, alien, vaguely contaminated.

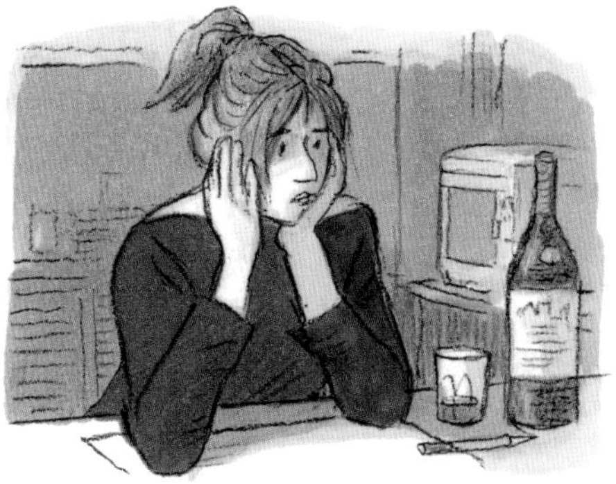

Outside, walking the pug, things were better. She felt more focused. She strolled the neighbourhood taking photos and looking up local house prices on her phone. (Before the market stalled, Cassandra's was worth £8 million.) Sloane Street was always worth a look for the limos and facelifts, the security men and the shoppers popping out for a few odds and ends at their local Dior. Everything was as Nicki expected, the smell of money hanging about like a gas. The only real money she saw was in Cassandra's petty cash drawer.

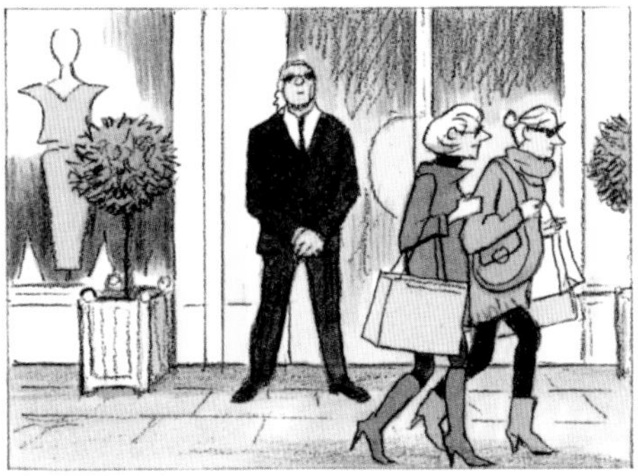

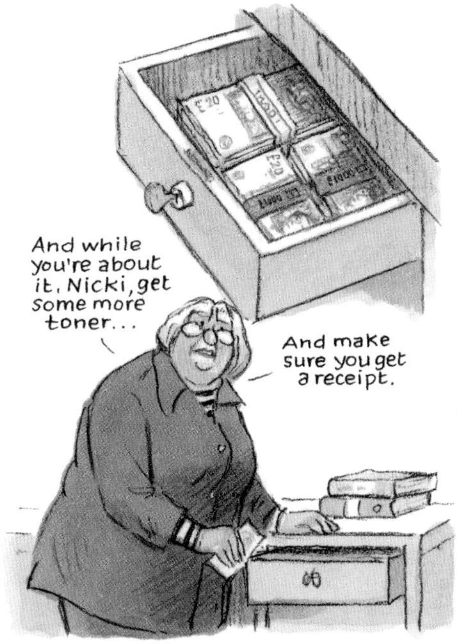
And while you're about it, Nicki, get some more toner...
And make sure you get a receipt.

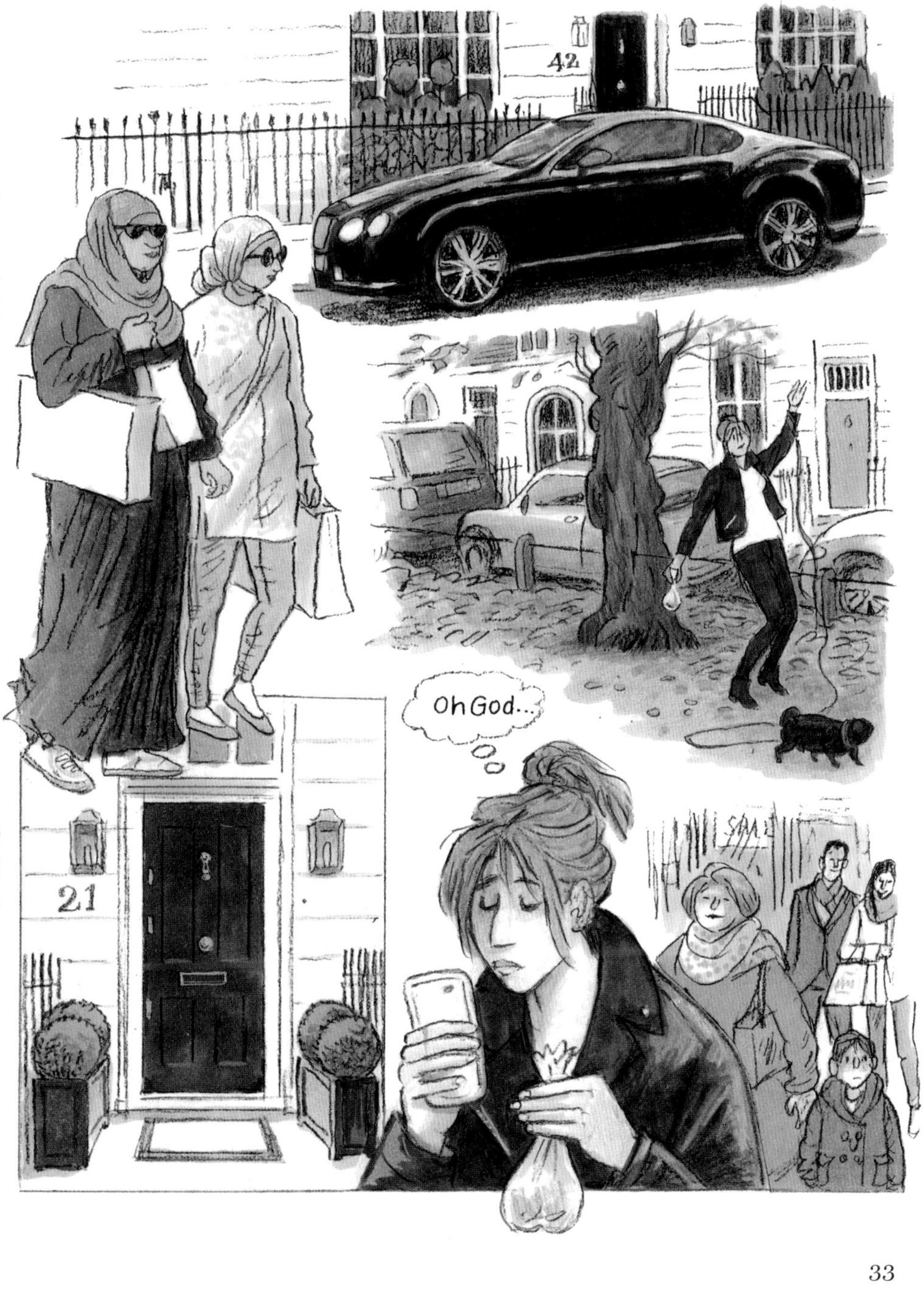
42
21
Oh God...

Nicki picked up after the dog, absently performed a shoulder shrug and was reminded of the horrible evening ahead. Mia's hen party. There would be a Champagne Burlesque session, true. But on her phone there was a thread she'd largely ignored, organising further details – details of Mia's Big Night. Vile, all of them.

Not going to the party was impossible. Mia would have created, even though she and Nicki were no longer close, no longer partners in crime. The days of "Abused Nudes" were over. When Mia took up with Luke, she found a proper job with a cancer charity, stopped smoking, started saving for a flat. She became distant, hard to get.

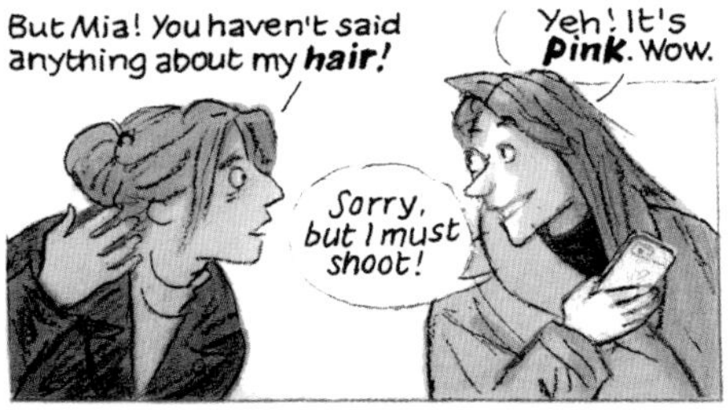
But Mia! You haven't said anything about my *hair!*
Yeh! It's **pink**. Wow.
Sorry, but I must shoot!

And as Mia stopped asking her advice (unthinkable in the past), Nicki didn't put her right about Luke.

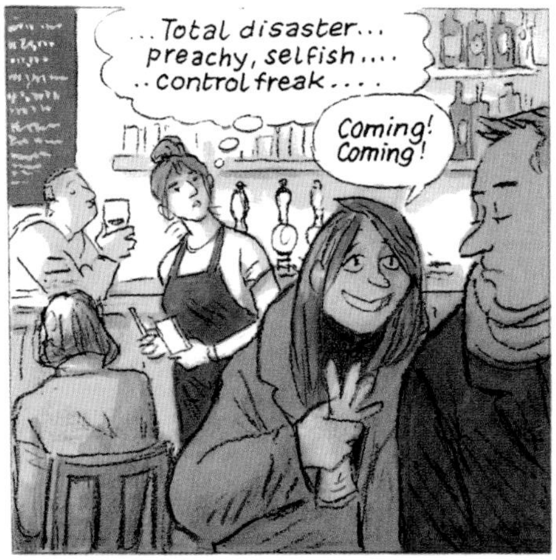
...Total disaster... preachy, selfish.... ..control freak....
Coming! Coming!

Now it was too late. Mia was about to screw up her life and Nicki was going to spend the evening looking pleased (in some ropey bar, wearing a cowboy hat and not much else).

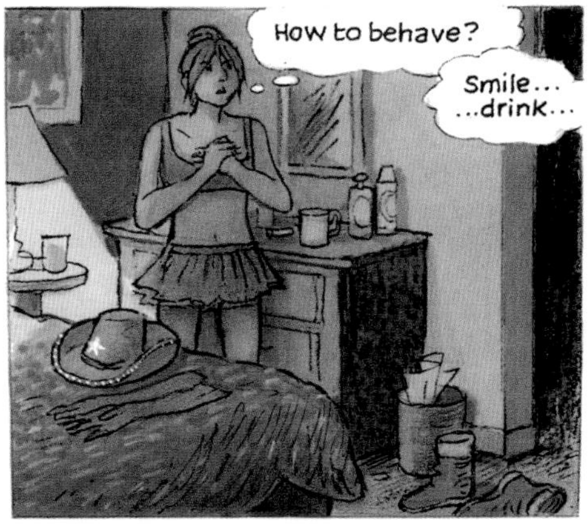
How to behave?
Smile... ...drink...

There was another reason to feel depressed. Mia had booked a burlesque session to start the evening. A reminder of the days when she was up for anything, when she and Nicki went to classes and learned how to dance and pose and peel off clothes. Eight of them gathered at Shimmy's, a dance place near King's Cross.

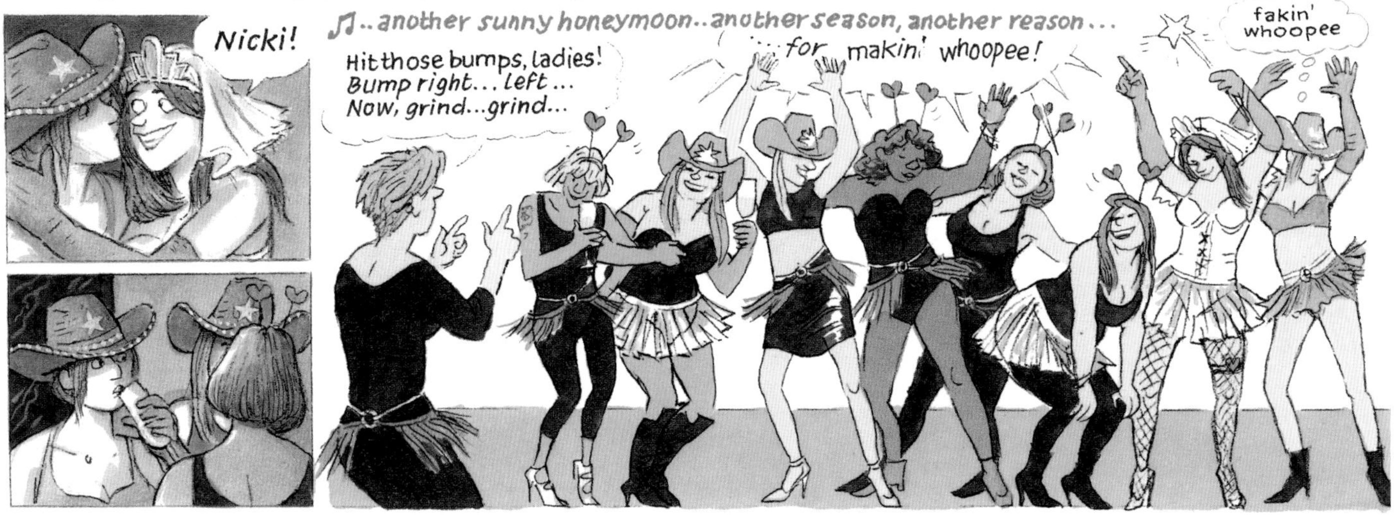
Nicki!
♫ ..another sunny honeymoon..another season, another reason...
...for makin' whoopee!
Hit those bumps, ladies! Bump right... left... Now, grind...grind...
fakin' whoopee

It was hard to keep a low profile – the thing about burlesque is showmanship, showing off and va-va-voom ...

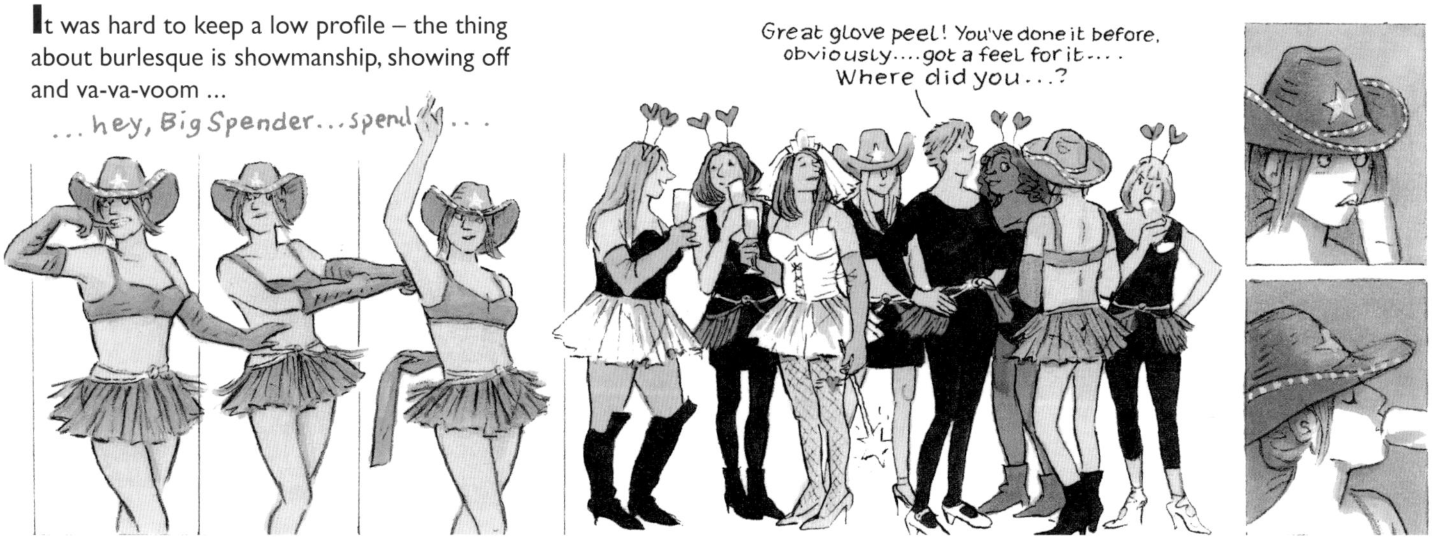
...hey, Big Spender...spend...
Great glove peel! You've done it before, obviously....got a feel for it.... Where did you...?

There was a brief bar crawl on the way to the evening's main venue ...

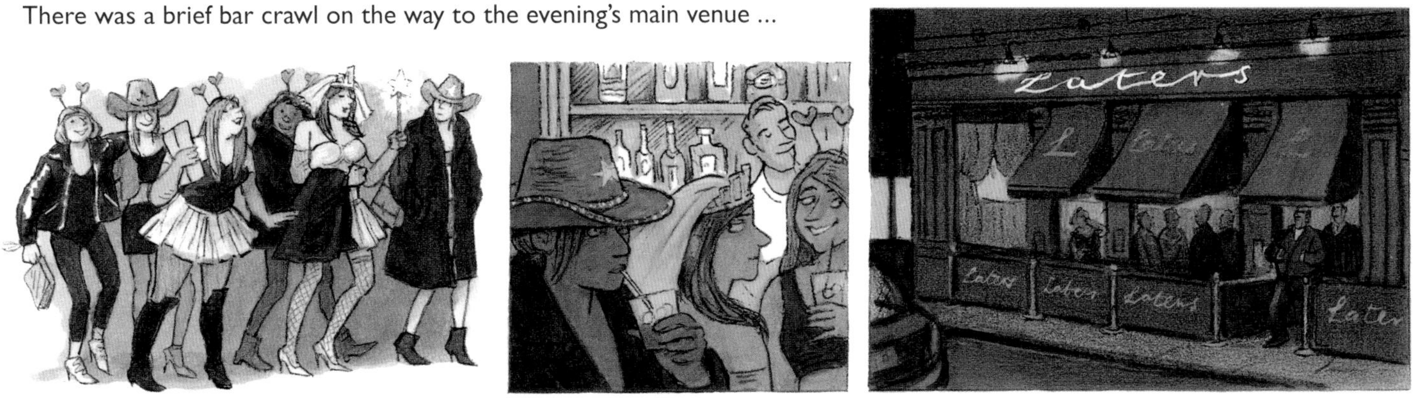
Laters

Then more drinks, toasts, downings-in-one, freak-out dancing, finger food, photos, hen-party accessories ...

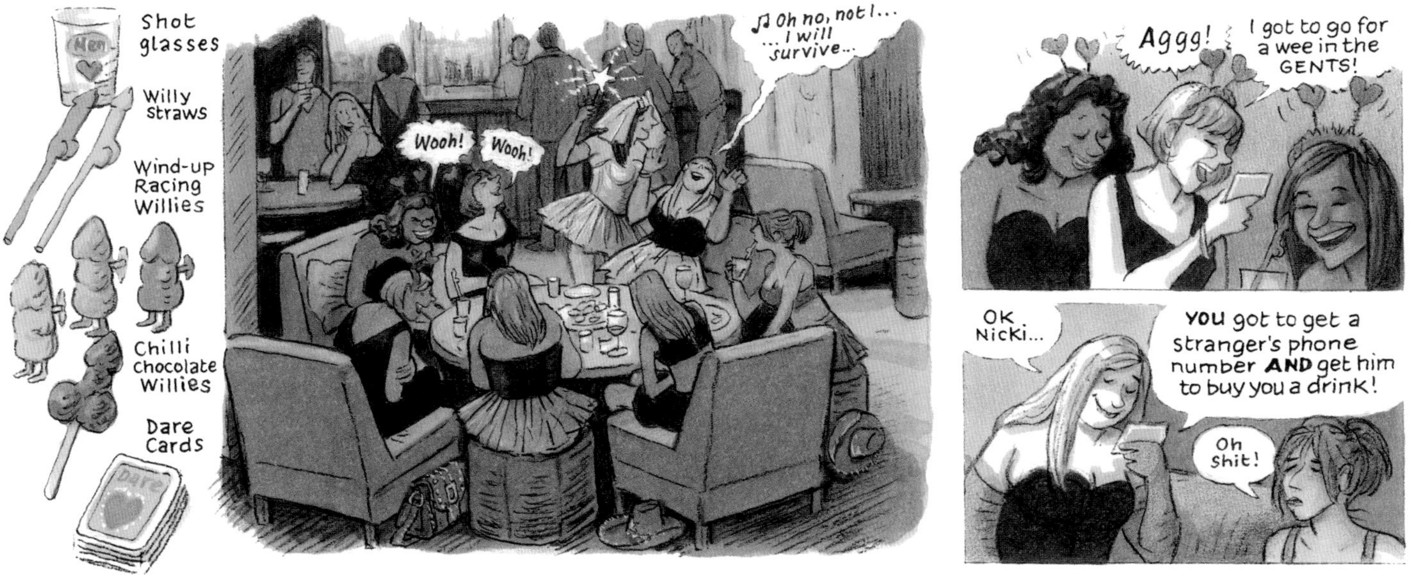
Shot glasses
Willy Straws
Wind-up Racing Willies
Chilli chocolate Willies
Dare Cards
Wooh!
Wooh!
♫ Oh no, not I... ...I will survive...
Aggg!
I got to go for a wee in the GENTS!
OK Nicki...
YOU got to get a stranger's phone number AND get him to buy you a drink!
Oh shit!

There were visits to the Ladies ...

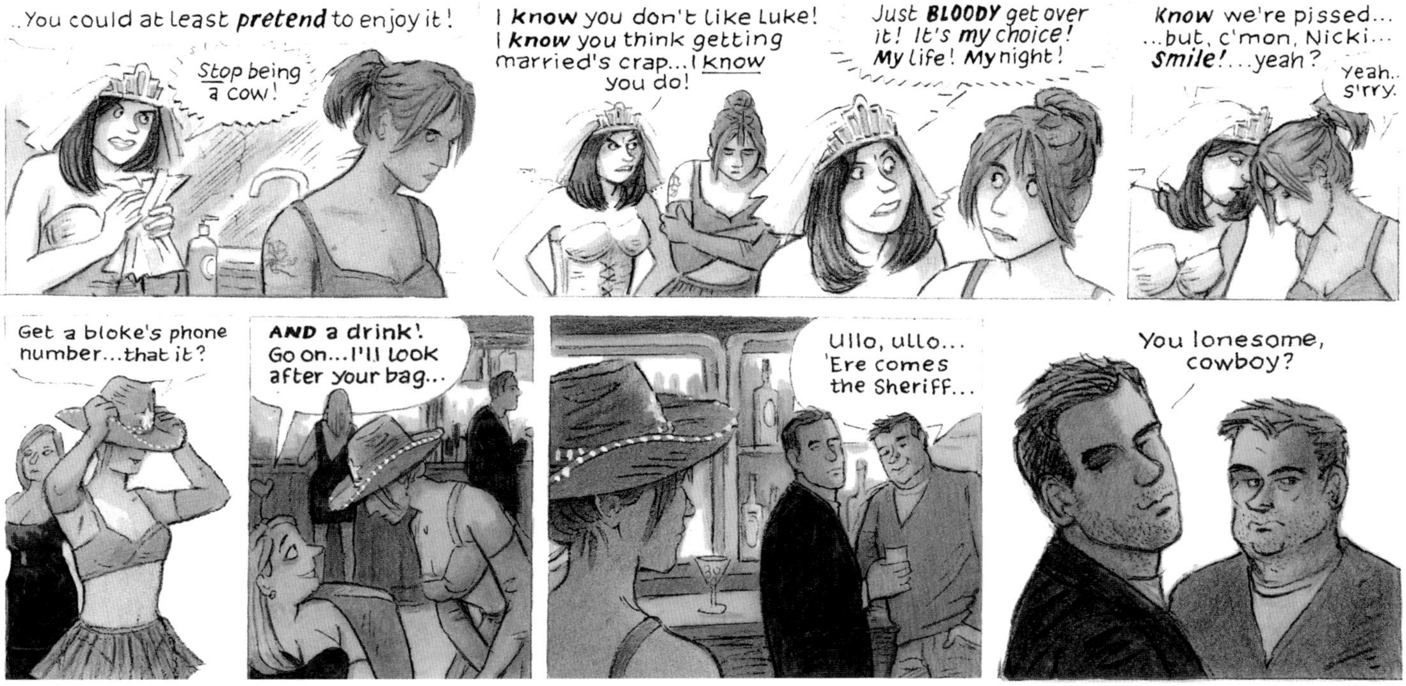
..You could at least pretend to enjoy it!
Stop being a cow!
I know you don't like Luke! I know you think getting married's crap...I know you do!
Just BLOODY get over it! It's my choice! My life! My night!
Know we're pissed... ...but, c'mon, Nicki... Smile!...yeah?
Yeah.. S'rry.
Get a bloke's phone number...that it?
AND a drink! Go on...I'll look after your bag...
Ullo, ullo... 'Ere comes the Sheriff...
You lonesome, cowboy?

The fit one was cool about buying a drink. But less keen to share his phone number.
And Nicki was not so drunk as to give *hers*.

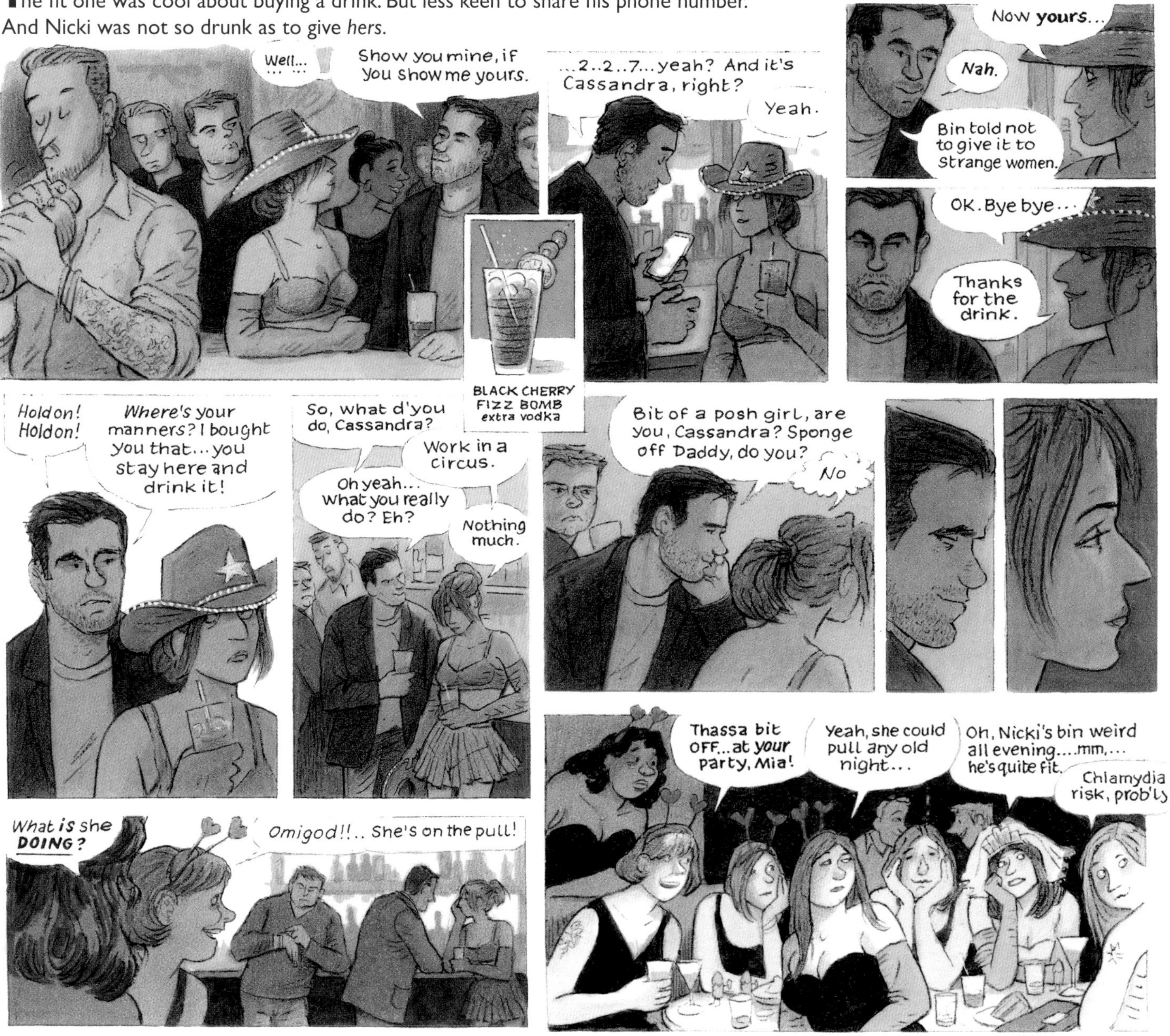
Well...
Show you mine, if you show me yours.
...2..2..7...yeah? And it's Cassandra, right?
Yeah.
BLACK CHERRY FIZZ BOMB extra vodka
Holdon! Holdon!
Where's your manners? I bought you that...you stay here and drink it!
So, what d'you do, Cassandra?
Work in a circus.
Oh yeah... what you really do? Eh?
Nothing much.
What is she DOING?
Omigod!!.. She's on the pull!
Bit of a posh girl, are you, Cassandra? Sponge off Daddy, do you?
No
Thassa bit OFF...at your party, Mia!
Yeah, she could pull any old night...
Oh, Nicki's bin weird all evening....mm,... he's quite fit.
Chlamydia risk, prob'ly
Now yours...
Nah.
Bin told not to give it to strange women.
OK. Bye bye...
Thanks for the drink.

Another cocktail arrived. This one made Nicki's eyeballs lock, put life on hold for seconds – or minutes. It was hard to tell.
Then her elbow would skid on the bar and she seemed to drop several floors in a lift.

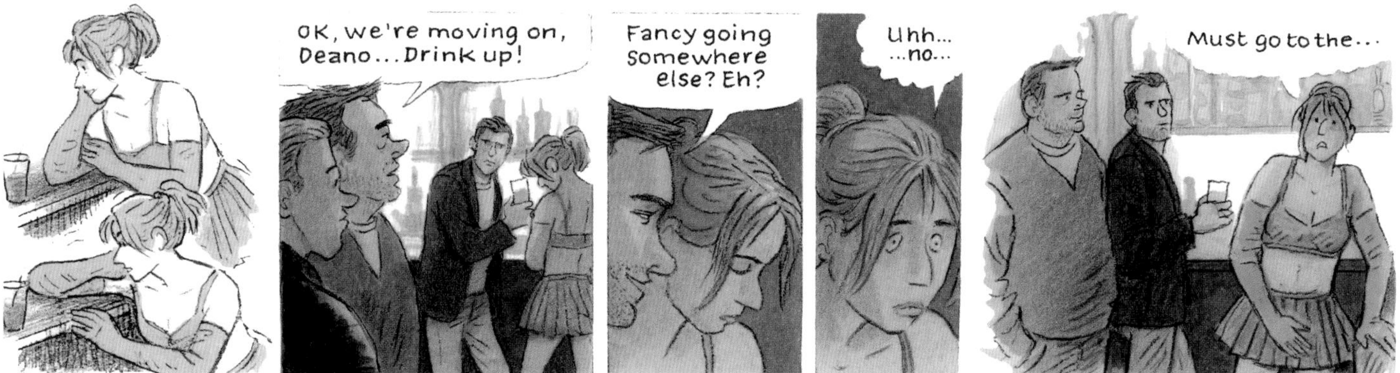
OK, we're moving on, Deano...Drink up!
Fancy going somewhere else? Eh?
Uhh... ...no...
Must go to the...

The way to the Ladies seemed to have been rearranged ...

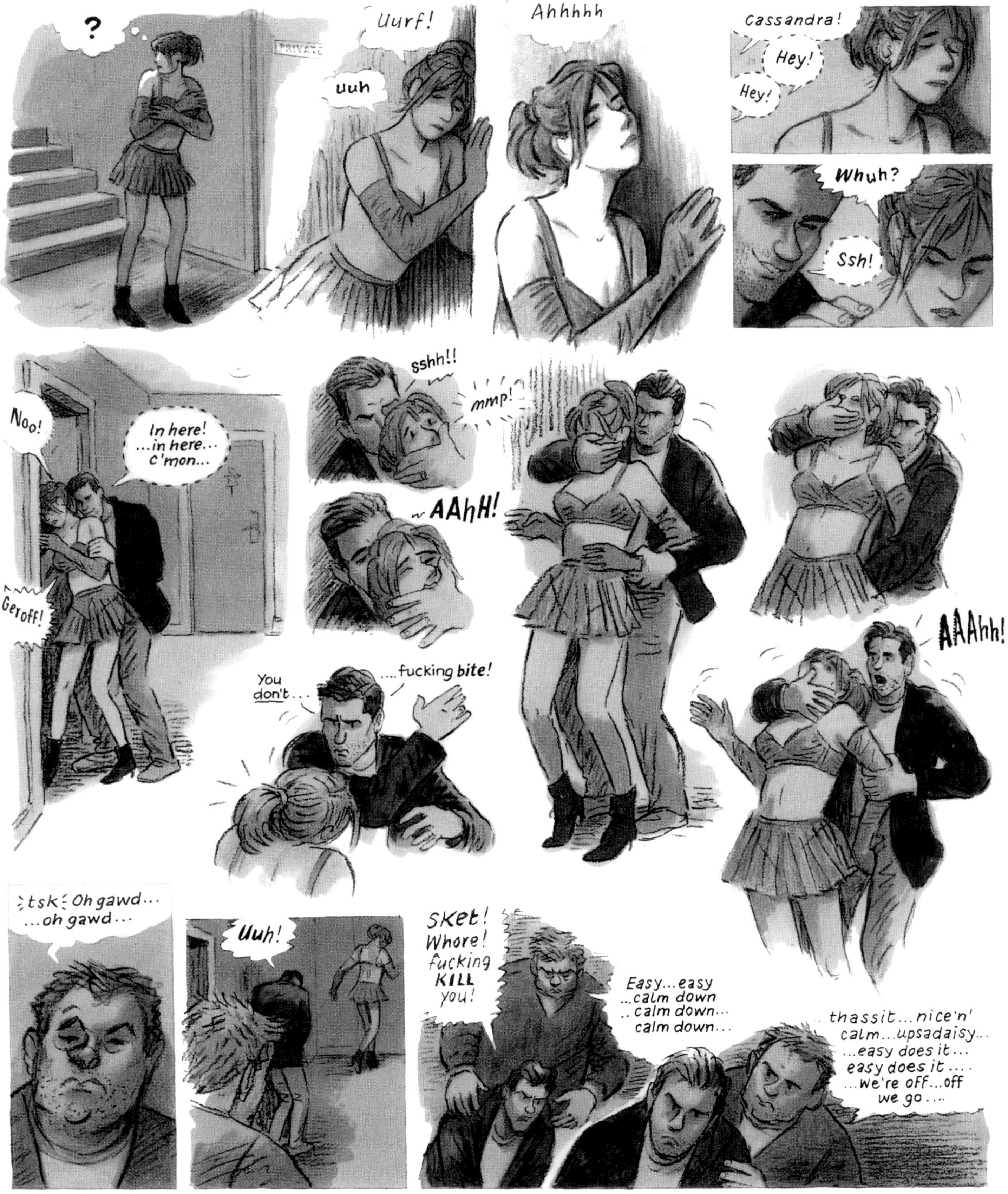
?
PRIVATE
Uurf!
uuh
Ahhhhh
Cassandra!
Hey!
Hey!
Whuh?
Ssh!
Noo!
In here!
...in here...
c'mon...
Geroff!
sshh!!
mmp!
AAhH!
You don't...
...fucking bite!
AAAhh!
tsk Oh gawd...
...oh gawd...
Uuh!
Sket!
Whore!
fucking
KILL
you!
Easy...easy
..calm down
..calm down...
calm down...
..thassit...nice'n'
calm...upsadaisy..
...easy does it...
easy does it....
...we're off...off
we go...

Holed up in the ladies, Nicki waited for him and his mate to kick the door in. Time passed. She emerged from the cubicle, examined the mark on her cheek, shouted 'Stupid!' at her reflection. Alex and Mia arrived, then the others, who stood near the washbasins rolling their eyes, making her breach of hen etiquette plain – stealing the limelight from the bride to be. And other charges, of snobbery and party-pooping. There were also sisterly and sympathetic noises, but these Nicki found hard to bear. They made her feel like a victim.

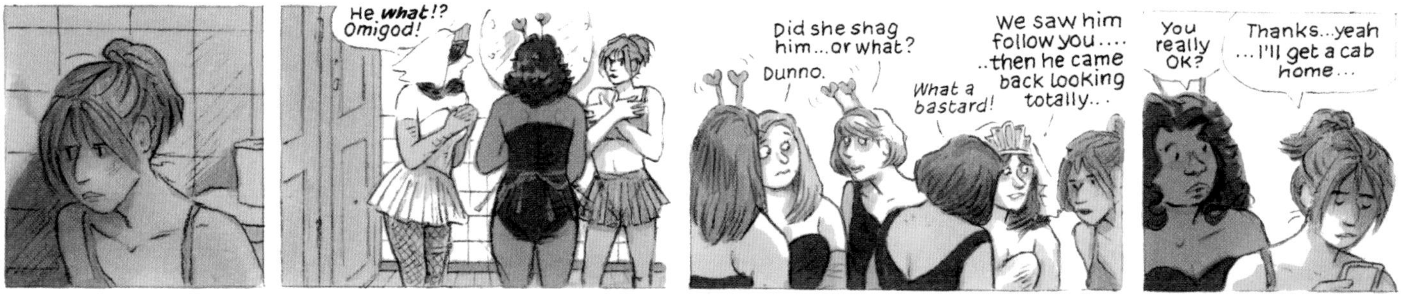
He what!? Omigod!
Did she shag him...or what?
Dunno.
We saw him follow you.... ..then he came back looking totally...
What a bastard!
You really OK?
Thanks...yeah ...I'll get a cab home...

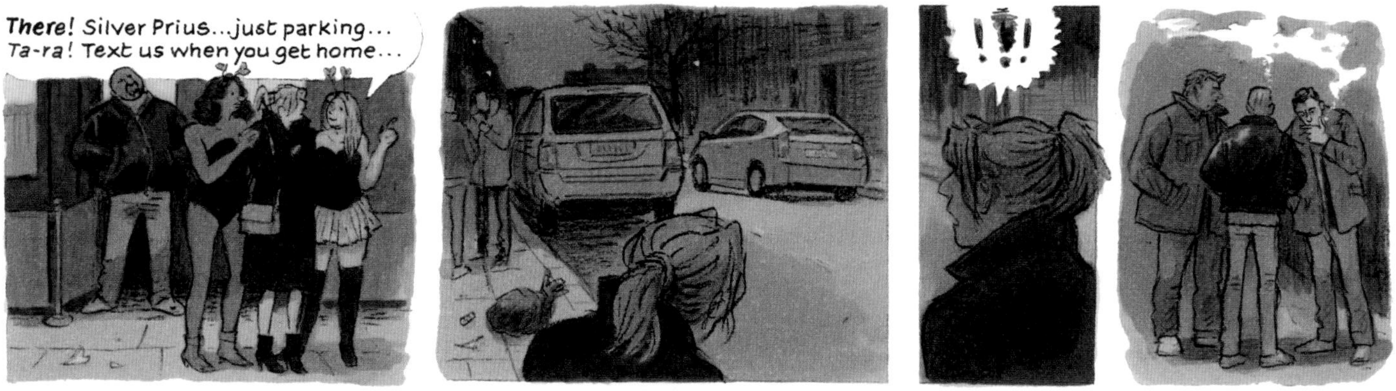
There! Silver Prius...just parking... Ta-ra! Text us when you get home...
!!!

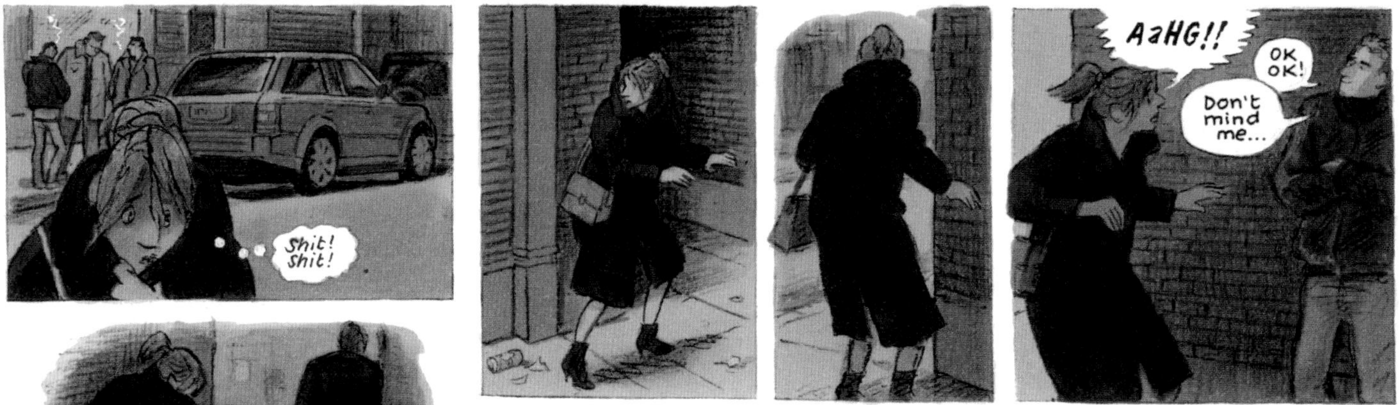
Shit! Shit!
AaHG!!
OK OK!
Don't mind me...

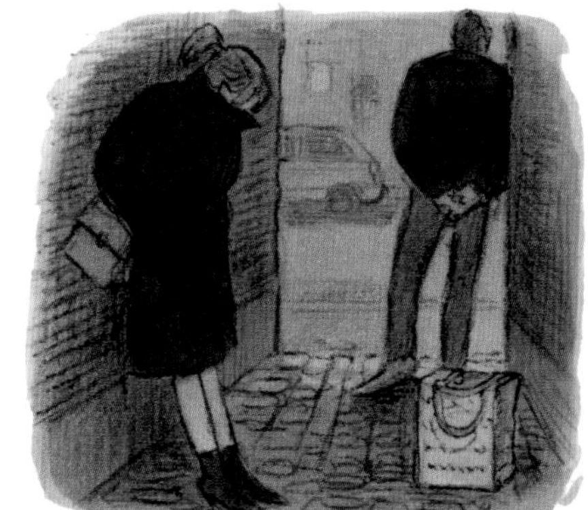

The alley smelled strongly of pee.
There was a Hamleys bag.
The presence of toys was strangely calming. She closed her eyes.

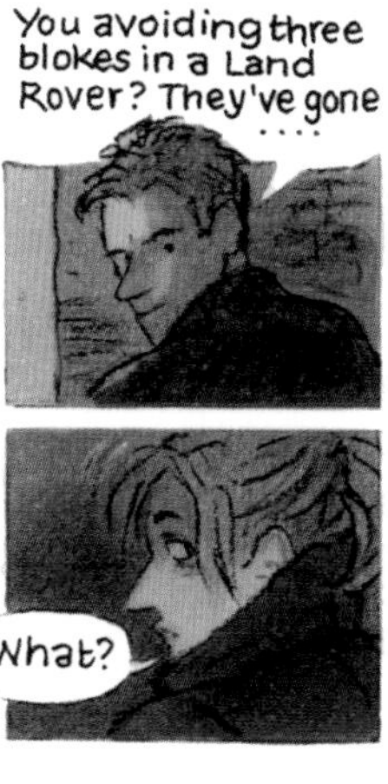
You avoiding three blokes in a Land Rover? They've gone ....
What?

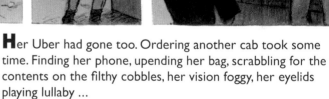

Her Uber had gone too. Ordering another cab took some time. Finding her phone, upending her bag, scrabbling for the contents on the filthy cobbles, her vision foggy, her eyelids playing lullaby ...

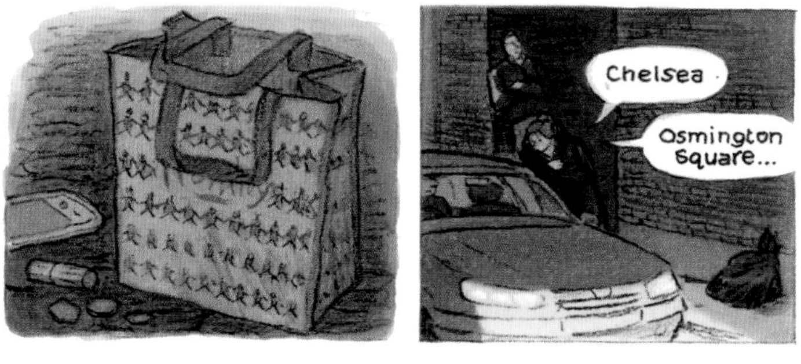
Chelsea
Osmington Square...

I can pinpoint the time when Nicki started to irritate me ...

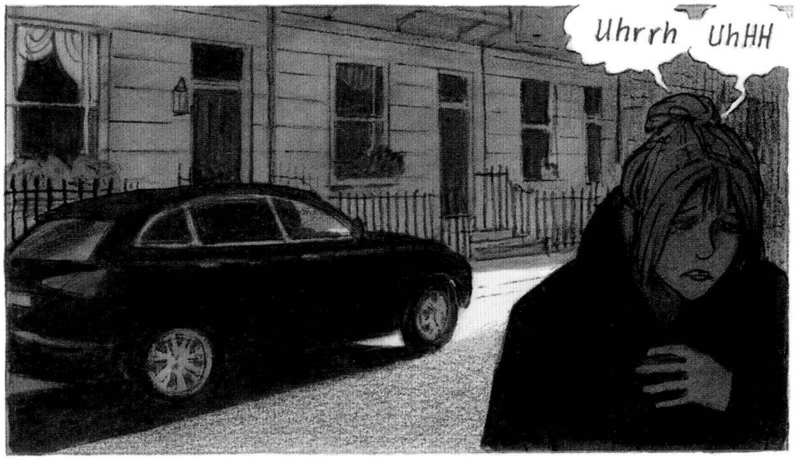
Uhrrh UhHH

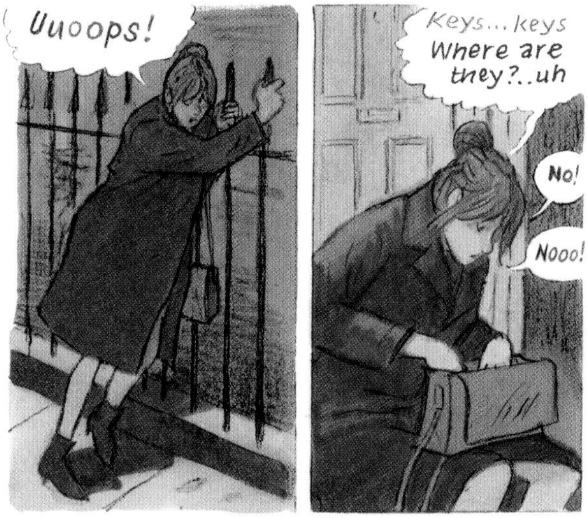
Uuoops!
Keys... keys
Where are they?..uh
No!
Nooo!

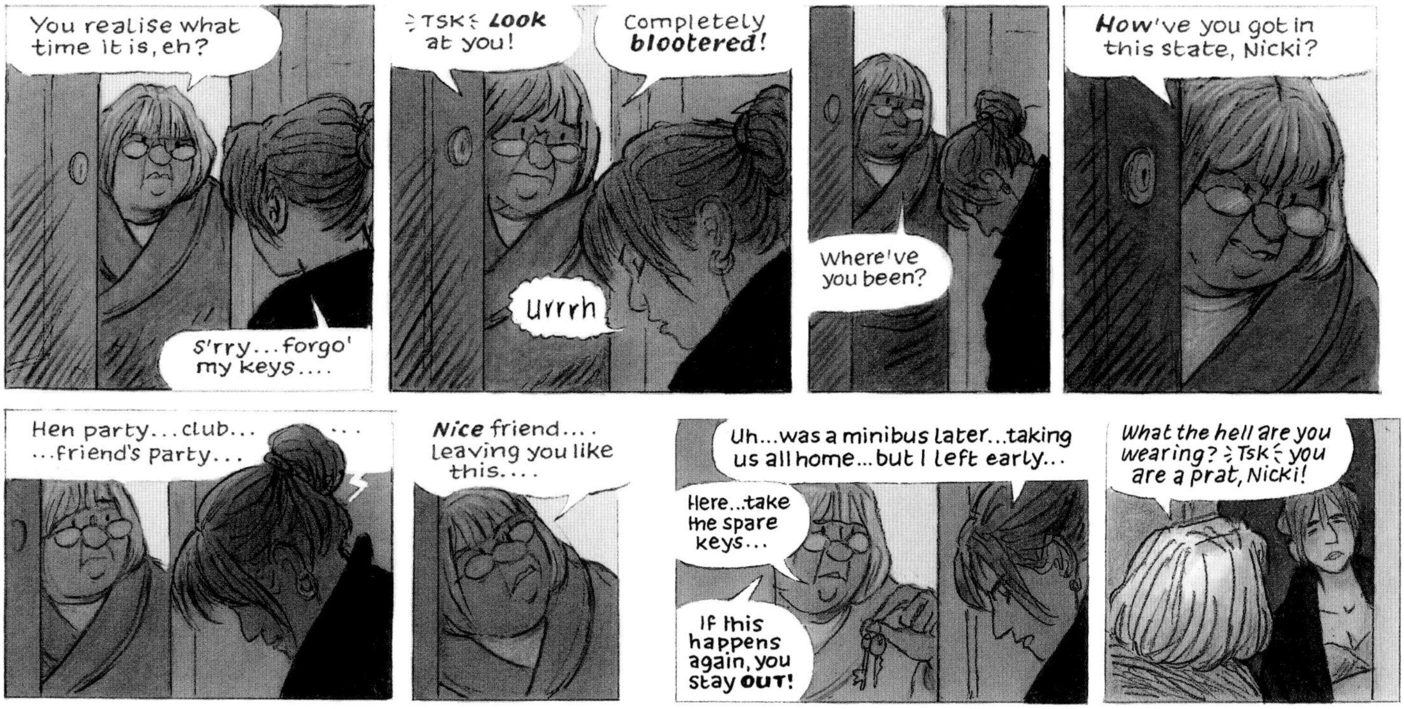
You realise what time it is, eh?
S'rry...forgo' my keys....
TSK Look at you!
Completely blootered!
Urrrh
Where've you been?
How've you got in this state, Nicki?
Hen party...club... ...friend's party...
...
Nice friend.... Leaving you like this....
Uh...was a minibus later...taking us all home...but I left early...
Here...take the spare keys...
If this happens again, you stay OUT!
What the hell are you wearing? Tsk you are a prat, Nicki!

Of course the next day she didn't turn up, meaning that I had to deal with the dog.

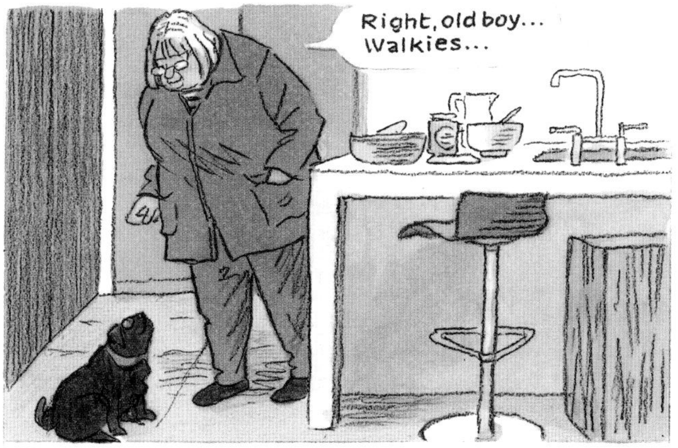
Right, old boy... Walkies...

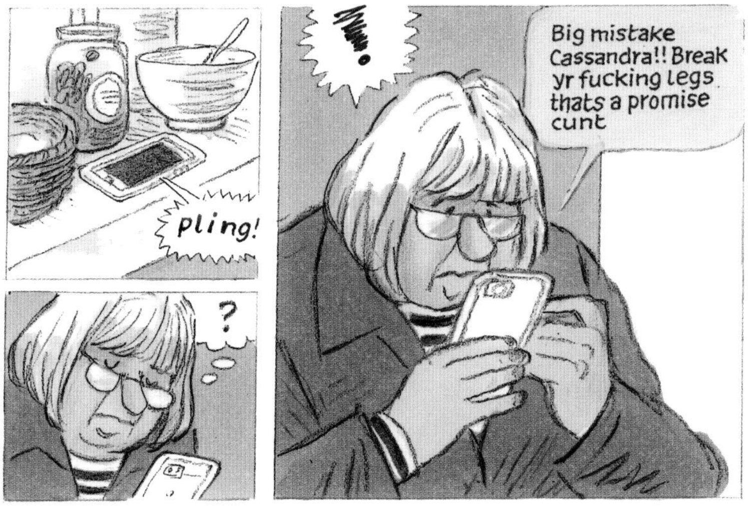
Pling!
?
Big mistake Cassandra!! Break yr fucking legs thats a promise cunt

I immediately assumed the text was sent by a friend and fellow art dealer, Teddy Wood, during one of his benders. I was used to his messages, usually accusations of blanking him or stinginess, or of knowing bugger all about Cubism. I didn't recognise the number, but then I could never keep track of Teddy's mobiles. His language *was* fruitier than usual. And as for threatening me with violence – me, twice his size in all directions, little twerp – I couldn't think what I'd done to deserve it.
Then I remembered the day before some fool had come into the gallery and showed me a painting he was interested in …

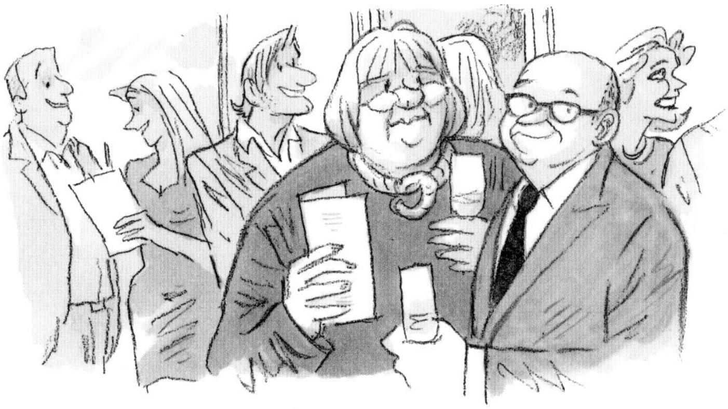

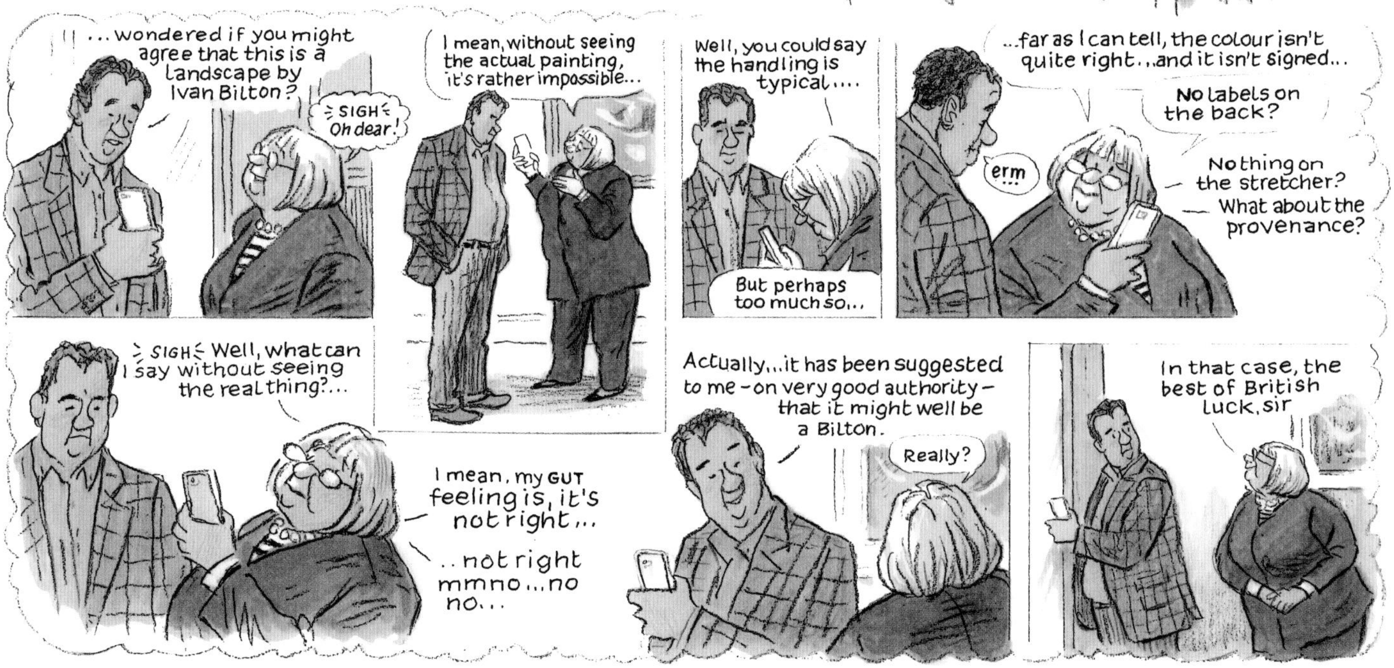

... wondered if you might agree that this is a landscape by Ivan Bilton?
SIGH Oh dear!
I mean, without seeing the actual painting, it's rather impossible...
Well, you could say the handling is typical....
But perhaps too much so...
...far as I can tell, the colour isn't quite right...and it isn't signed...
erm
No labels on the back?
Nothing on the stretcher?
What about the provenance?
SIGH Well, what can I say without seeing the real thing?...
I mean, my GUT feeling is, it's not right...
..not right mmno...no no...
Actually...it has been suggested to me – on very good authority – that it might well be a Bilton.
Really?
In that case, the best of British luck, sir

I remember thinking, someone's trying to sell him a pup. That someone had to be Teddy, now furious with me for queering his pitch with a potential buyer. I'm a fine one to talk, but Teddy can be a bit naughty. He's a great ensnarer of the unwary, wonderful at suggesting that something might be genuine, when he knows it's not.
I replied in kind.

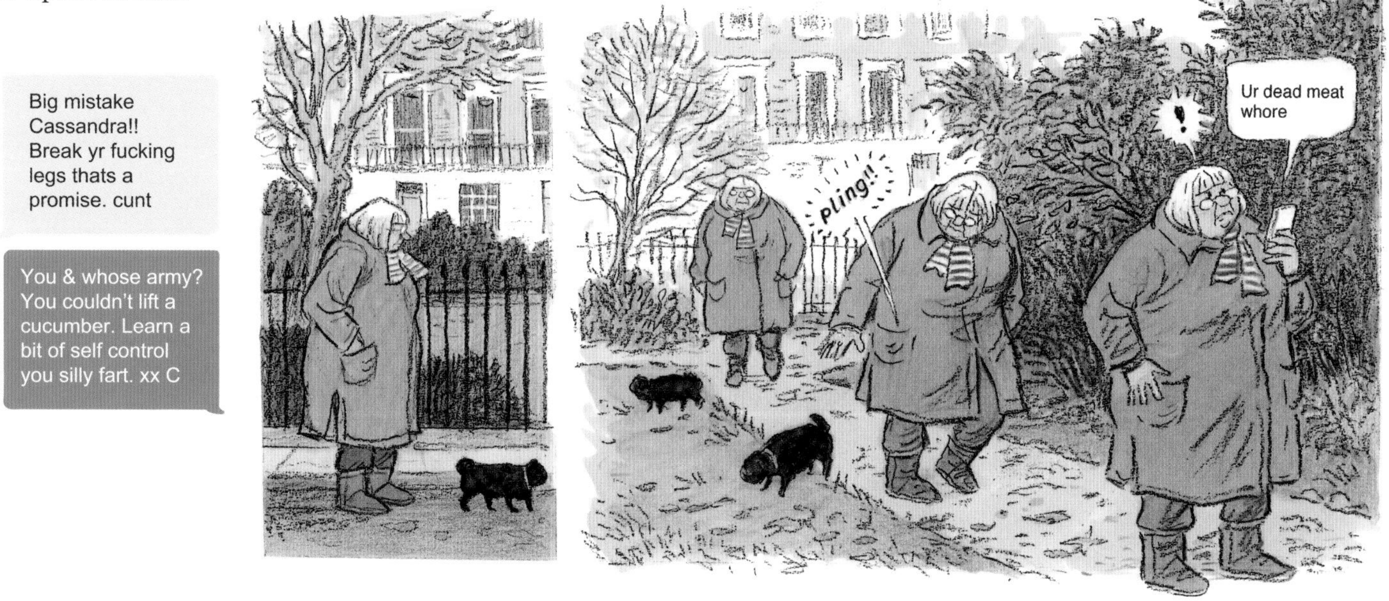

Big mistake Cassandra!! Break yr fucking legs thats a promise. cunt
You & whose army? You couldn't lift a cucumber. Learn a bit of self control you silly fart. xx C
pling!!
Ur dead meat whore

On my return ...

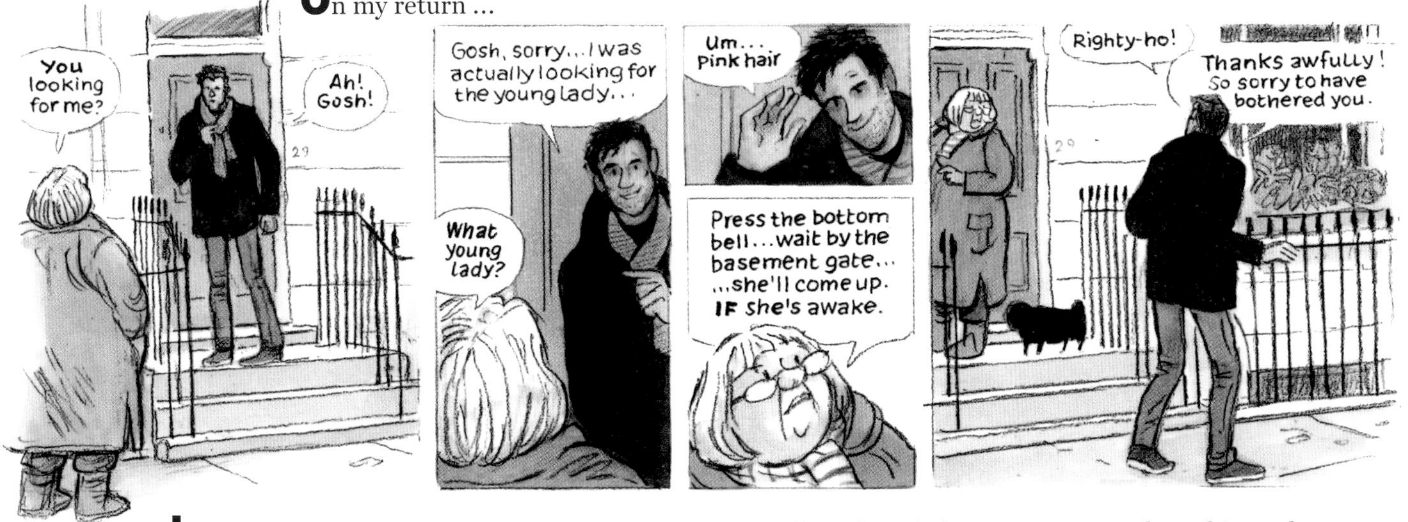
You looking for me?
Ah! Gosh!
Gosh, sorry... I was actually looking for the young lady...
What young lady?
Um... Pink hair
Press the bottom bell... wait by the basement gate... ...she'll come up. IF she's awake.
Righty-ho!
Thanks awfully! So sorry to have bothered you.

I rang Teddy's number in vain – he'd turned the thing off. And so I left messages everywhere, his work number, e-mail and landline. While doing this, I saw Nicki and her visitor walk through the square, Nicki moving very slowly. Hungover, of course. As Elsa didn't come at weekends, I fixed myself lunch. And waited.

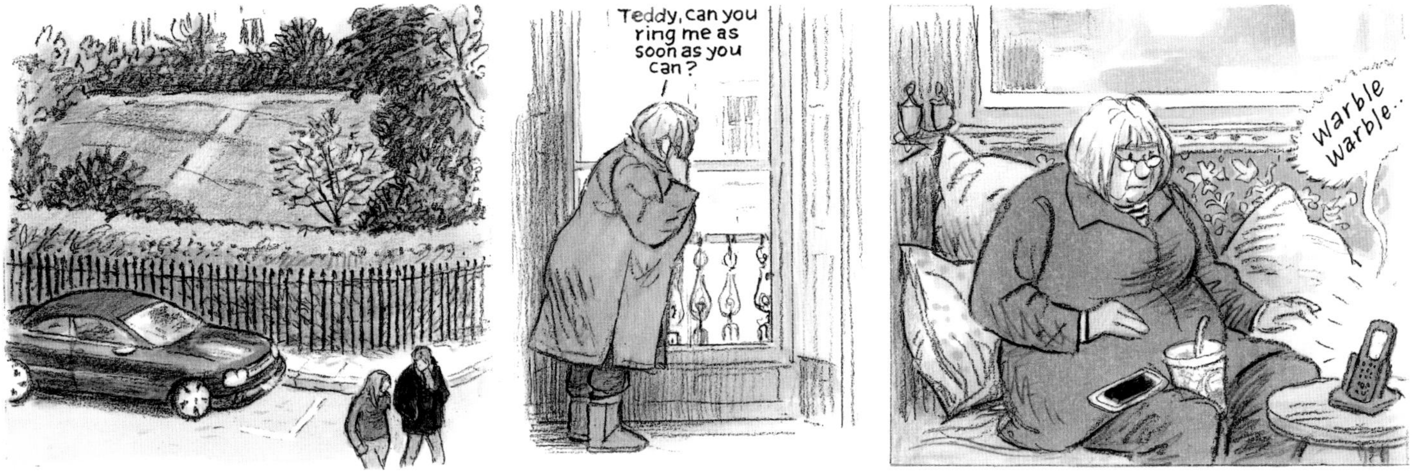
Teddy, can you ring me as soon as you can?
warble warble...

At first, Teddy was outraged that I'd suspected him. He swore his innocence. Then, because another text had arrived, he was all ears ...

You don't shit on people and get away with it Cassandra. Be afraid.

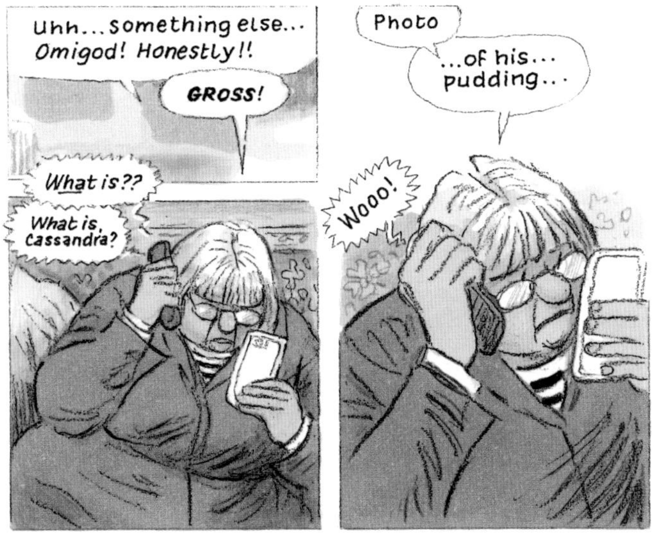
Uhh... something else... Omigod! Honestly!!
GROSS!
What is??
What is, Cassandra?
Photo
...of his... pudding...
Wooo!

Teddy's take was to ignore the texts and block the number. He said it was normal, people sent each other "dick pics" and death threats every day.
No big deal.
But I smelled the first whiff of Shit Creek.
Someone had rumbled me.

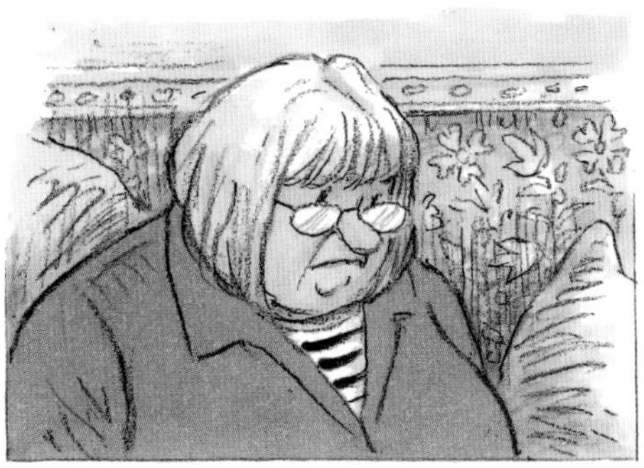

I was surprised when much later Nicki turned up to walk the dog. She was damp from the rain with an ominously moony look about her, for which I guessed her visitor was responsible. Whether the bruise on her face was his doing I never discovered.

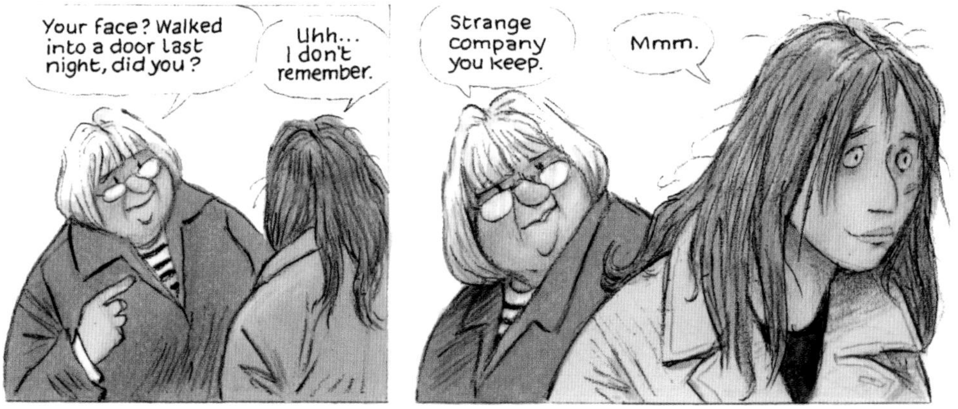

Your face? Walked into a door last night, did you?
Uhh... I don't remember.
Strange company you keep.
Mmm.

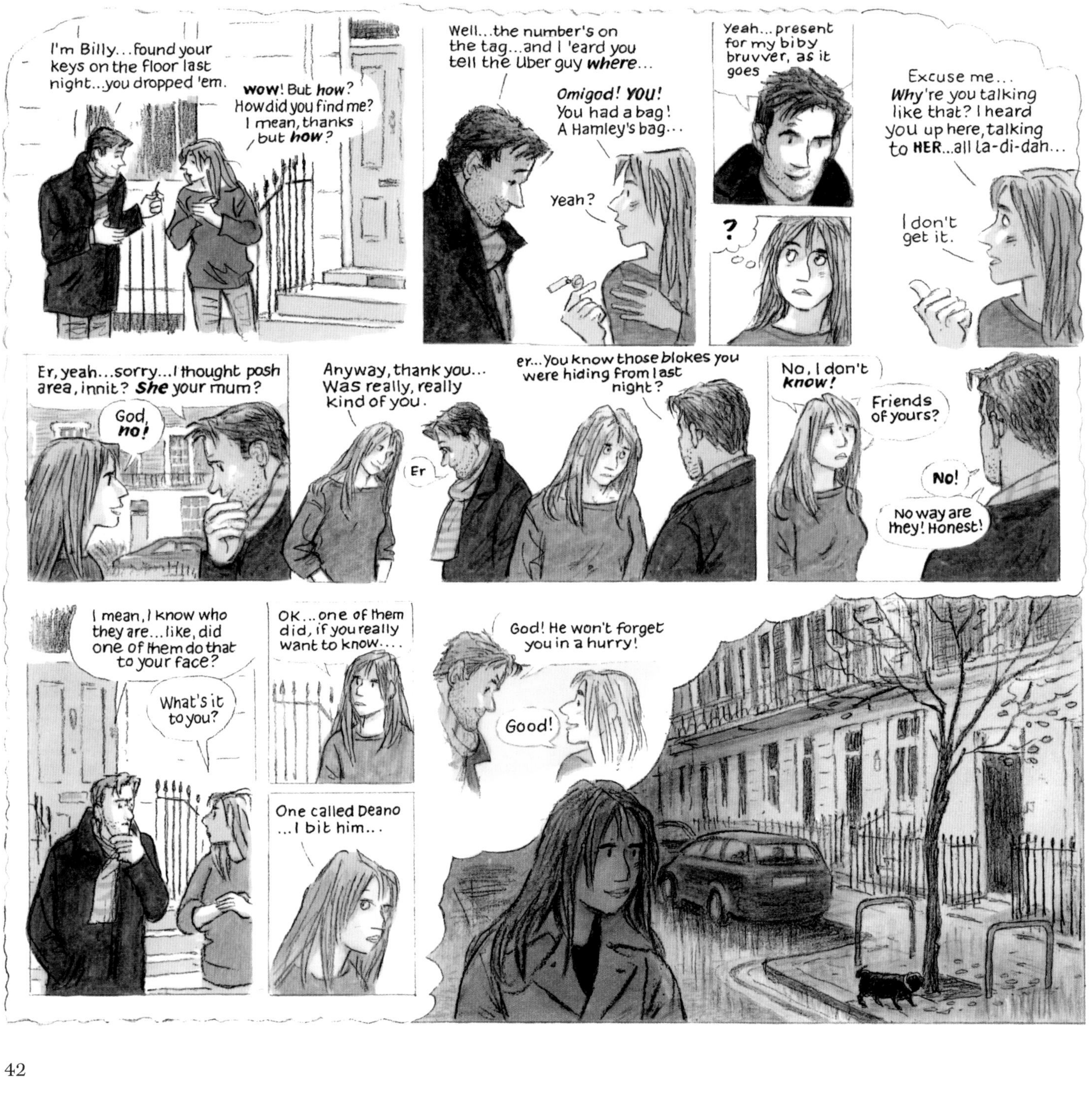

I'm Billy...found your keys on the floor last night...you dropped 'em.
WOW! But how? How did you find me? I mean, thanks but how?
Well...the number's on the tag...and I 'eard you tell the Uber guy where...
Omigod! YOU! You had a bag! A Hamley's bag...
Yeah?
Yeah...present for my biby bruvver, as it goes
?
Excuse me... Why're you talking like that? I heard you up here, talking to HER...all la-di-dah...
I don't get it.
Er, yeah...sorry...I thought posh area, innit? She your mum?
God, no!
Anyway, thank you... Was really, really kind of you.
Er
er...You know those blokes you were hiding from last night?
No, I don't know!
Friends of yours?
No!
No way are they! Honest!
I mean, I know who they are...like, did one of them do that to your face?
What's it to you?
OK...one of them did, if you really want to know....
One called Deano ...I bit him...
God! He won't forget you in a hurry!
Good!

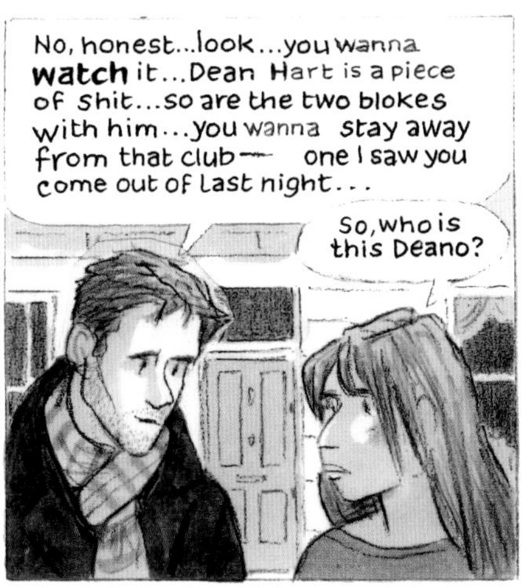
No, honest...look...you wanna **watch** it...Dean Hart is a piece of shit...so are the two blokes with him...you wanna stay away from that club— one I saw you come out of last night...
So, who is this Deano?

Billy said: OK, maybe Deano couldn't help it because he's on medication, but he was a bastard with women all the same. One time he was nearly done for assault, except the girl backed off. Or was persuaded to, that was the gossip. The two blokes with him were his cousin Pete and his uncle Grant, known as Nanny, because he minded Deano. The three of them liked bars that did hen nights ...

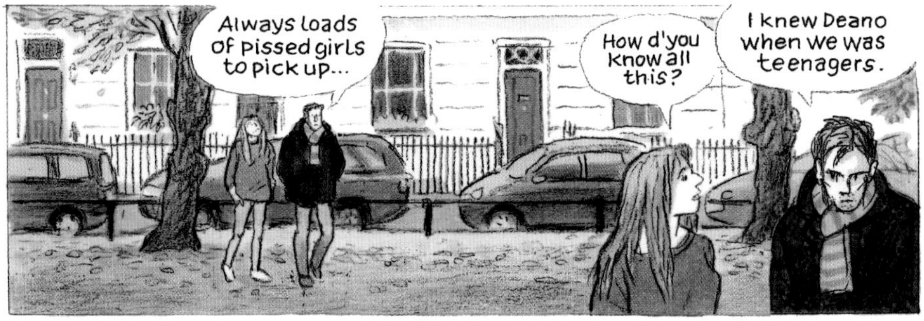
Always loads of pissed girls to pick up...
How d'you know all this?
I knew Deano when we was teenagers.

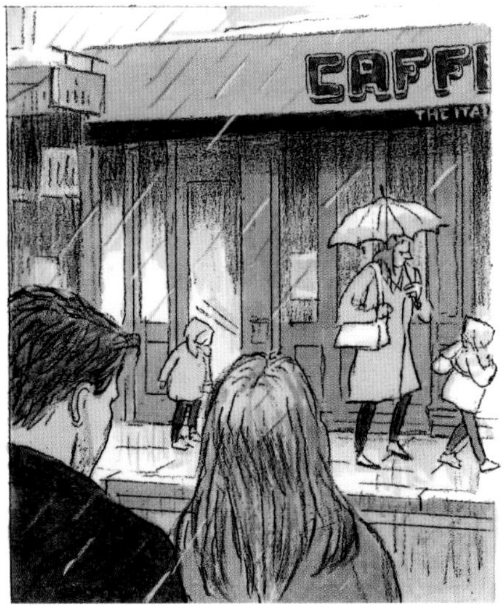
CAFFE

Billy said: He and Deano were north London boys, went to the same school and started off working for the electrical firm where Billy's dad was. Which is why Billy is now in the movies, sort of, part of a lighting crew, heavy lifting, running cables.

Billy said: Deano behaved a bit weird even then. He had mood swings. They were sort of mates for a bit. They did graffiti together, called themselves the "Prick Men", spraying pricks on walls in subways, mainly, some of them running the whole length. Deano was shorter so he did the nuts and the bottom line; Billy did the top and the bishop.

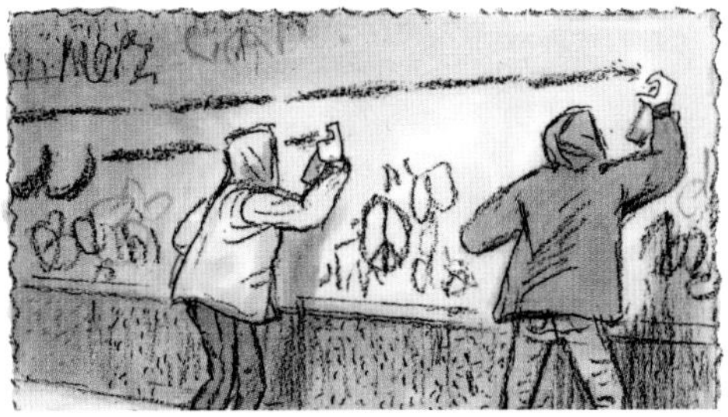

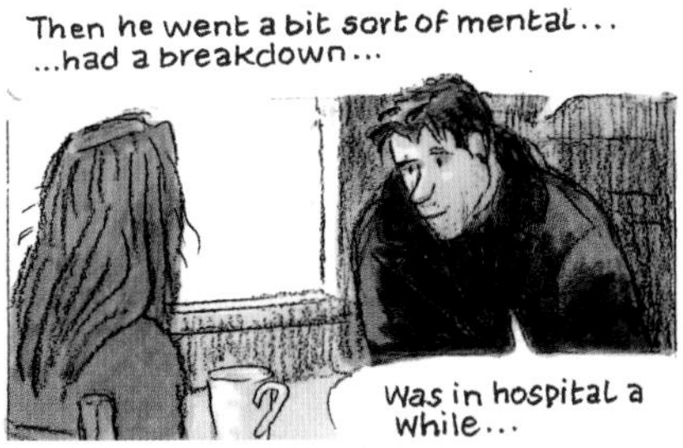
Then he went a bit sort of mental... ...had a breakdown...
Was in hospital a while...

Billy said: He didn't really see Deano after that. He heard that Deano never did much except play video games, snort coke, bet on horses and chase women. He supposed Deano's family could afford to look after him. They lived well, the Harts. They had a big scrap metal yard off the Eastland Road, but most of their money, you didn't ask where it came from. Deano's dad had done time and now lived in Spain, like a gent. It was common knowledge some of the family were basically a bit evil.

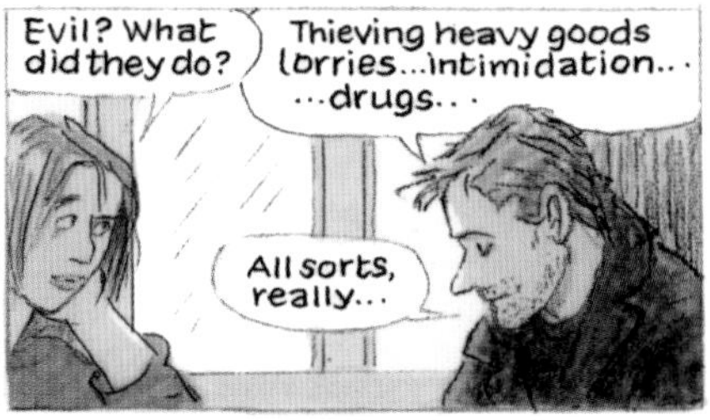
Evil? What did they do?
Thieving heavy goods lorries...intimidation... ...drugs...
All sorts, really...

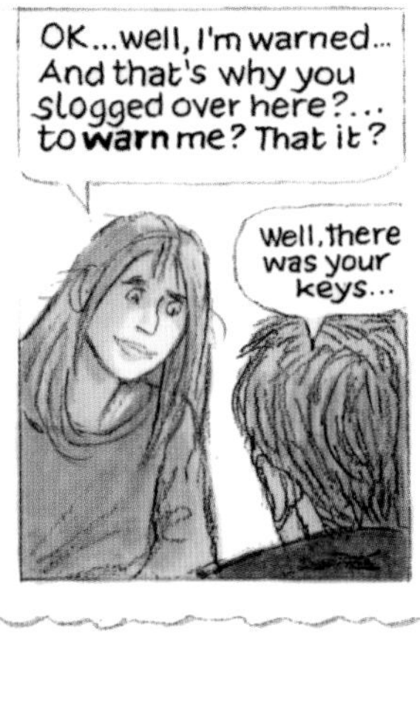
OK...well, I'm warned... And that's why you slogged over here?... to **warn** me? That it?
Well, there was your keys...

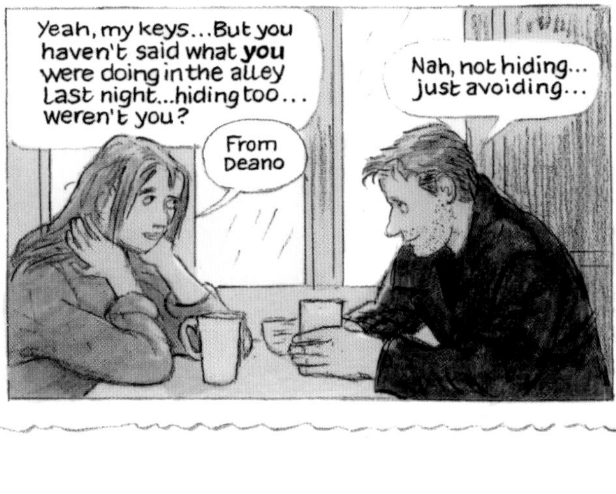
Yeah, my keys...But you haven't said what **you** were doing in the alley last night...hiding too... weren't you?
From Deano
Nah, not hiding... just avoiding...

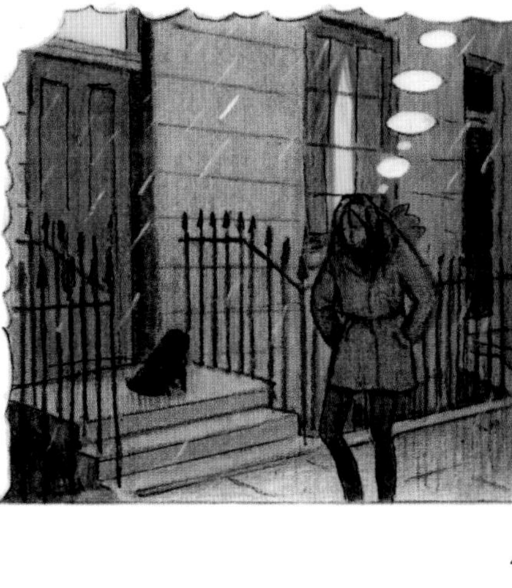

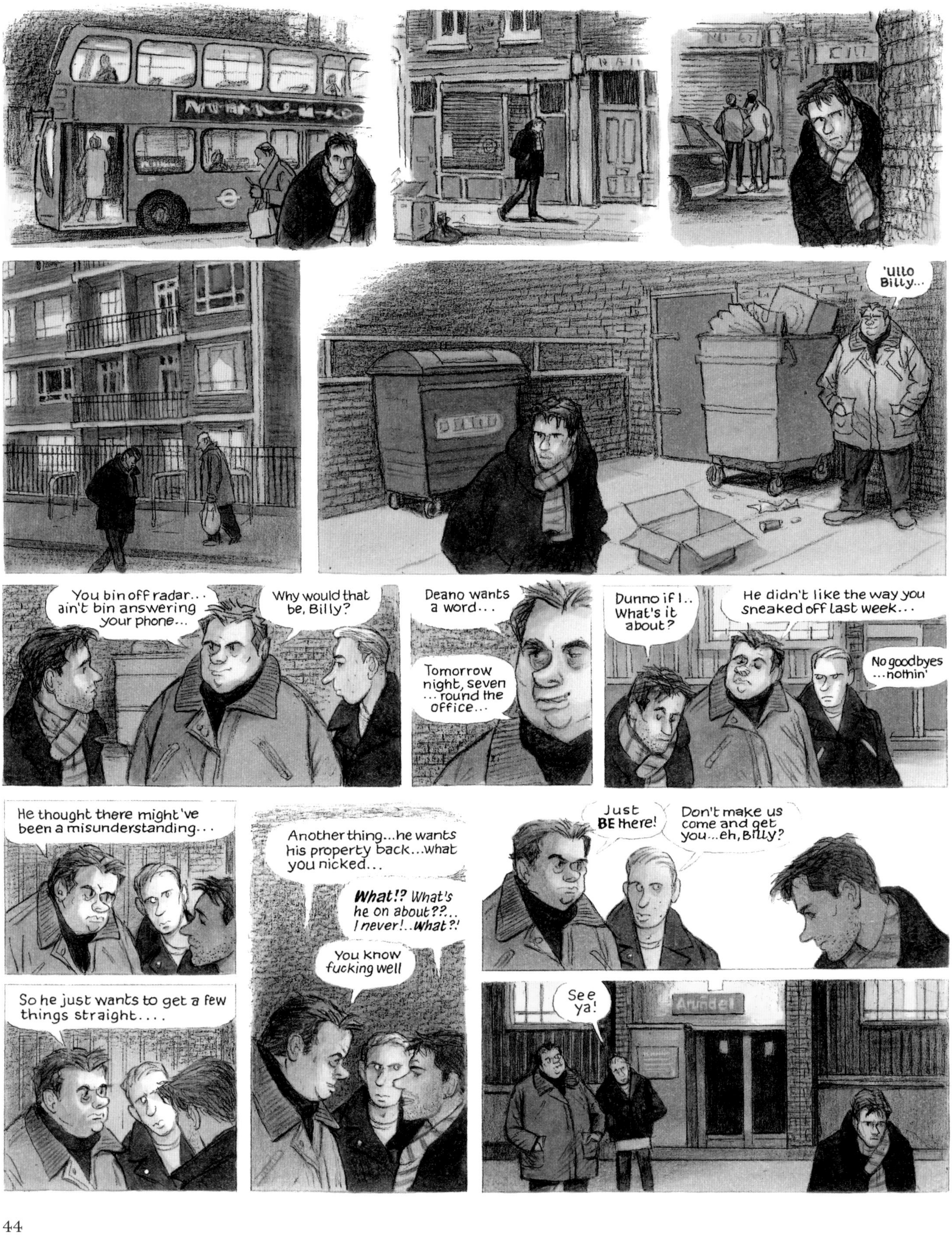
'Ullo Billy...
You bin off radar... ain't bin answering your phone...
Why would that be, Billy?
Deano wants a word...
Tomorrow night, seven ...round the office...
Dunno if I.. What's it about?
He didn't like the way you sneaked off last week...
No goodbyes ...nothin'
He thought there might've been a misunderstanding...
So he just wants to get a few things straight....
Another thing...he wants his property back...what you nicked...
What!? What's he on about??... I never!..**What**?!
You know fucking well
Just **BE** there!
Don't make us come and get you...eh, Billy?
See ya!

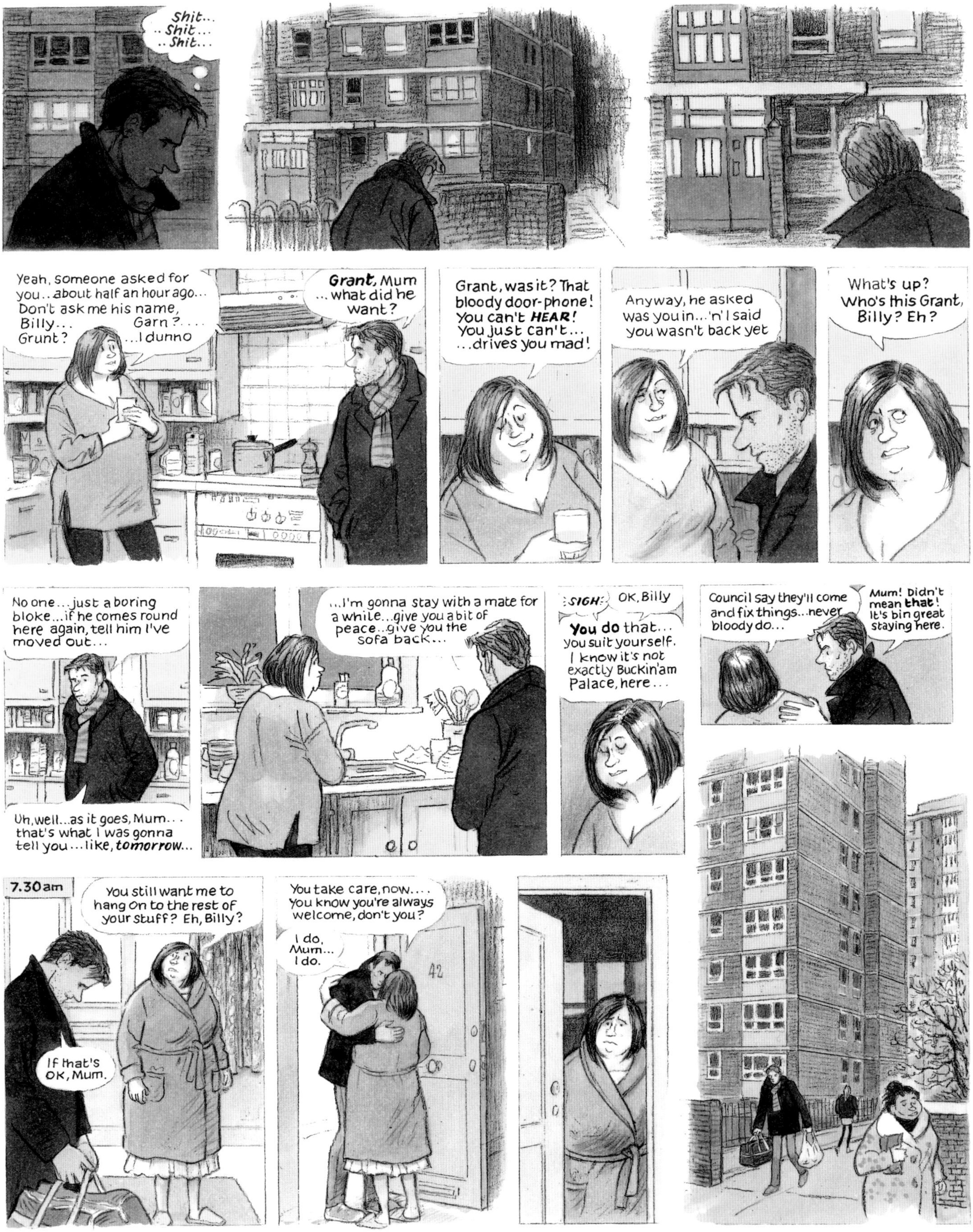
Shit...
..Shit...
..Shit...
Yeah, someone asked for you.. about half an hour ago... Don't ask me his name, Billy... Garn?... Grunt? ...I dunno
Grant, Mum ...what did he want?
Grant, was it? That bloody door-phone! You can't HEAR! You just can't... ...drives you mad!
Anyway, he asked was you in...'n' I said you wasn't back yet
What's up? Who's this Grant, Billy? Eh?
No one... just a boring bloke... if he comes round here again, tell him I've moved out...
Uh, well...as it goes, Mum... that's what I was gonna tell you... like, tomorrow...
...I'm gonna stay with a mate for a while...give you a bit of peace...give you the sofa back...
SIGH
OK, Billy
You do that... you suit yourself. I know it's not exactly Buckin'am Palace, here...
Council say they'll come and fix things...never bloody do...
Mum! Didn't mean that! It's bin great staying here.
7.30 am
You still want me to hang on to the rest of your stuff? Eh, Billy?
If that's OK, Mum.
You take care, now.... You know you're always welcome, don't you?
I do, Mum... I do.
42

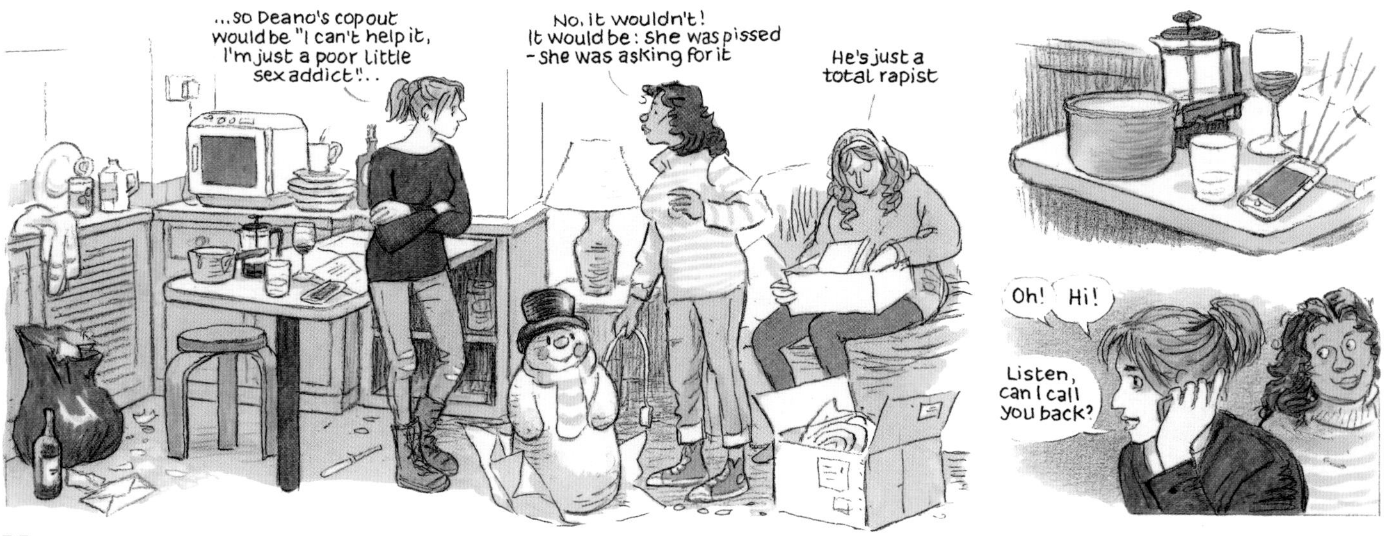
...so Deano's copout would be "I can't help it, I'm just a poor little sex addict"!..
No, it wouldn't! It would be: she was pissed - she was asking for it
He's just a total rapist
Oh!
Hi!
Listen, can I call you back?

Nicki's mates Alex and Annie thought it was in Billy's favour that he'd phoned instead of simply turning up on the doorstep and also that he gave her time to consider his big ask. About some new bother with Deano. Billy needed somewhere to lie low for a night or so. Staying with his mum wasn't on, his ex-partner Dee didn't want to know and a mate's sofa was no longer free. He was entirely house-trained, he told Nicki, could kip anywhere, in a chair, on the floor.
Of course Nicki guessed that Billy had another motive – he fancied her, she knew he did from the looks he gave her when they last met. This prospect was not unwelcome. Weeks had passed since her affair with an ex-housemate had fizzled out.

Nicki joined Billy in a nearby pub. Their eyes met for a moment too long, making for an awkwardness, making Nicki gabble about her new project, which involved trawling eBay and junkshops. She told him about slaving for Cassandra, about her student debt and how she couldn't afford anywhere to live. Having started she couldn't stop. She told Billy how she couldn't face asking her parents for money, how her father was slowly dying and how she couldn't take her mother's martyrdom.

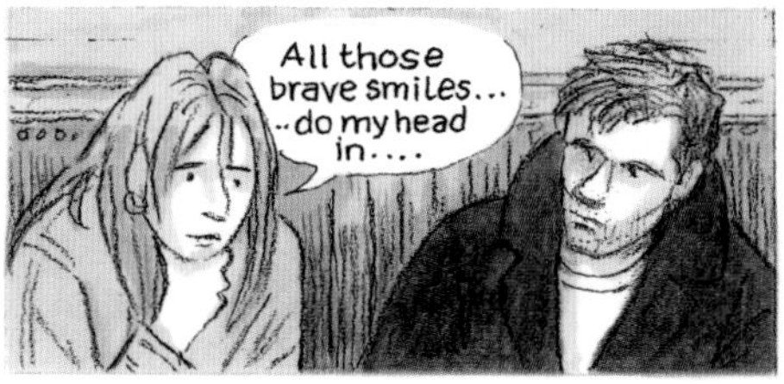
All those brave smiles... ..do my head in....

At which point she realised that he should be telling her things. What was going on? What had he done? Why was Deano mad with him? Billy said there were two reasons. One, because he'd stood Deano up. Two, because he'd nicked something of Deano's, sort of on purpose, but without really thinking.

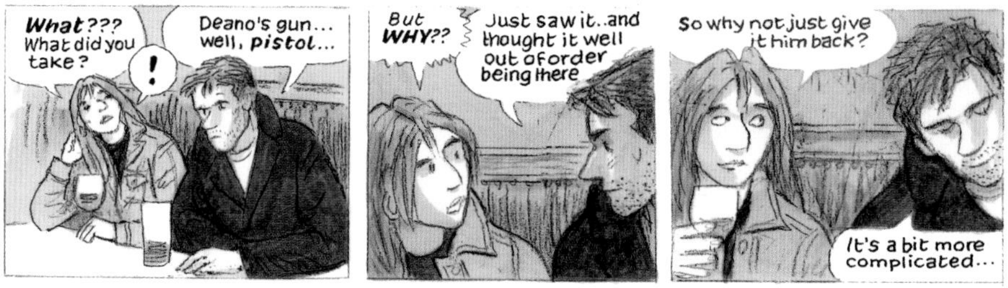
What??? What did you take?
Deano's gun... well, pistol...
!
But WHY??
Just saw it..and thought it well out of order being there
So why not just give it him back?
It's a bit more complicated...

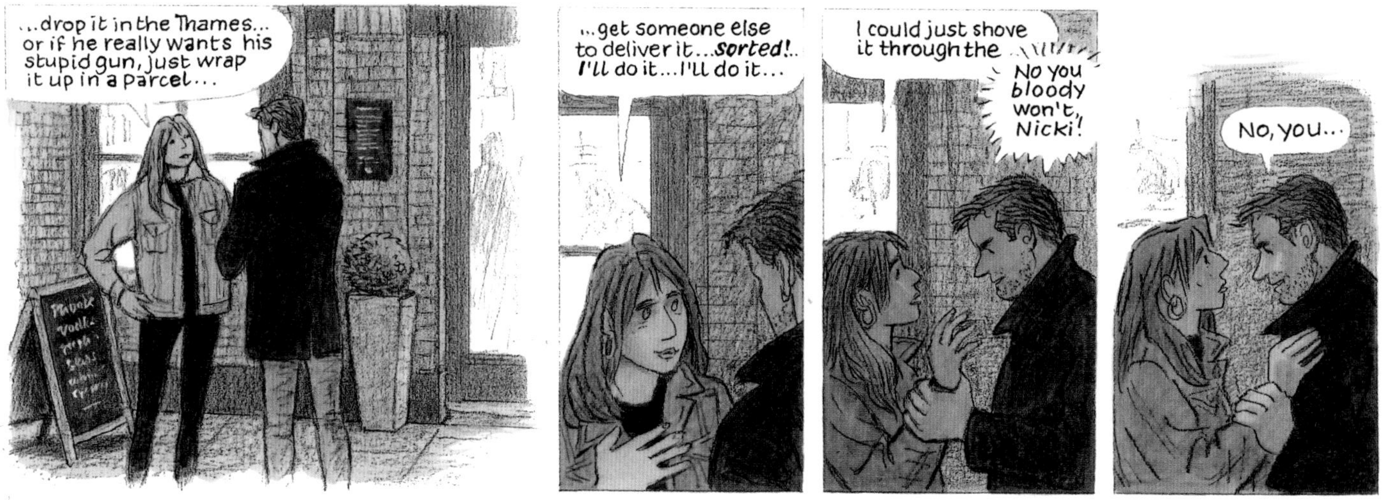
...drop it in the Thames... or if he really wants his stupid gun, just wrap it up in a parcel...
...get someone else to deliver it...sorted!.. I'll do it...I'll do it...
I could just shove it through the
No you bloody won't, Nicki!
No, you...

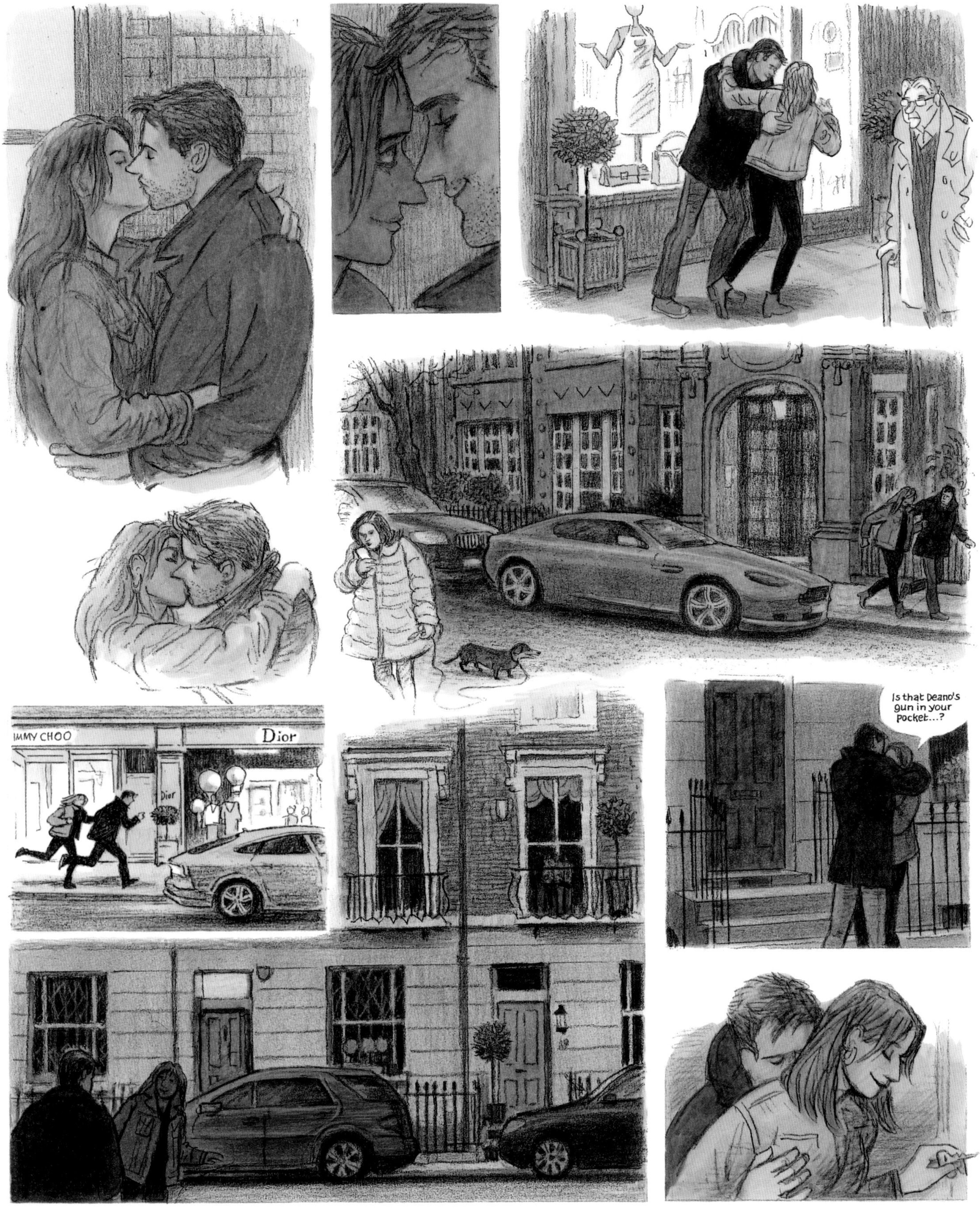
IMMY CHOO
Dior
Dior
Is that Deano's gun in your pocket...?

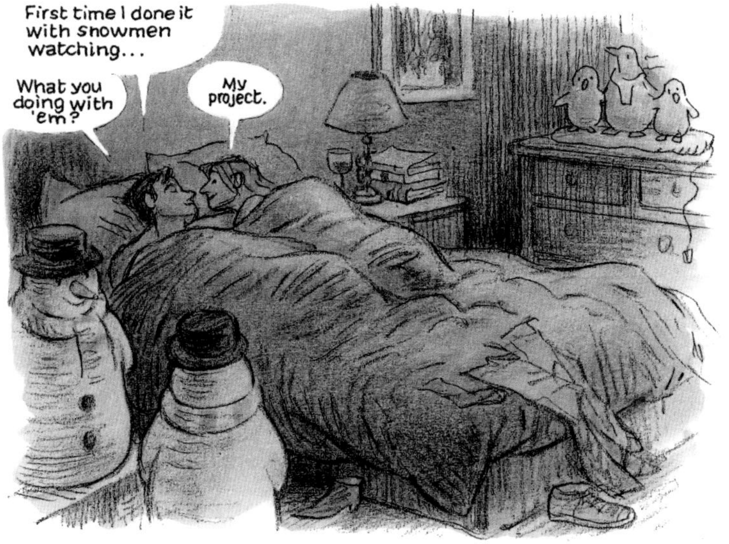
First time I done it with snowmen watching...
What you doing with 'em?
My project.

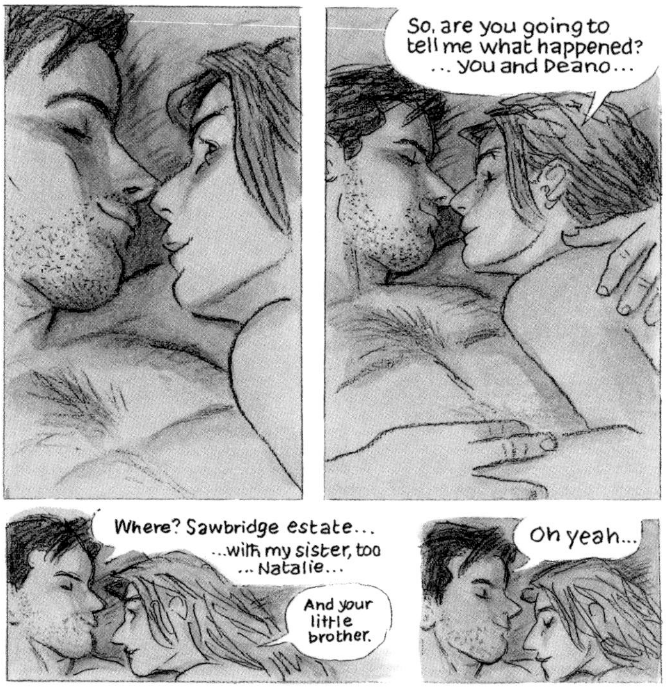
So, are you going to tell me what happened? ... you and Deano...
Where? Sawbridge estate... ...with my sister, too ... Natalie...
And your little brother.
Oh yeah...

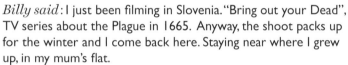

Billy said: I just been filming in Slovenia. "Bring out your Dead", TV series about the Plague in 1665. Anyway, the shoot packs up for the winter and I come back here. Staying near where I grew up, in my mum's flat.

So I'm in the pub when Deano comes in. He goes "Yo, Prickman!" like I'm his long-lost brother. And we have a few pints. Then he says do I want to come racing with him and Nanny at Newbury the next day. So I says yes, 'cos I'm a bit spare – and fucking stupid. So we drive there and I lose a few quid. But Nanny and Deano's bets come good. Then Deano gets bored and we leave before the fourth race. So Deano's driving and Nanny's directing him to some boozer he knows near Kintbury. Weather got all murky and we missed the turning. Then middle of fucking nowhere, there's this girl, hitching a lift.

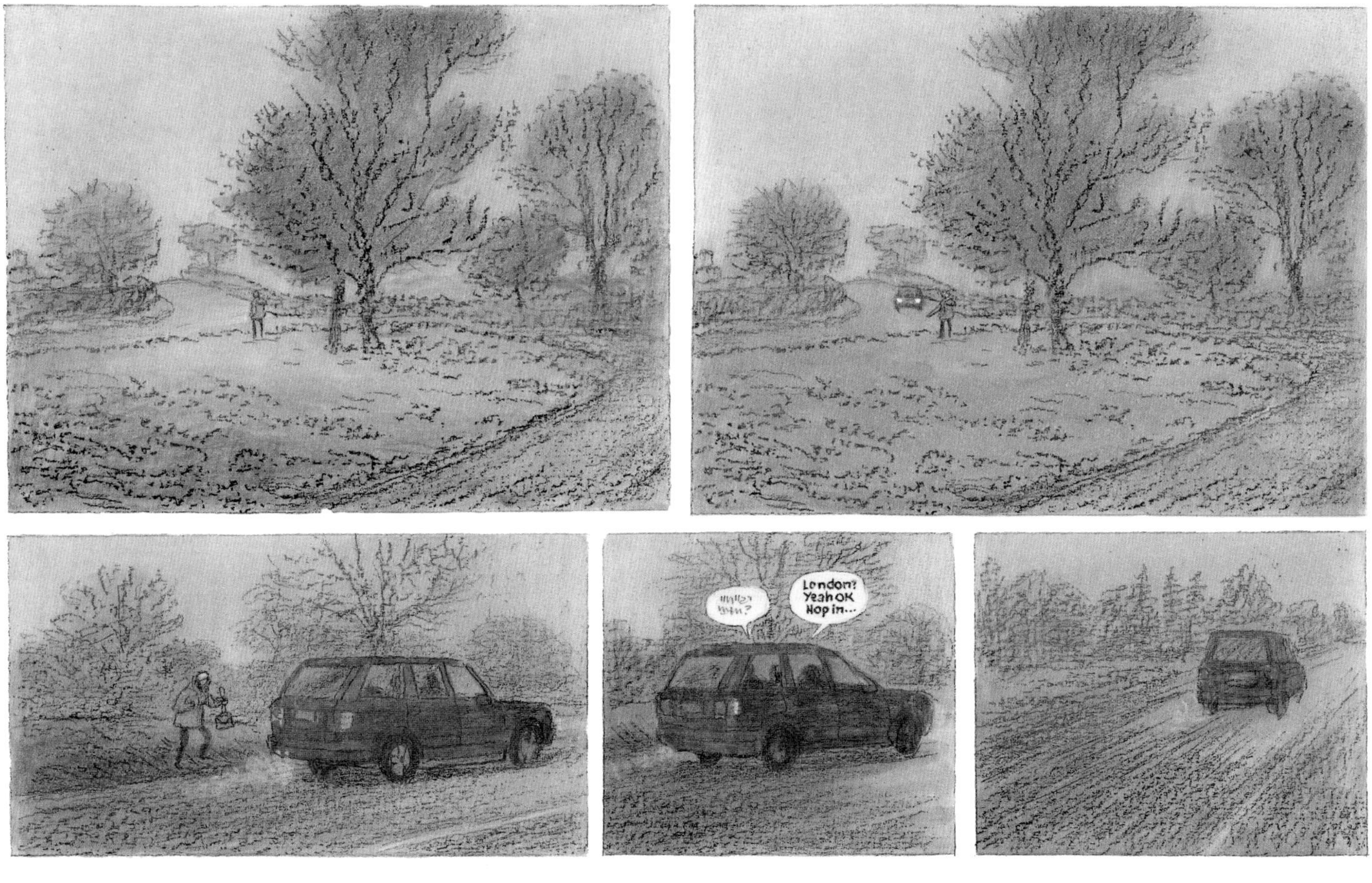
London? Yeah OK Hop in...

The girl sits in the back with me. Foreign. Pissed off. Didn't say her name. In fact, said nothing, except she was cold, and she "had ride from Bristol"... until "truck driver tell her to get the hell out", near where Deano picked her up.

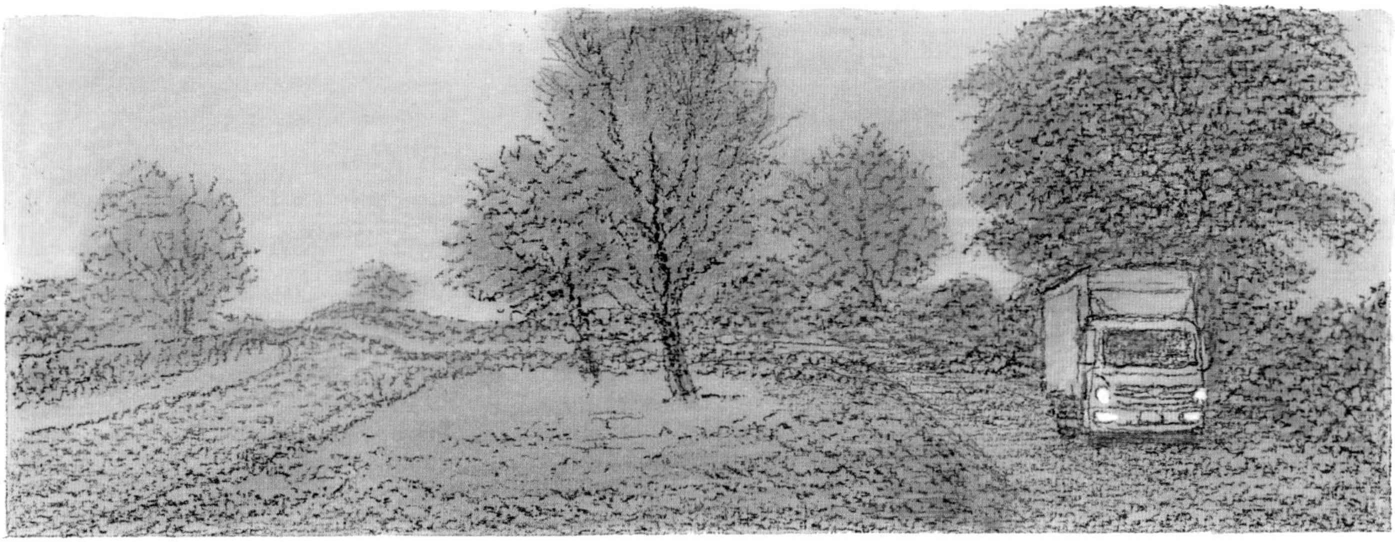

We stop for petrol and Deano says for her to sit next to him in the front. Me and Nanny have a kip in the back and when I wakes up we're back in town. God knows what crap Deano's told her but the girl's all smiles. Got her hand on his knee and is totally up for a drink with him – or drugs maybe it was. Deano doesn't go the normal way to Eastland Road, he goes all round the houses, parks up, inside some gates near the railway. Turns out it's near the back of the Harts' scrap yard. You go up this little alley to the office and main entrance on Brignall Way.

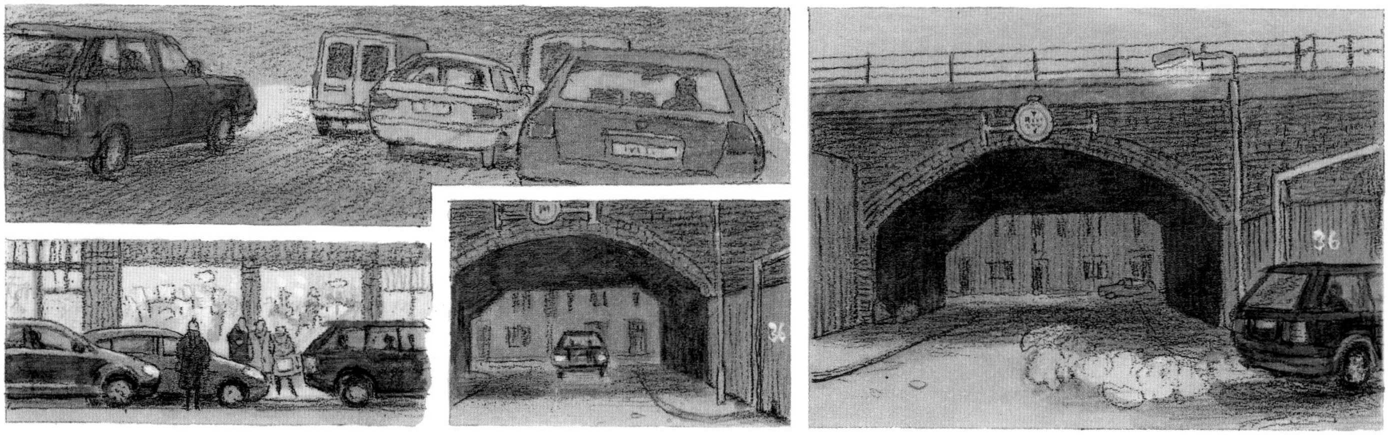

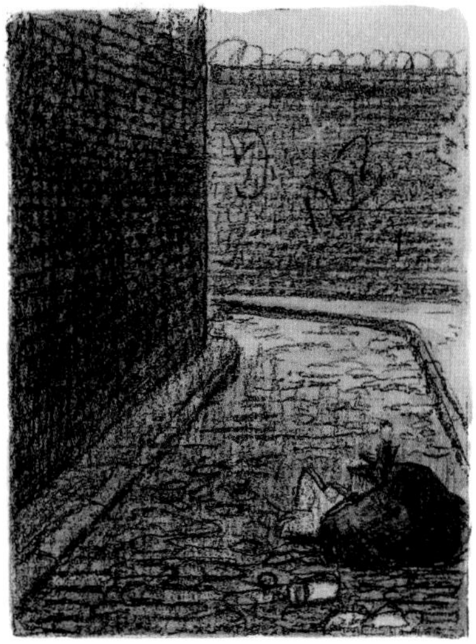

So Deano goes round the passenger side of the car, helps the lady out all gentleman-like. Nanny and me, we're like shutting the gates. Deano comes over, totally ignores me, says to Nanny something about bringing Deano's fags and the tripod out the boot. Then he and the girl go skipping off up the alley.

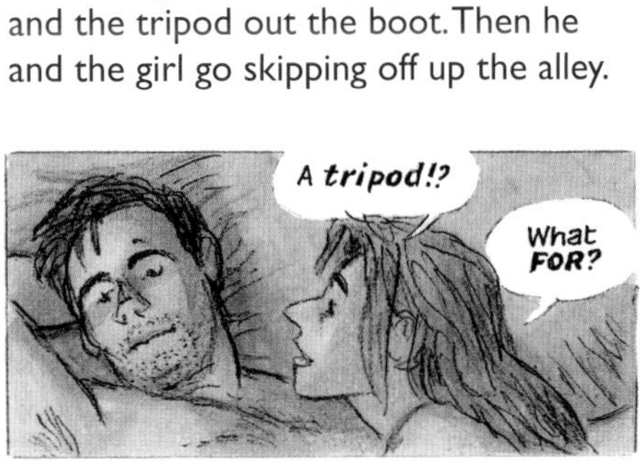
A ***tripod!?***
What ***FOR?***

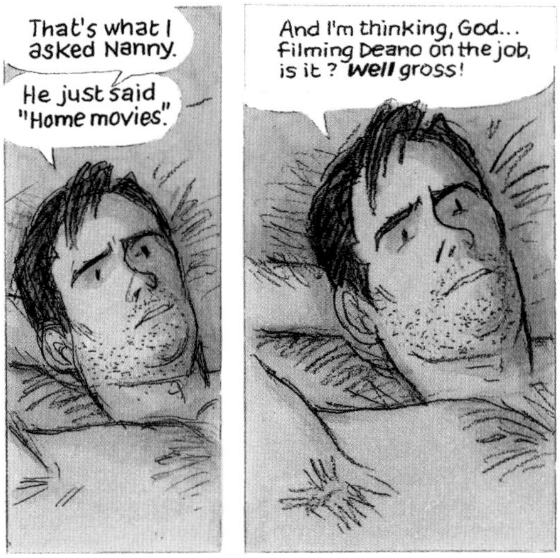
That's what I asked Nanny.
He just said "Home movies".
And I'm thinking, God... filming Deano on the job, is it? ***Well*** gross!

Billy said: While Nanny was round by the boot, I'm inside the car, looking everywhere for Deano's fags. On the back seat I see a glove the girl's left behind, and a little make-up bag. Which I put in my pocket to give her. Shoved under the driver's seat there's this body warmer. Man-size. A dead weight inside the poacher pocket. And it sure ain't fags. What I feel is a gun.

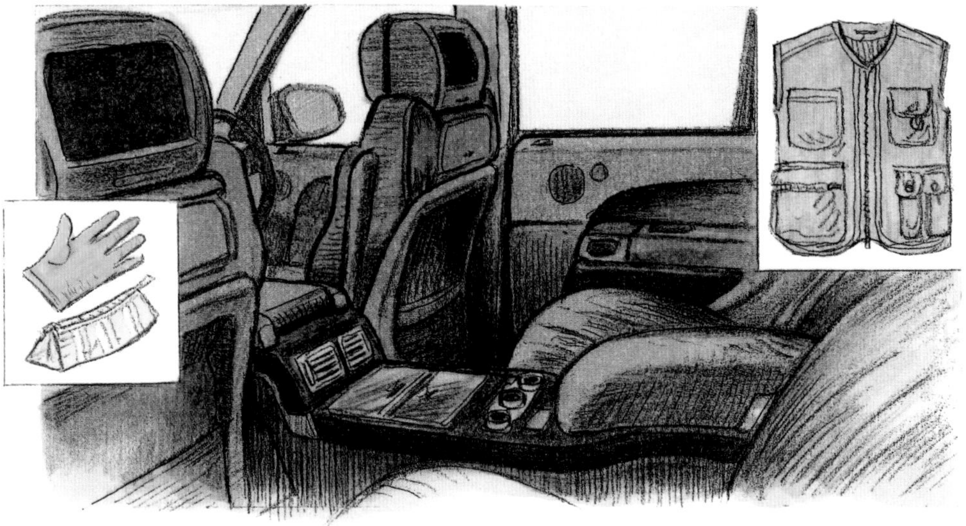

My first reaction is like "Bloody Deano!" Drives like a maniac – what if we'd been stopped by the road cops? What the fuck was he doing with it!? Then I think What the fuck am I doing with him!? I just wanted out. I was also mad at Deano for ignoring me, behaving like a macho prat. I pocketed his gun and a clip of bullets. Nanny's waiting by the alley and when I gets out he locks the motor with the remote, and walks off. I suppose I'm meant to follow with Deano's fags, but I was like fuck it. Deano's forgotten all about me. So, when Nanny disappeared round the corner, I legged it.

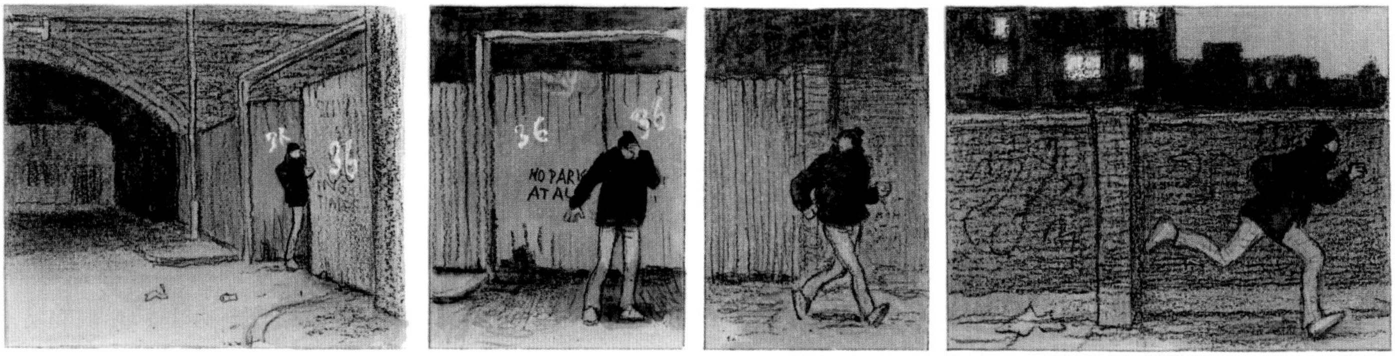

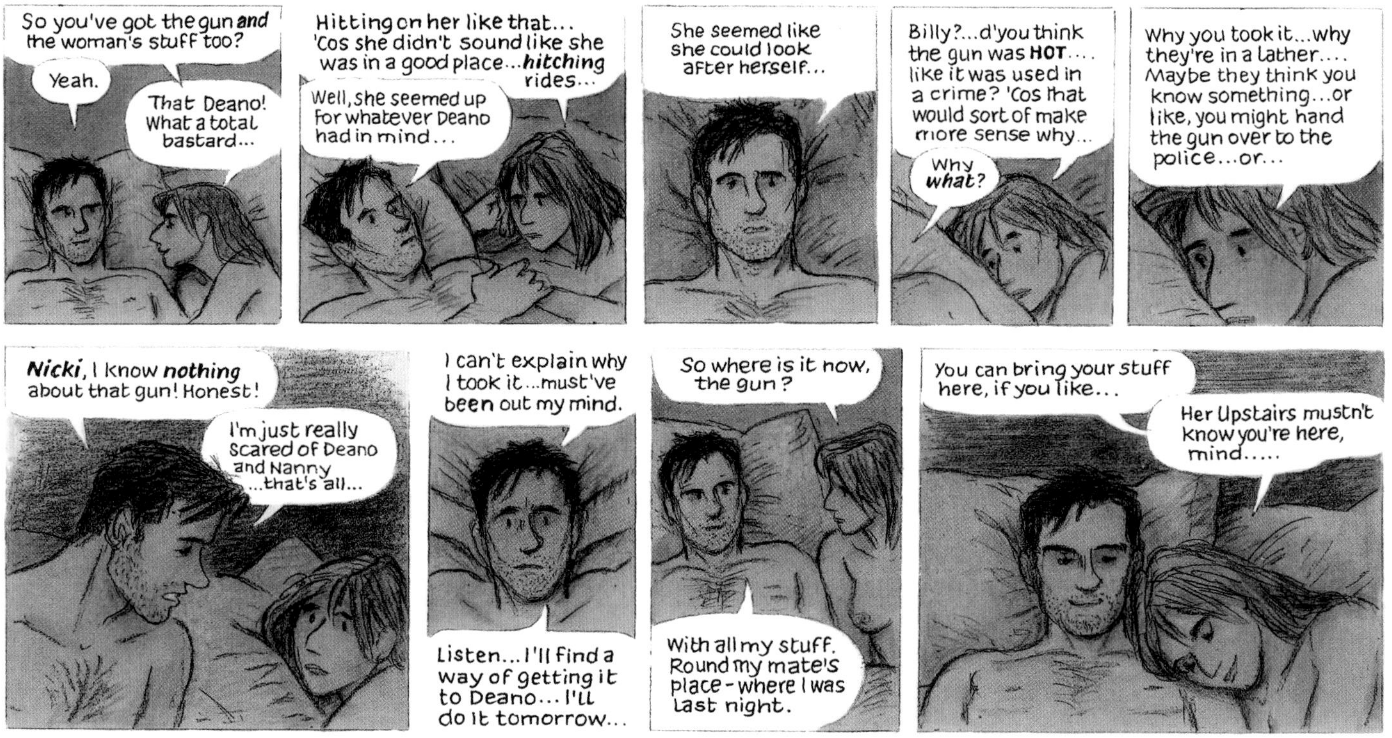
So you've got the gun and the woman's stuff too?
Yeah.
That Deano! What a total bastard...
Hitting on her like that... 'Cos she didn't sound like she was in a good place...hitching rides...
Well, she seemed up for whatever Deano had in mind...
She seemed like she could look after herself...
Billy?...d'you think the gun was HOT.... like it was used in a crime? 'Cos that would sort of make more sense why...
Why what?
Why you took it...why they're in a lather.... Maybe they think you know something...or like, you might hand the gun over to the police...or...
Nicki, I know nothing about that gun! Honest!
I'm just really scared of Deano and Nanny ...that's all...
I can't explain why I took it...must've been out my mind.
Listen...I'll find a way of getting it to Deano... I'll do it tomorrow...
So where is it now, the gun?
With all my stuff. Round my mate's place - where I was last night.
You can bring your stuff here, if you like...
Her Upstairs mustn't know you're here, mind.....

After I had blocked the obscene texter's number there were no further messages. No threats via my other devices, no poison pen letters. Nothing. Despite this I spent the rest of that autumn peering over my shoulder, paranoid that the texter (who surely had to be one of my duped clients) was about to break my legs, or at least denounce me in public. But which of them was it?

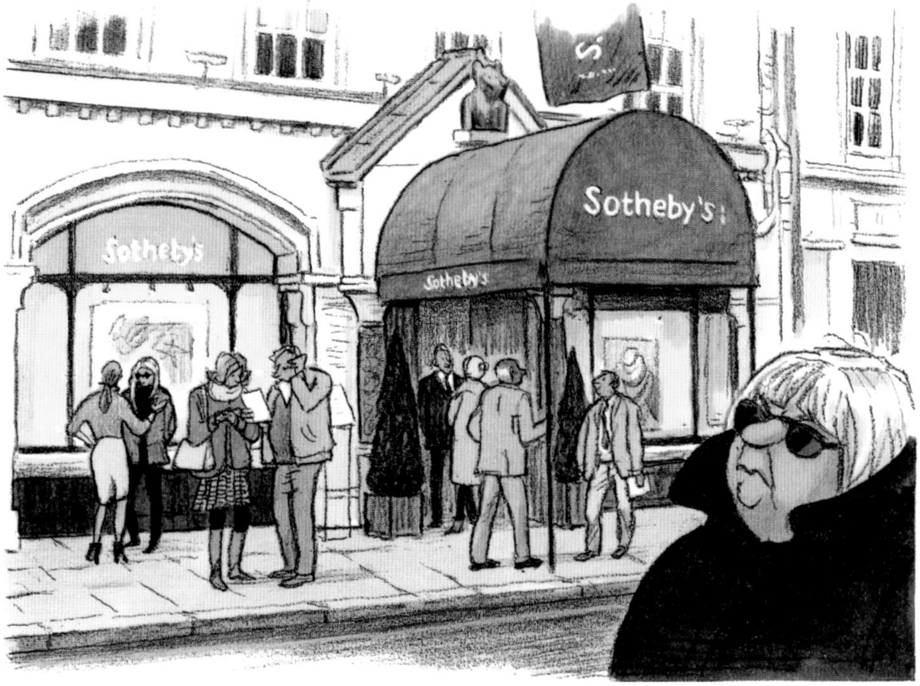
Sotheby's

I engineered chance meetings with three of the parties, who could not have been more beaming and amicable. I rang Kimberley Chaffham (notorious for snubs) and listened to her gush about the Lucian Freud she was buying. I went to Hampstead and lunched with Jane McMullen, just in case someone had planted suspicion in her woolly head. I found her out the back, in her pottery studio, wire-brushing a piece of rusty drainpipe.

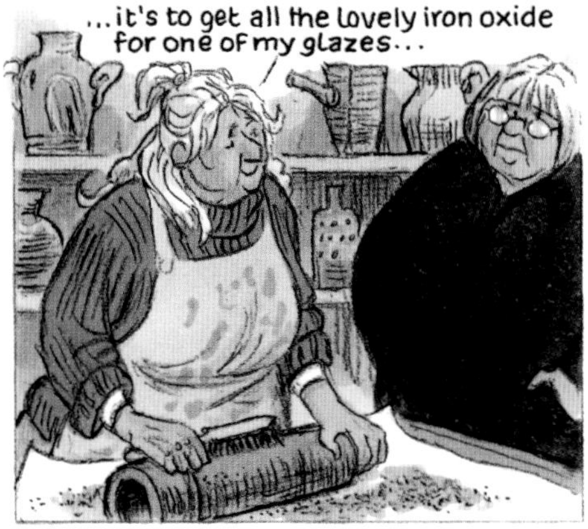
...it's to get all the lovely iron oxide for one of my glazes...

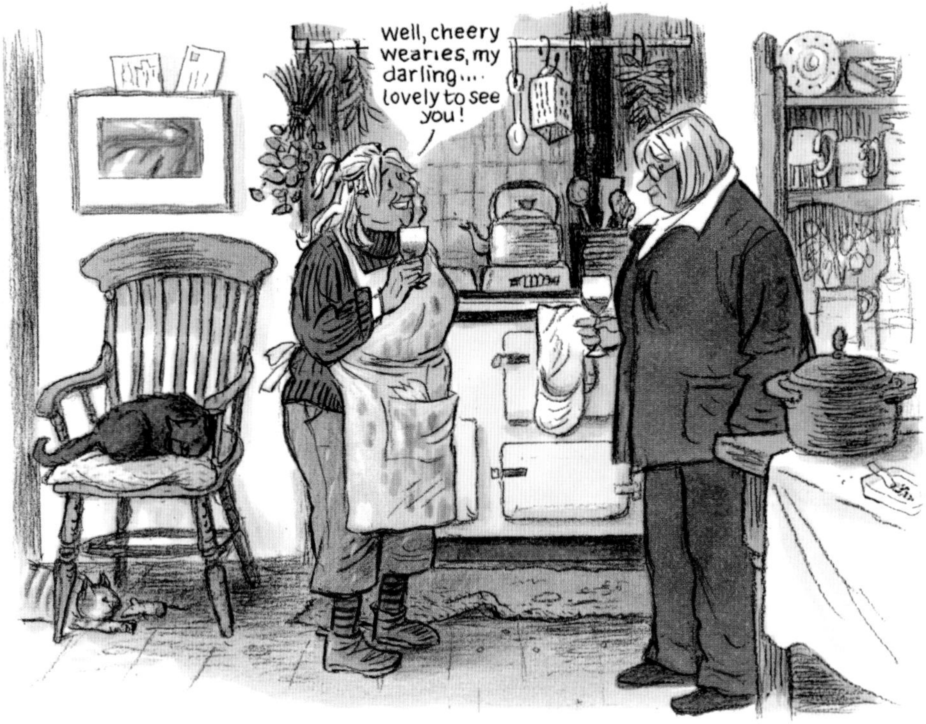
Well, cheery wearies, my darling... lovely to see you!

I needed a drink and fortunately Jane had opened a rather decent claret. Clearly she'd heard nothing (as yet) about my sleights of hand in the selling of Ken McMullen's work. We talked of old times, of Freddie, of her late husband. She said how eternally grateful she was to Frederick Boult for looking after Ken's estate so well. She was so trusting, absurdly pleased to see me. I did feel perfidious. And uncomfortable, not helped by the plateful of something beige Jane served, which made me fart all afternoon. I remember having to blame it on the dog.

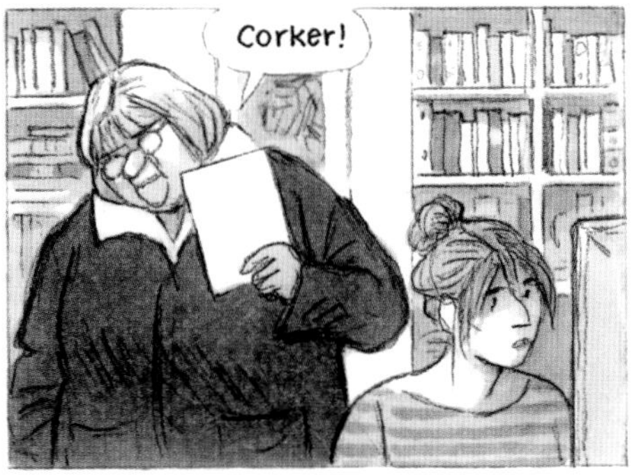
Corker!

As for Nicki, from her behaviour in art galleries, I knew she was quite capable of playing silly buggers and for a moment I did nurse suspicions about her being behind the texts, but soon dismissed them. After all, she enjoyed my generosity. Why would she want to annoy me? Why spit in a well she was drinking out of?

The one positive effect of the text business was to make me more watchful at home. For instance I hadn't noticed just how matey Nicki and Elsa had become. I was now aware of them murmuring in the kitchen, Nicki trying out her dreadful Italian. It seemed she'd spent family holidays near La Spezia where Elsa grew up.
Until I noticed Nicki carrying Tupperware boxes, I'd been unaware that Elsa was giving Nicki the leftovers of meals she cooked for me. I mean prime steak, osso buco, turbot, tiramisu. I put a stop to it.
Buggered if I was feeding the girl as well as housing her.

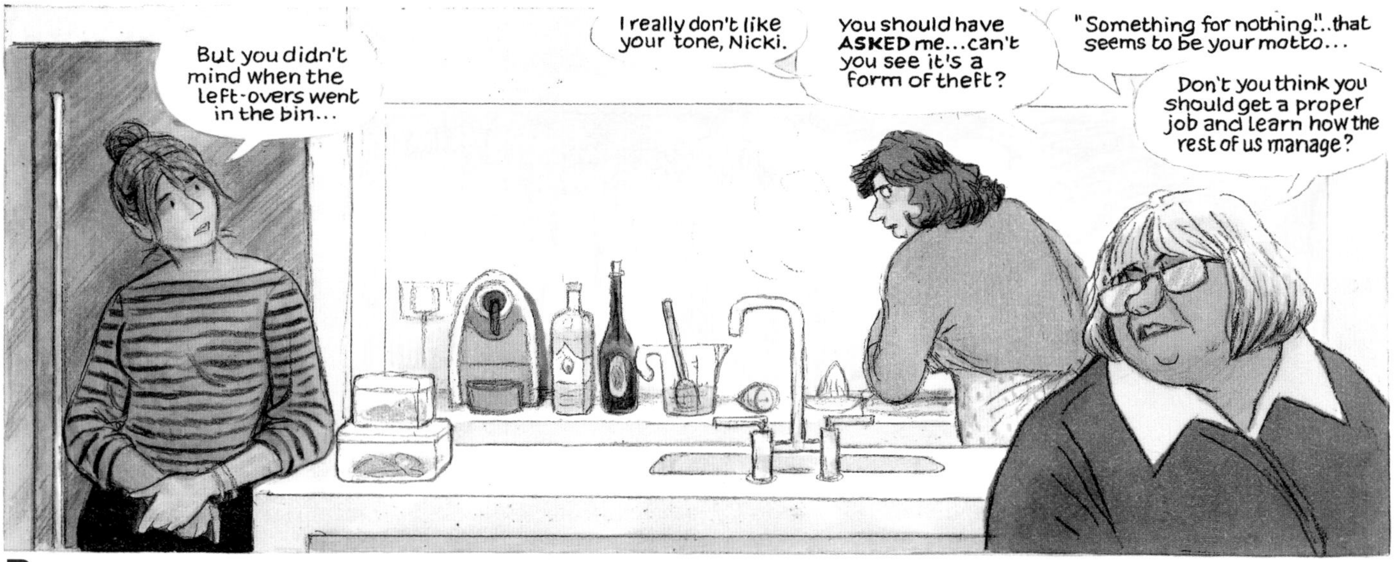

But you didn't mind when the left-overs went in the bin...
I really don't like your tone, Nicki.
You should have ASKED me...can't you see it's a form of theft?
"Something for nothing"...that seems to be your motto...
Don't you think you should get a proper job and learn how the rest of us manage?

Perhaps something I said rubbed off on Nicki. She expressed an interest in the world of art dealing, asking questions and wanting to come with me to the salerooms. I told her how I began my career working as a counter girl at Sotheby's in the late Sixties. Dealing with queues bringing their worthless oleographs, bits of silver and so on. I told her how occcasionally I would spot something very good – my eye often proving keener than some of the experts in the building.

Then I asked Nicki about the project she was supposed to be working on (for which I had lent her £1,000). She of course got out her bloody iPad.

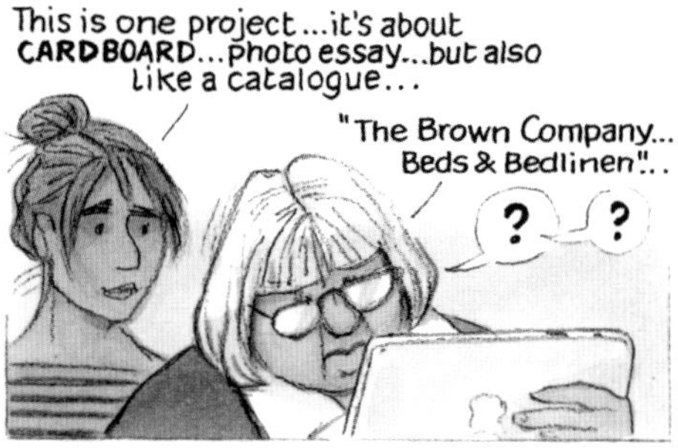

This is one project...it's about CARDBOARD...photo essay...but also like a catalogue...
"The Brown Company... Beds & Bedlinen"...
? ?

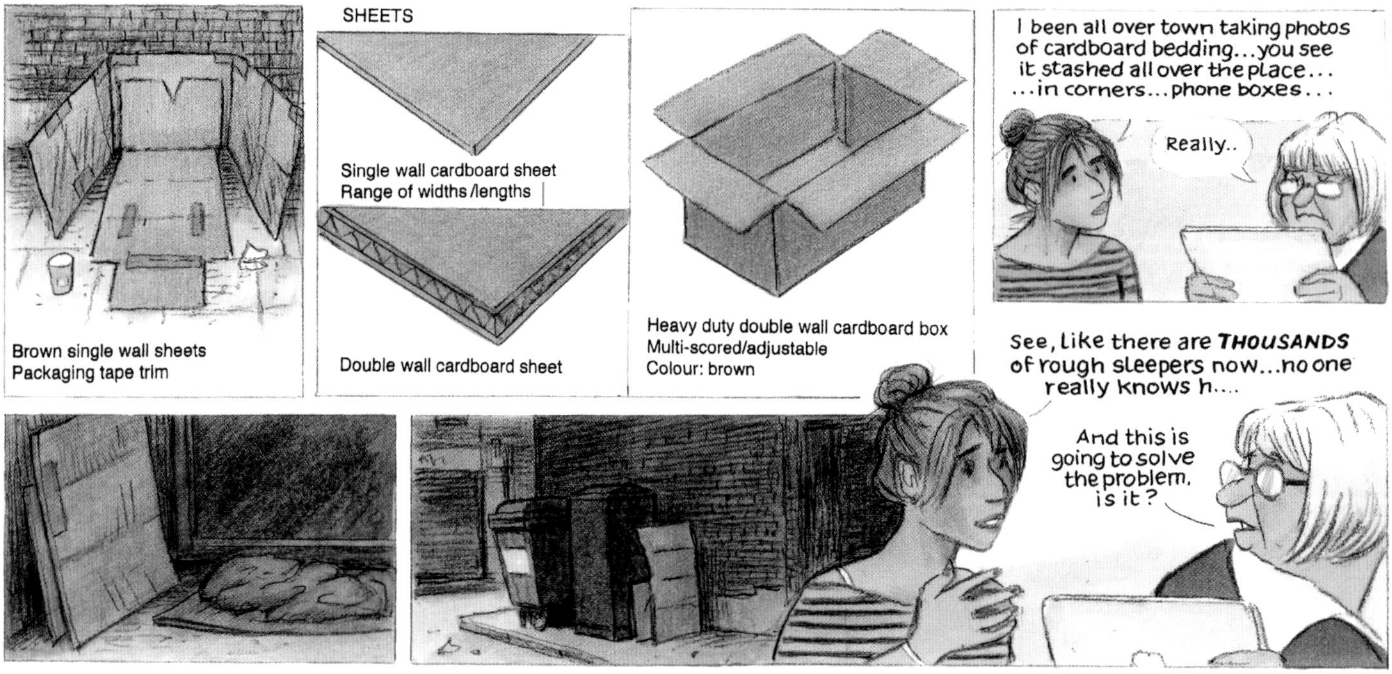

Brown single wall sheets
Packaging tape trim
SHEETS
Single wall cardboard sheet
Range of widths /lengths
Double wall cardboard sheet
Heavy duty double wall cardboard box
Multi-scored/adjustable
Colour: brown
I been all over town taking photos of cardboard bedding...you see it stashed all over the place... ...in corners...phone boxes...
Really..
See, like there are THOUSANDS of rough sleepers now...no one really knows h....
And this is going to solve the problem, is it?

November 26th

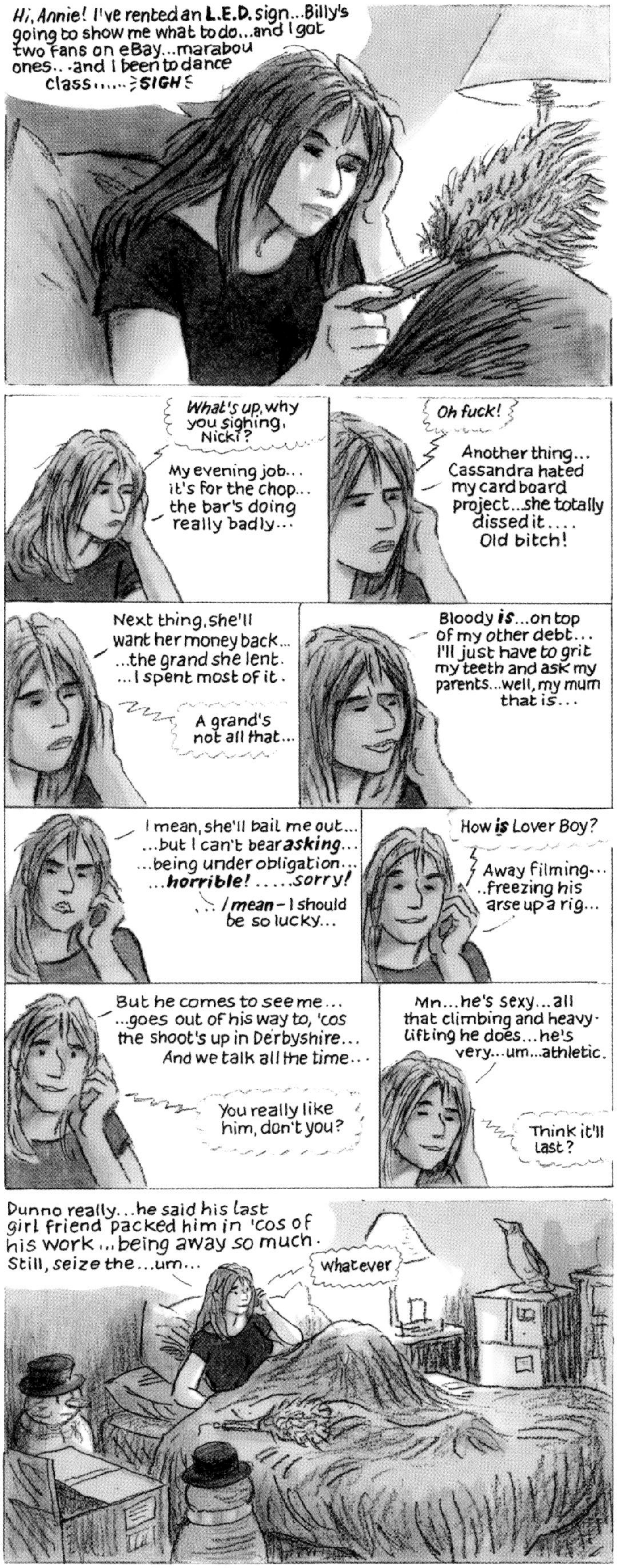

Hi, Annie! I've rented an L.E.D. sign...Billy's going to show me what to do...and I got two fans on eBay...marabou ones...and I been to dance class...... SIGH
What's up, why you sighing, Nicki?
My evening job... it's for the chop... the bar's doing really badly...
Oh fuck!
Another thing... Cassandra hated my card board project...she totally dissed it.... Old bitch!
Next thing, she'll want her money back... ...the grand she lent. ...I spent most of it.
A grand's not all that...
Bloody is...on top of my other debt... I'll just have to grit my teeth and ask my parents...well, my mum that is...
I mean, she'll bail me out... ...but I can't bear asking... ...being under obligation... ...horrible!.....sorry!
...I mean - I should be so lucky...
How is Lover Boy?
Away filming... ..freezing his arse up a rig...
But he comes to see me... ...goes out of his way to, 'cos the shoot's up in Derbyshire... And we talk all the time...
You really like him, don't you?
Mn...he's sexy...all that climbing and heavy-lifting he does...he's very...um...athletic.
Think it'll last?
Dunno really...he said his last girl friend packed him in 'cos of his work...being away so much. Still, seize the...um...
whatever

December 4th

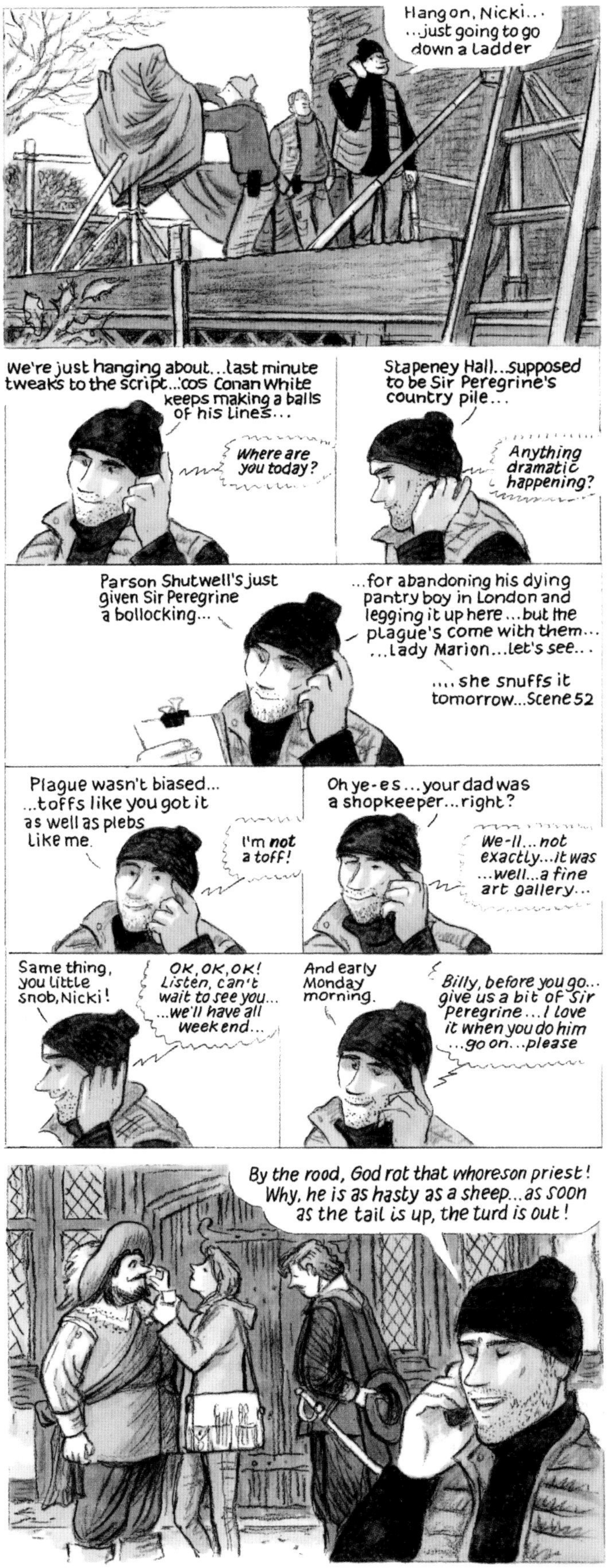

Hang on, Nicki... ...just going to go down a ladder
We're just hanging about...last minute tweaks to the script...'cos Conan White keeps making a balls of his lines...
Where are you today?
Stapeney Hall...supposed to be Sir Peregrine's country pile...
Anything dramatic happening?
Parson Shutwell's just given Sir Peregrine a bollocking...
...for abandoning his dying pantry boy in London and legging it up here...but the plague's come with them... ...Lady Marion...let's see...
....she snuffs it tomorrow...Scene 52
Plague wasn't biased... ...toffs like you got it as well as plebs like me.
I'm not a toff!
Oh ye-es...your dad was a shopkeeper...right?
We-ll...not exactly...it was ...well...a fine art gallery...
Same thing, you little snob, Nicki!
OK, OK, OK! Listen, can't wait to see you... ...we'll have all weekend...
And early Monday morning.
Billy, before you go... give us a bit of Sir Peregrine...I love it when you do him ...go on...please
By the rood, God rot that whoreson priest! Why, he is as hasty as a sheep...as soon as the tail is up, the turd is out!

By the end of last November, I had decided that Nicki must go. She had become sloppy, inattentive, yawned the whole time. As for her righteousness, one wanted to vomit, the way she paraded her virtue in her art. (If one could call it art – when it required no skill, no precision, no aesthetic content and reeked of bourgeois shame).

Christmas seemed the best time to tell her as by then she would have finished transcribing my book, including the footnotes. There was also another job I'd asked her to do. I was going away for a week, as I usually did in December. My house in Brittany being uncomfortable in winter, I'd booked into a hotel in Biarritz.
The girls in the gallery, Elsa, Milena, Nicki and my driver had all had plenty of warning of the dates. Elsa was to come in daily to check the house and, as I deplored the cost of kennels, Nicki had agreed to look after Corker.

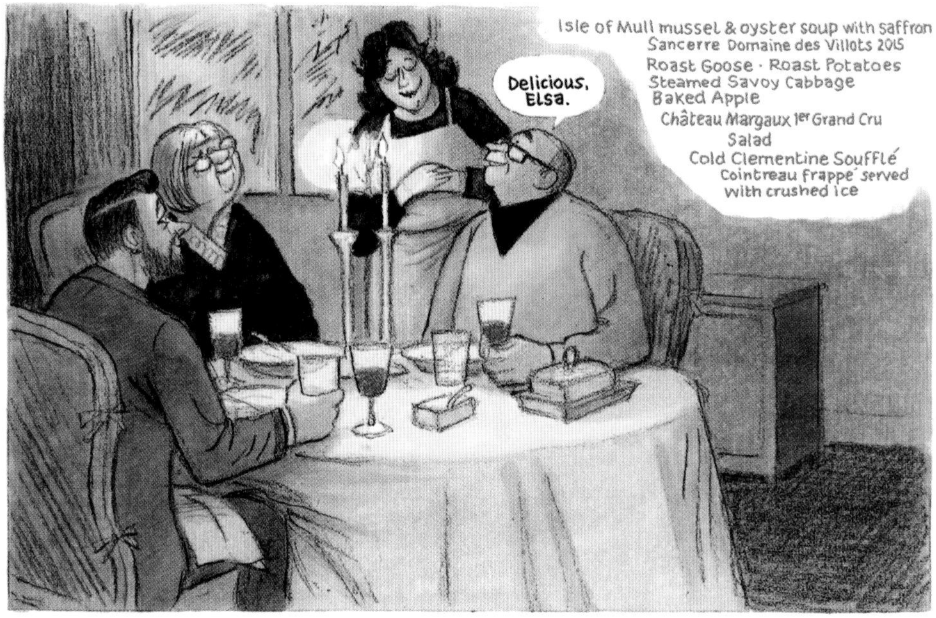
Isle of Mull mussel & oyster soup with saffron
Sancerre Domaine des Villots 2015
Roast Goose · Roast Potatoes
Steamed Savoy Cabbage
Baked Apple
Château Margaux 1er Grand Cru
Salad
Cold Clementine Soufflé
Cointreau frappé served with crushed ice
Delicious, Elsa.

A day or two before my departure I had invited Teddy Wood and his partner, Yves, to dinner. The dining area on the ground floor was rarely used.
I entertained very little and in the ordinary way ate upstairs in the evening, watching TV. Elsa would prepare a tray and leave things to be heated.
That evening Elsa had cooked a magnificent dinner which was quite ruined (for me anyway) by the noises coming up from the basement …

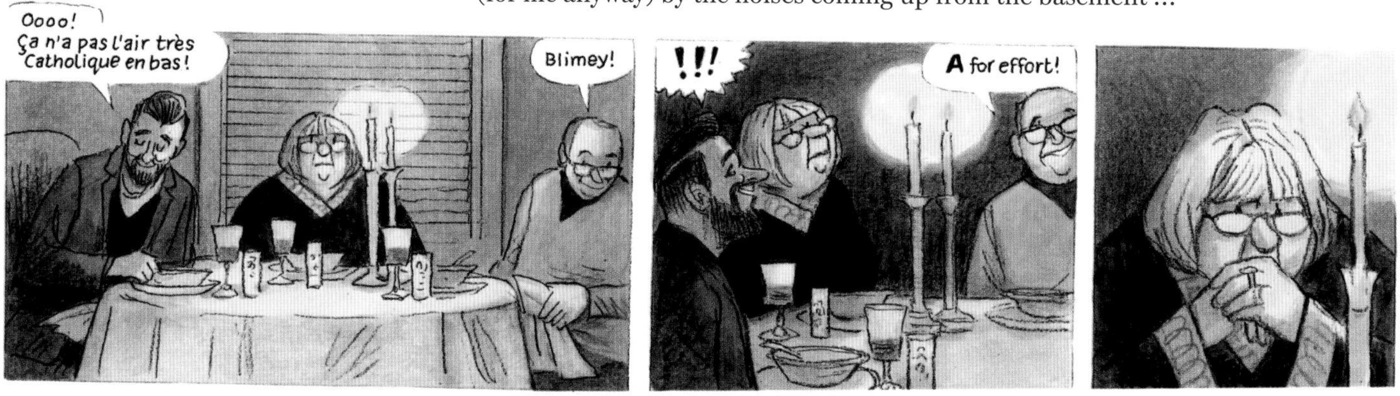
Oooo! Ça n'a pas l'air très Catholique en bas!
Blimey!
!!!
A for effort!

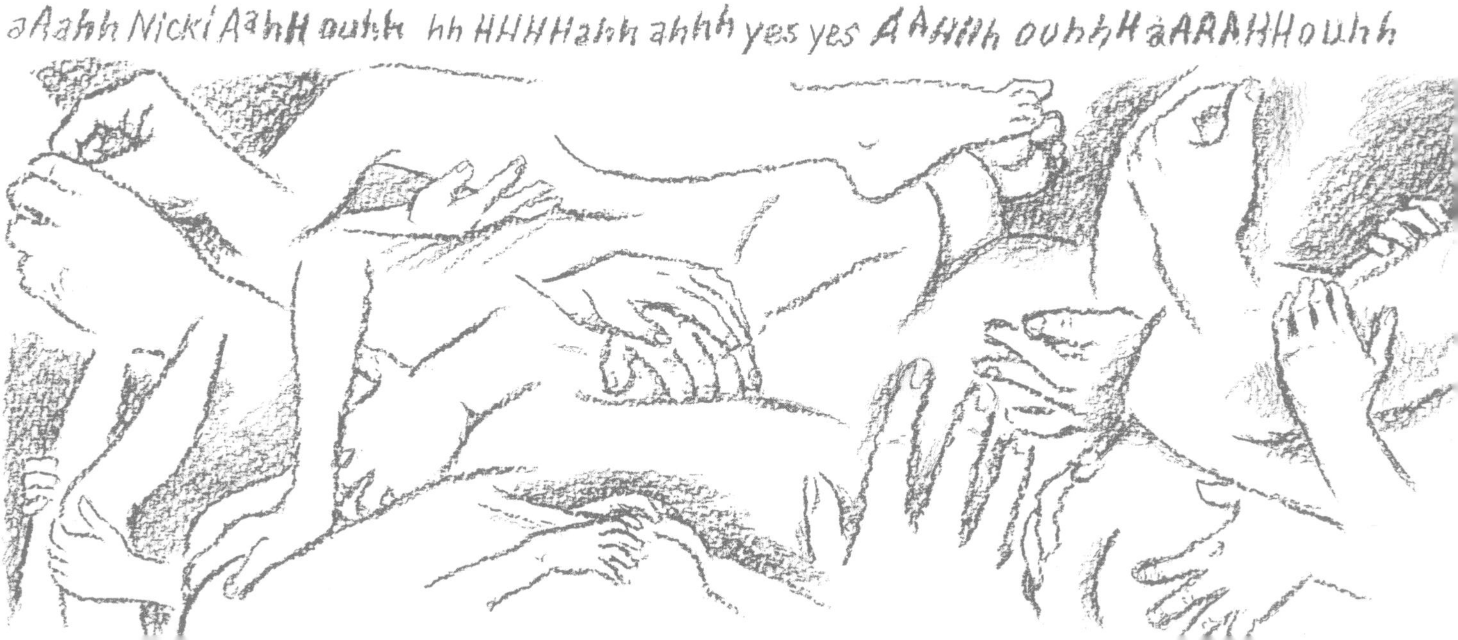
aAahh Nicki AahH ouhh hh HHHHahh ahhh yes yes AAHHh ouhhHaARAHHouhh

I am not a prude. Nicki Boult was entitled to a sex life. Albeit in my basement, but that was not the cause of my anguish during the small hours.

I had been married and divorced but otherwise not much troubled by ardour. Something on which I once prided myself – other people's love life seemed so all-consuming and messy. Over the years I had one or two liaisons, but always disliked the power play between the sexes, the coercion, submission, the idea of being "had".

Of course at a cultural level I believed Love to be many-splendoured, in books, plays, poetry and its depiction in art – Indian temples, paintings by my favourite Giulio Romano, or Utamaro prints. But in practice, I could never stop thinking how utterly absurd the act was, no more sublime, say, than the pile of pigs I once saw on a country walk. The same squeals and grunts.

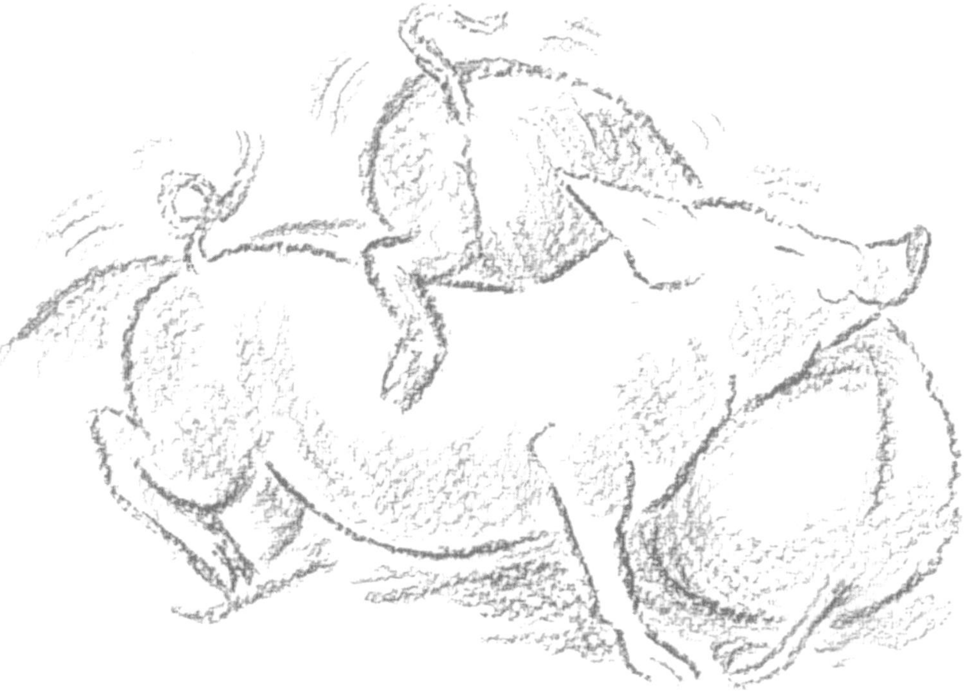

But the goings on in the basement played in my imagination. Long after my guests had gone I remember sitting overwhelmed by regret. It was the realisation that my diffidence in sexual matters had been just cowardice, the fear of losing control. I had denied myself pleasure. I had never lost myself in the steam of passion as I imagined Nicki had. Certainly no one had ever cried out my name as her lover did. (Although "Cassandra" is more of a mouthful to repeat at peak moments.)

And there I was, late in life, nursing plans for death and had barely lived, it seemed.

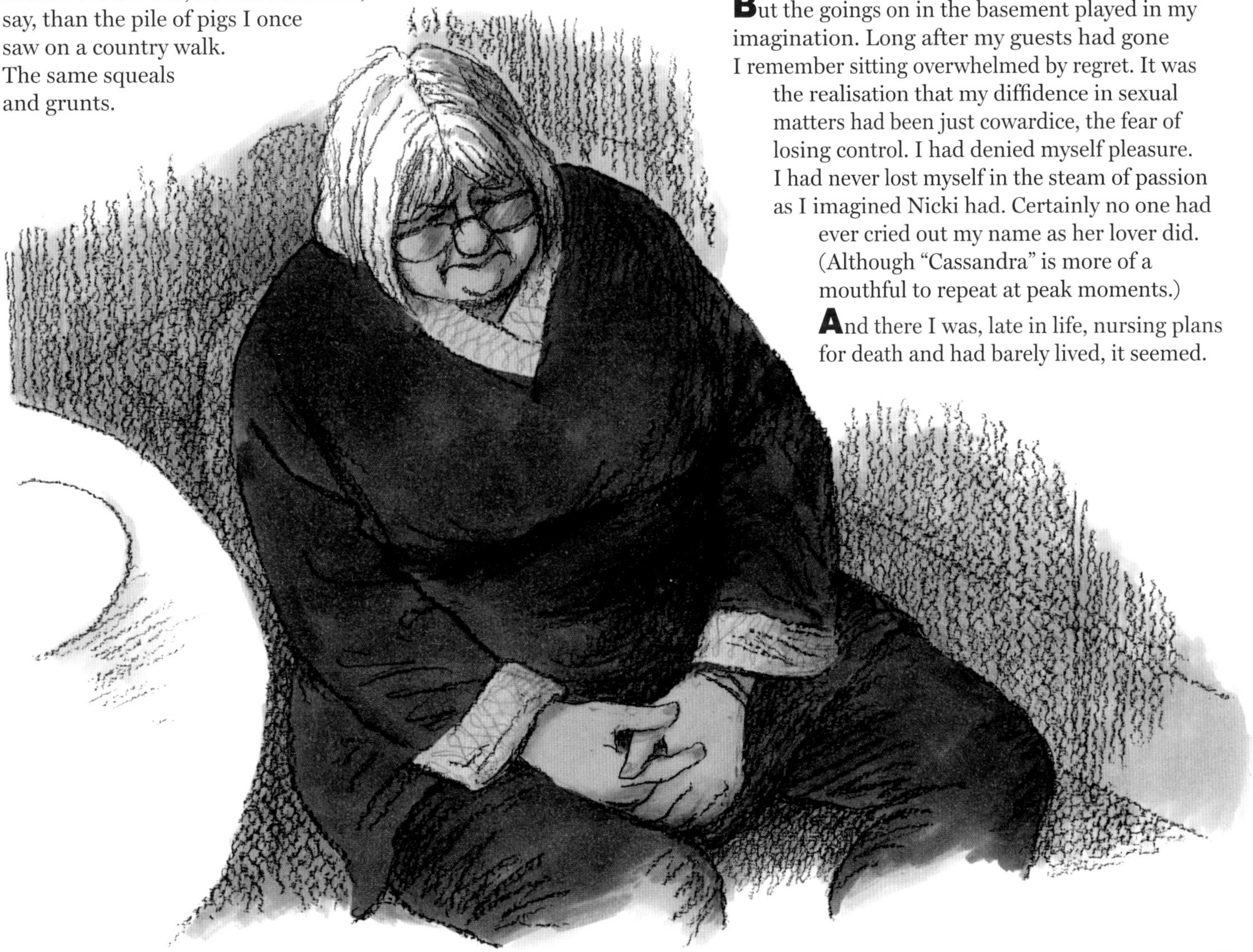

As Nicki had Sundays off, I was up early the next day to walk the dog and later sat over breakfast bung-eyed from lack of sleep.
I heard the whine of the basement gate. There were the two love-birds, the same man I'd once met on the doorstep, and Nicki, looking smarter than usual. (She'd mentioned she was going to the country to see her parents.) It occurred to me that if he was living down below he ought to pay some rent – Chelsea rates. I'd ask Elsa to keep tabs on the situation while I was away.

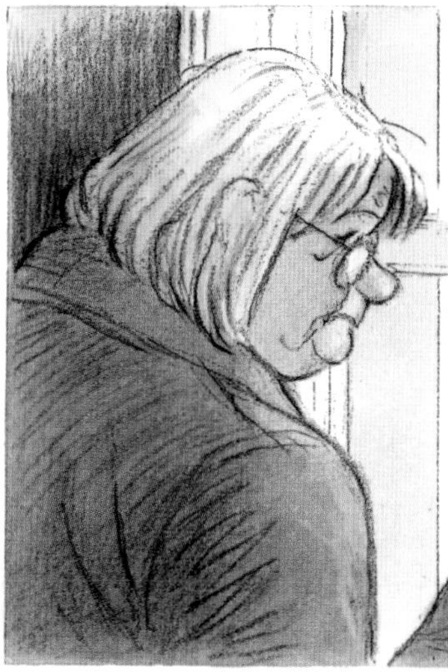

But perhaps their relationship was a bit wobbly. They seemed to be having an argument. Before they disappeared, I heard Nicki say quite clearly, "Why did you lie?"

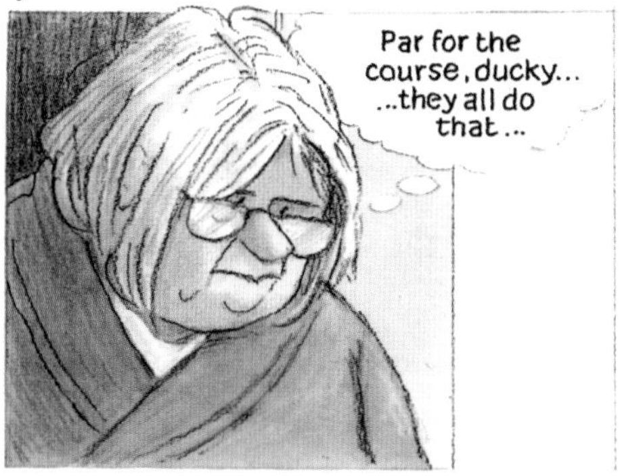

Par for the course, ducky... ...they all do that...

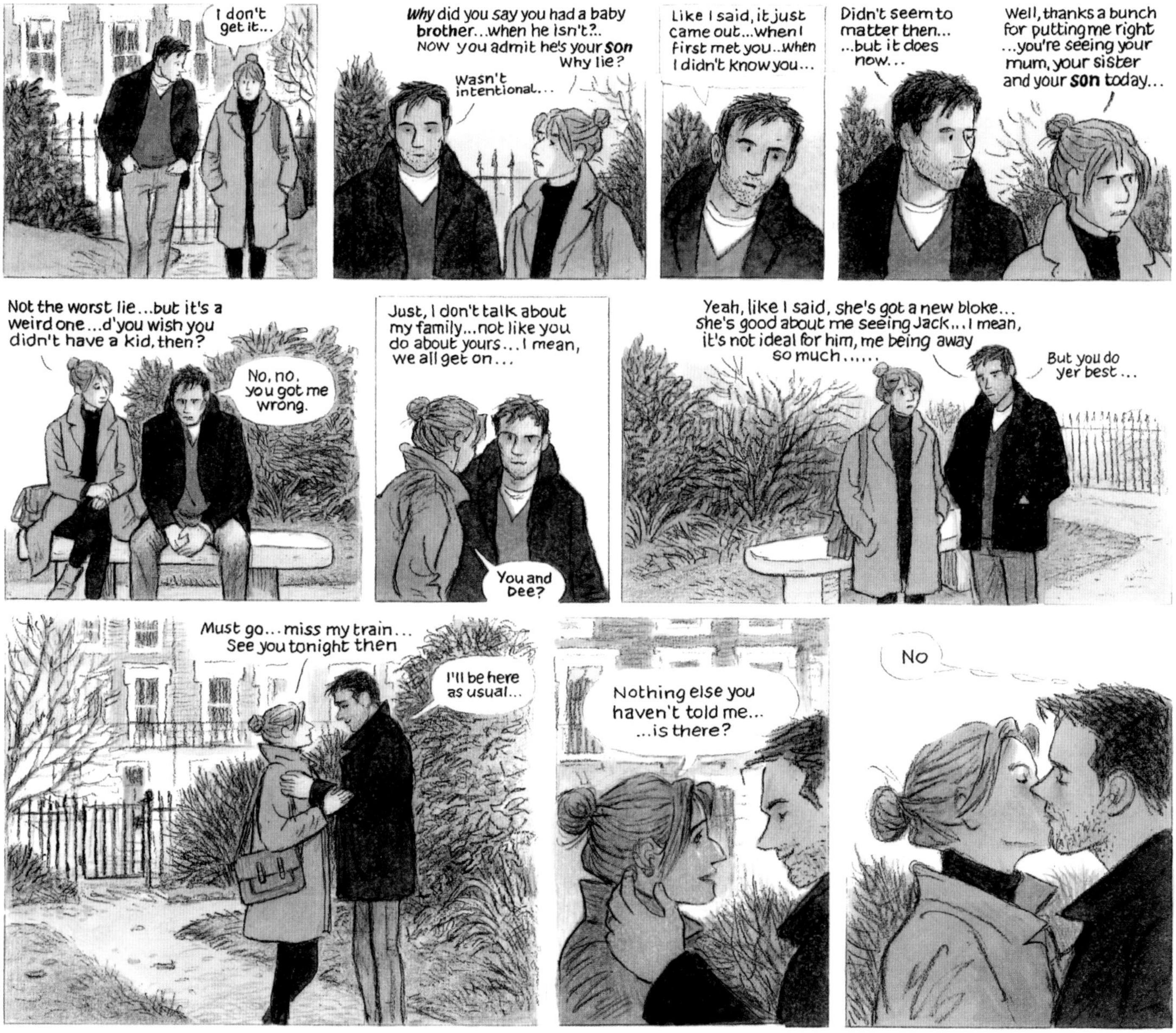

I don't get it...
Why did you say you had a baby brother...when he isn't?.. Now you admit he's your son Why lie?
Wasn't intentional...
Like I said, it just came out...when I first met you...when I didn't know you...
Didn't seem to matter then... ...but it does now...
Well, thanks a bunch for putting me right ...you're seeing your mum, your sister and your son today...
Not the worst lie...but it's a weird one...d'you wish you didn't have a kid, then?
No, no, you got me wrong.
Just, I don't talk about my family...not like you do about yours...I mean, we all get on...
You and Dee?
Yeah, like I said, she's got a new bloke... she's good about me seeing Jack... I mean, it's not ideal for him, me being away so much......
But you do yer best...
Must go... miss my train... See you tonight then
I'll be here as usual...
Nothing else you haven't told me... ...is there?
No

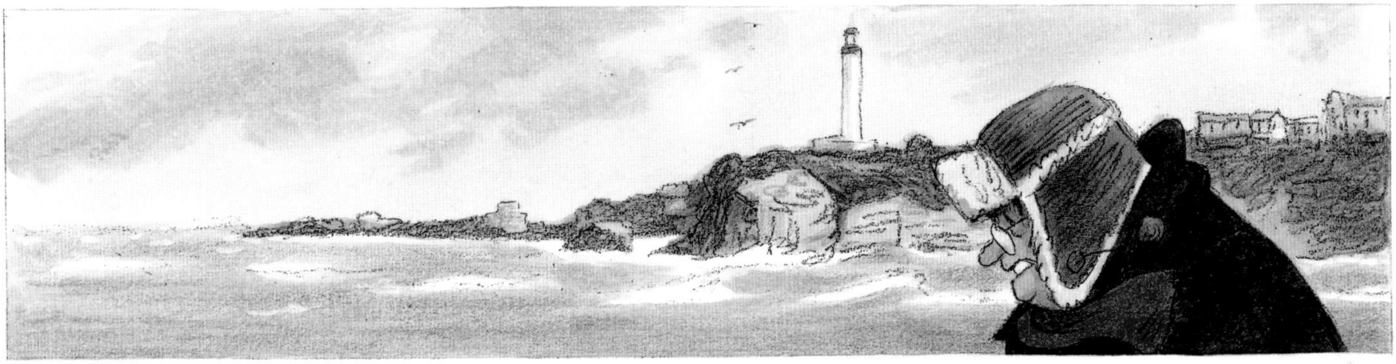

With hindsight, my choice of a 5-star hotel in Biarritz was crazy, but then I had no inkling that financial ruin was around the corner. I had stayed there several times, always in December, and found it perfect. The service was both attentive and discreet, the spaces large enough to avoid intimacy with other guests, beyond the odd "bonjour/bonsoir" in the lift. The only person I ever engaged with was the sommelier.

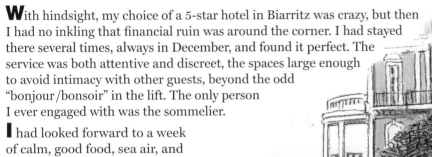

I had looked forward to a week of calm, good food, sea air, and the opportunity to revise a chapter of my book (one covering the British sculptors who showed at the Venice Biennale in 1952, and whose neurotic, contorted and melodramatic work I admired).

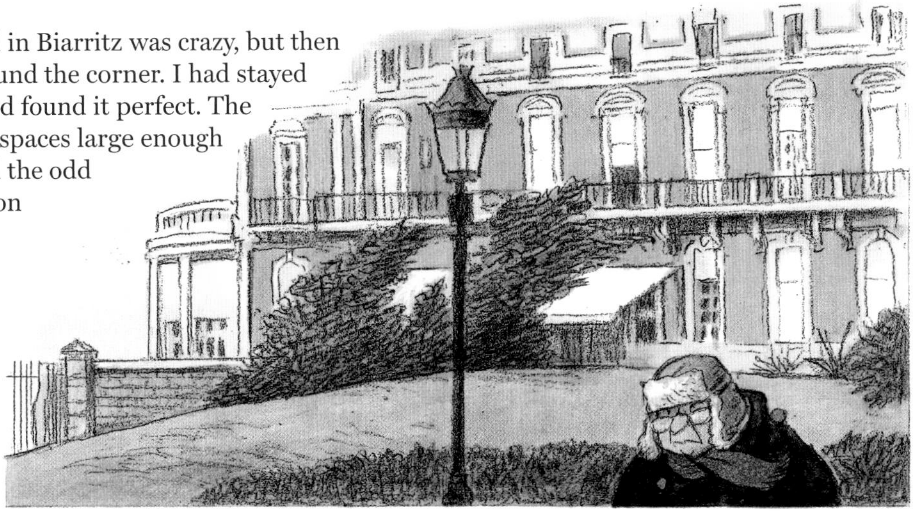

In the event I could not concentrate: distracted by the tick of my alarm clock, the creak of the chaise longue when I moved. Outside, in my favourite kind of weather, the wind scattered every consecutive thought. I was aware of time passing, it was like being in a waiting room for some unfixed appointment. Occasionally it was time for lunch, a nap, or a walk, but mostly it was time wasted, time gone. I was tense, suffered indigestion, slept badly.

On the third night of my stay I dreamed of Freddie. His younger self stood by the bed, glaring at me. He spoke once, a well-worn phrase of his ...

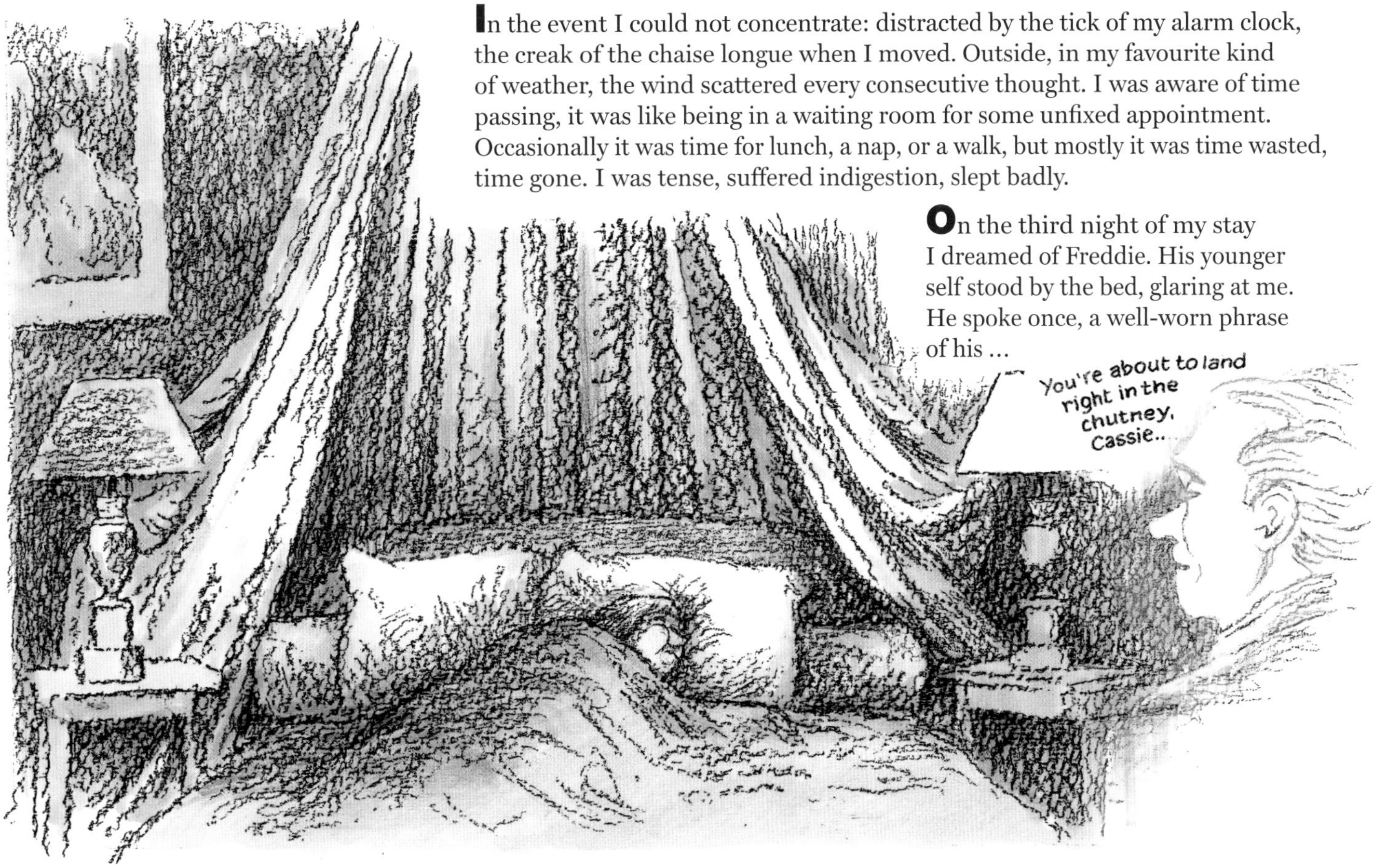
You're about to land right in the chutney, Cassie..

I cut short my stay in France, booked another flight and arrived back in Osmington Square in the late evening ...

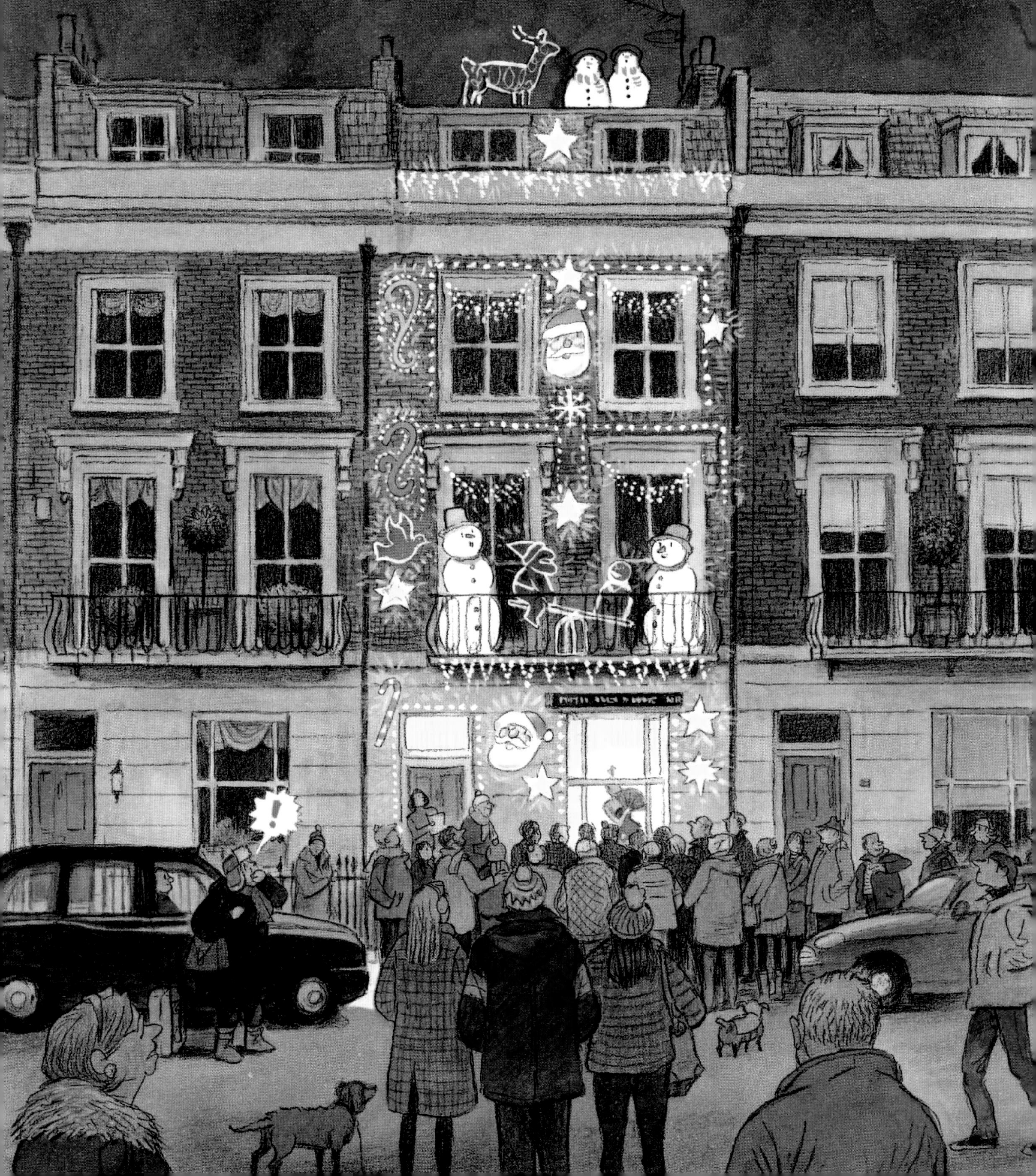
!

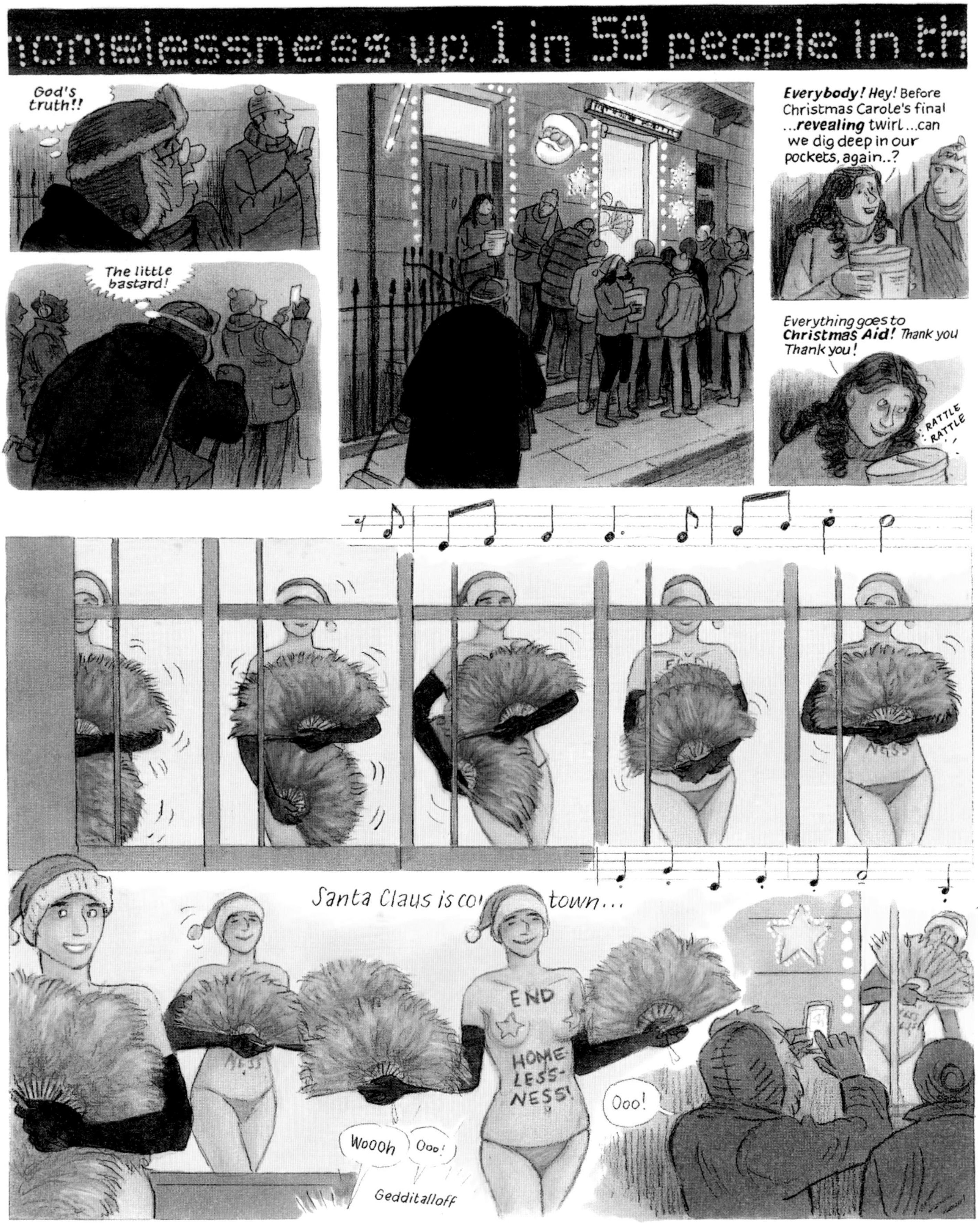
homelessness up. 1 in 59 people in th
God's truth!!
The little bastard!
Everybody! Hey! Before Christmas Carole's final ...revealing twirl...can we dig deep in our pockets, again..?
Everything goes to Christmas Aid! Thank you Thank you!
RATTLE RATTLE
Santa Claus is co town...
END
HOME-LESS-NESS!
Ooo!
Woooh
Ooo!
Gedditalloff

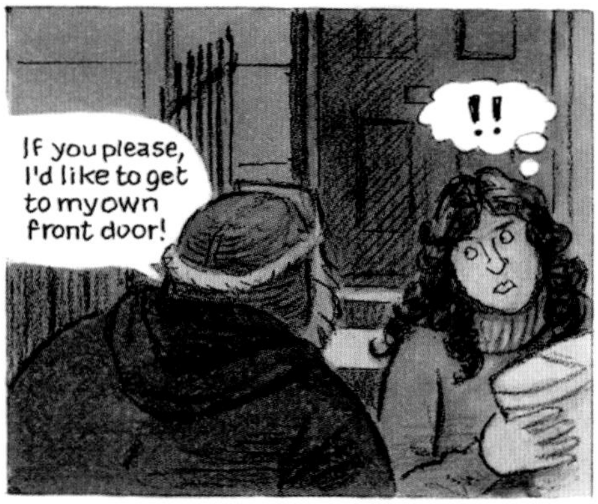
If you please, I'd like to get to my own front door!
!!

Inside the house I went straight to the fusebox and cut off the electricity. Darkness reigned.
I met Nicki in the hall, where I let fly ... at her deceit, contempt and betrayal of trust, at the theft of my electricity, her trespass inside the house and the defacement outside; at the tawdry public spectacle I'd witnessed, which had disturbed the entire neighbourhood. (Dodgy ground this, as there are few resident neighbours.) I wanted Nicki out of the basement and my loan repaid.

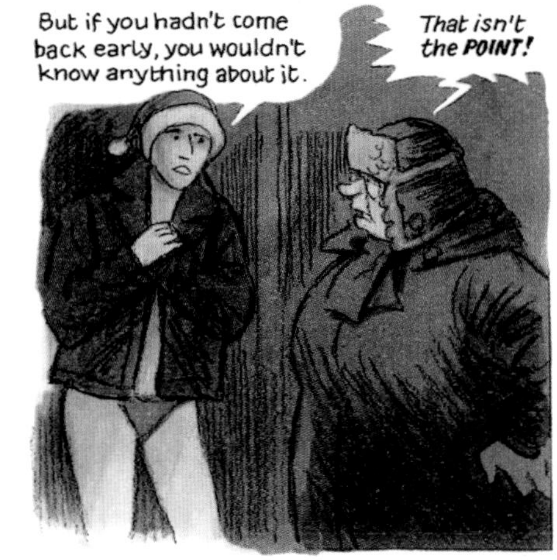
But if you hadn't come back early, you wouldn't know anything about it.
That isn't the POINT!

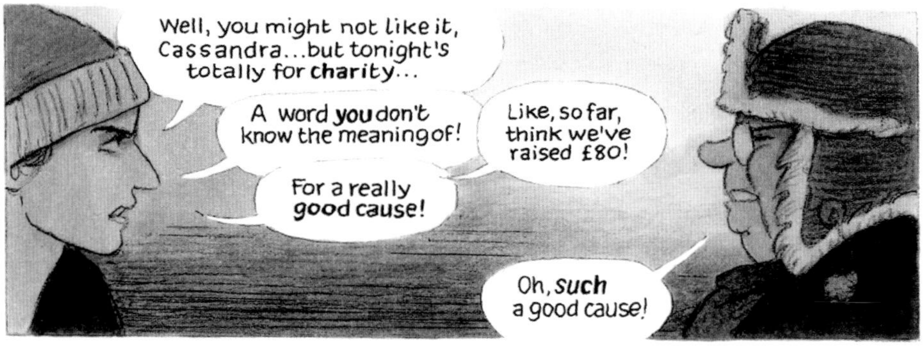
Well, you might not like it, Cassandra...but tonight's totally for charity...
A word you don't know the meaning of!
Like, so far, think we've raised £80!
For a really good cause!
Oh, such a good cause!

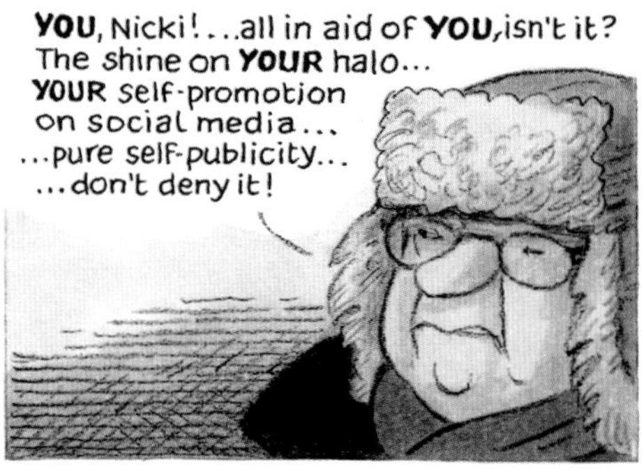
YOU, Nicki!...all in aid of YOU, isn't it? The shine on YOUR halo... YOUR self-promotion on social media... ...pure self-publicity... ...don't deny it!

The next morning Nicki appeared and I agreed to let her stay till Saturday, by which time she promised to have cleaned the basement and dismantled the Christmas junk on the house. I refused to feel bad about her – it wasn't as if she was being booted out on to the street. She would be going home to a Georgian farmhouse near Charlbury.
I received no apology for her deceit – and Elsa's too. During my absence Elsa had nipped off to Italy to see a new grandchild, leaving Nicki in charge of the house. The only thing that caused Nicki concern was my accusation of hypocrisy ...

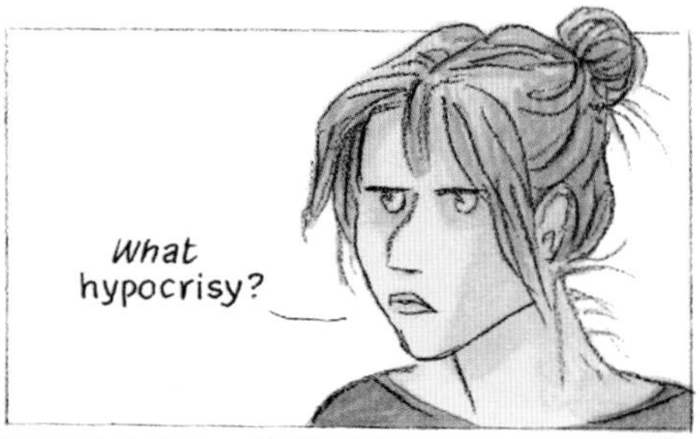
What hypocrisy?

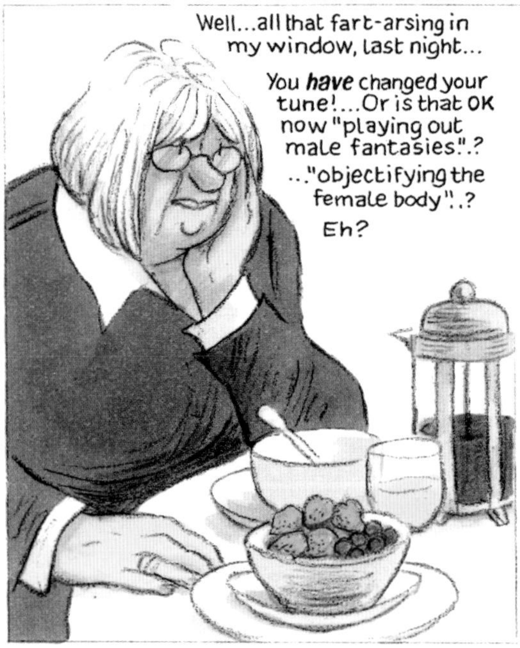
Well...all that fart-arsing in my window, last night...
You have changed your tune!...Or is that OK now "playing out male fantasies".? ..."objectifying the female body".? Eh?

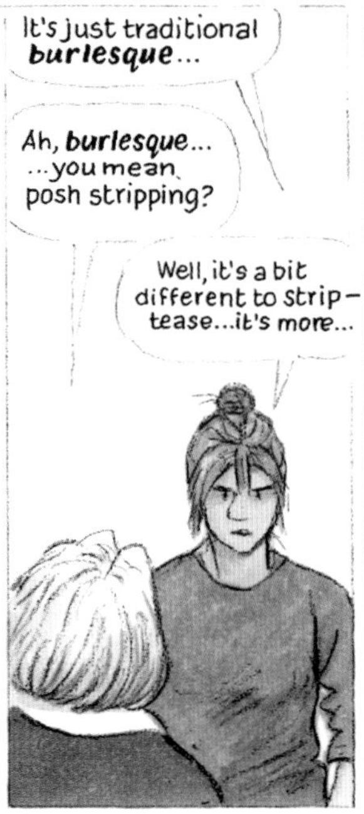
It's just traditional burlesque...
Ah, burlesque... ...you mean posh stripping?
Well, it's a bit different to strip-tease...it's more...

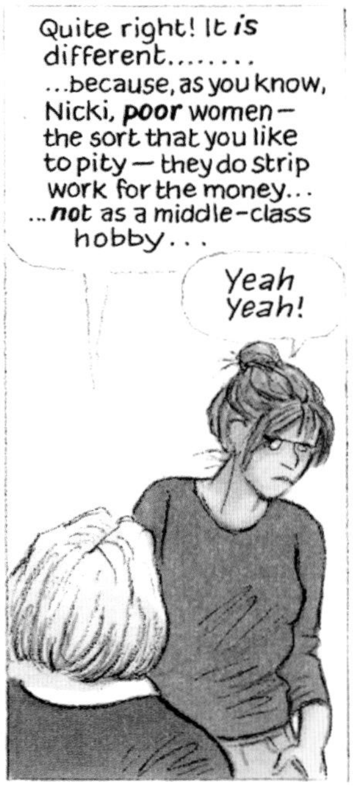
Quite right! It is different........ ...because, as you know, Nicki, poor women – the sort that you like to pity – they do strip work for the money... ...not as a middle-class hobby...
Yeah Yeah!

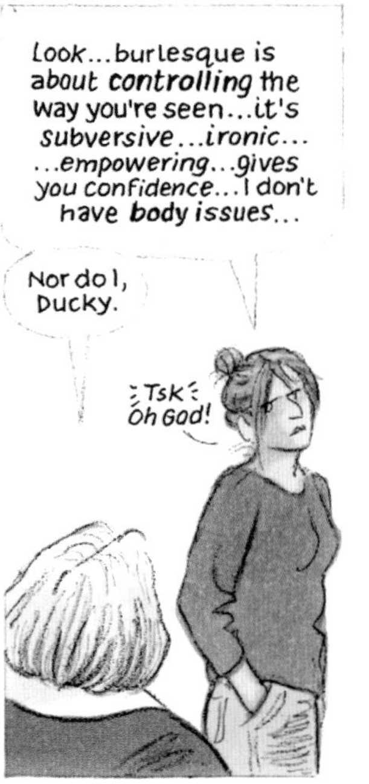
Look...burlesque is about controlling the way you're seen...it's subversive...ironic... ...empowering...gives you confidence...I don't have body issues...
Nor do I, Ducky.
Tsk Oh God!

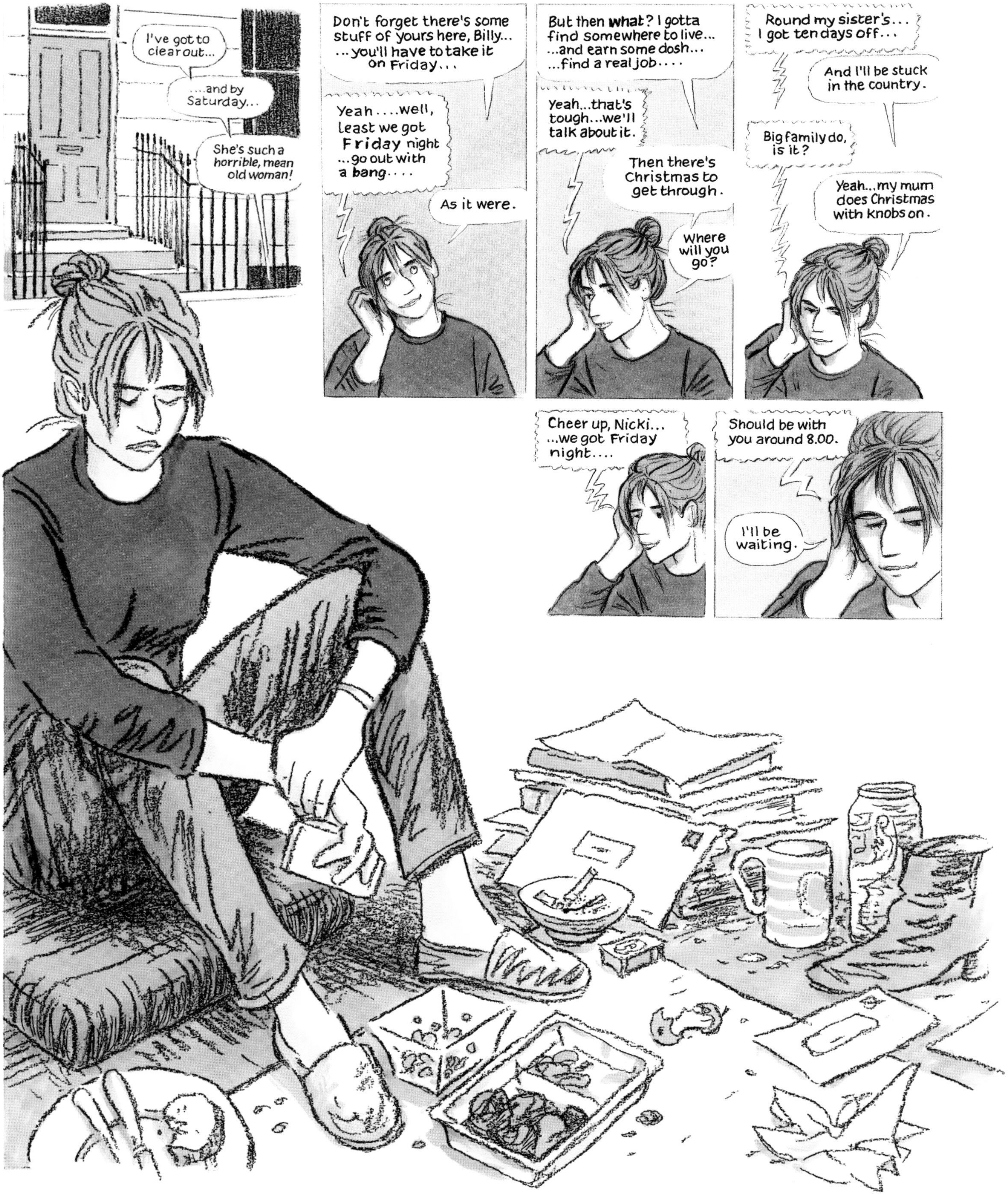
I've got to clear out...
....and by Saturday...
She's such a horrible, mean old woman!
Don't forget there's some stuff of yours here, Billy... ...you'll have to take it on Friday...
Yeah....well, least we got Friday night ...go out with a bang....
As it were.
But then what? I gotta find somewhere to live... ...and earn some dosh... ...find a real job....
Yeah...that's tough...we'll talk about it.
Then there's Christmas to get through.
Where will you go?
Round my sister's... I got ten days off...
And I'll be stuck in the country.
Big family do, is it?
Yeah...my mum does Christmas with knobs on.
Cheer up, Nicki... ...we got Friday night....
Should be with you around 8.00.
I'll be waiting.

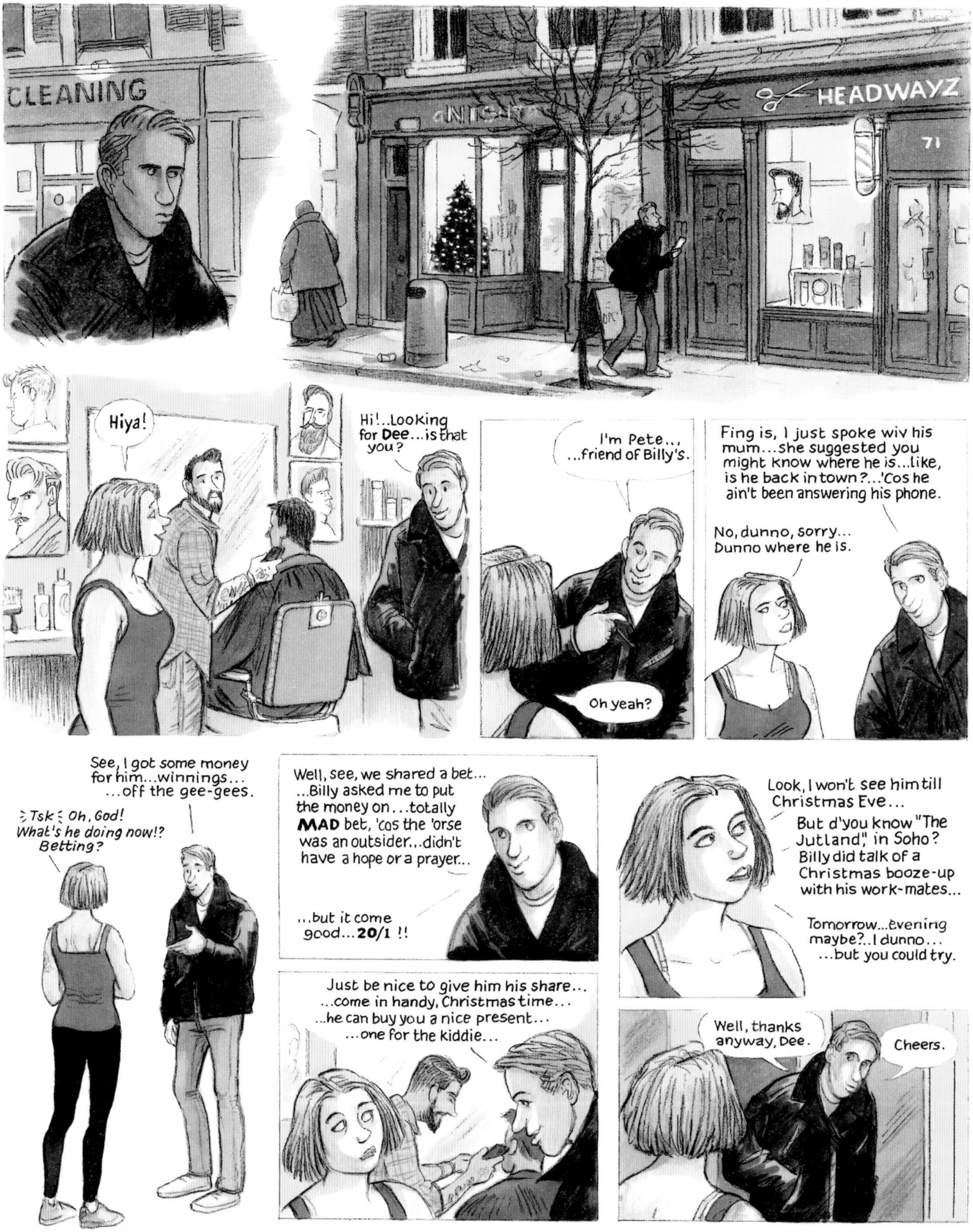
CLEANING
HEADWAYZ
71
Hiya!
Hi!..Looking for Dee...is that you?
I'm Pete... ...friend of Billy's.
Oh yeah?
Fing is, I just spoke wiv his mum...she suggested you might know where he is...like, is he back in town?...'Cos he ain't been answering his phone.
No, dunno, sorry... Dunno where he is.
See, I got some money for him...winnings... ...off the gee-gees.
Tsk Oh, God! What's he doing now!? Betting?
Well, see, we shared a bet... ...Billy asked me to put the money on...totally MAD bet, 'cos the 'orse was an outsider...didn't have a hope or a prayer...
...but it come good...20/1 !!
Look, I won't see him till Christmas Eve...
But d'you know "The Jutland," in Soho? Billy did talk of a Christmas booze-up with his work-mates...
Tomorrow...evening maybe?..I dunno... ...but you could try.
Just be nice to give him his share... ...come in handy, Christmas time... ...he can buy you a nice present... ...one for the kiddie...
Well, thanks anyway, Dee.
Cheers.

December 21st 20.15

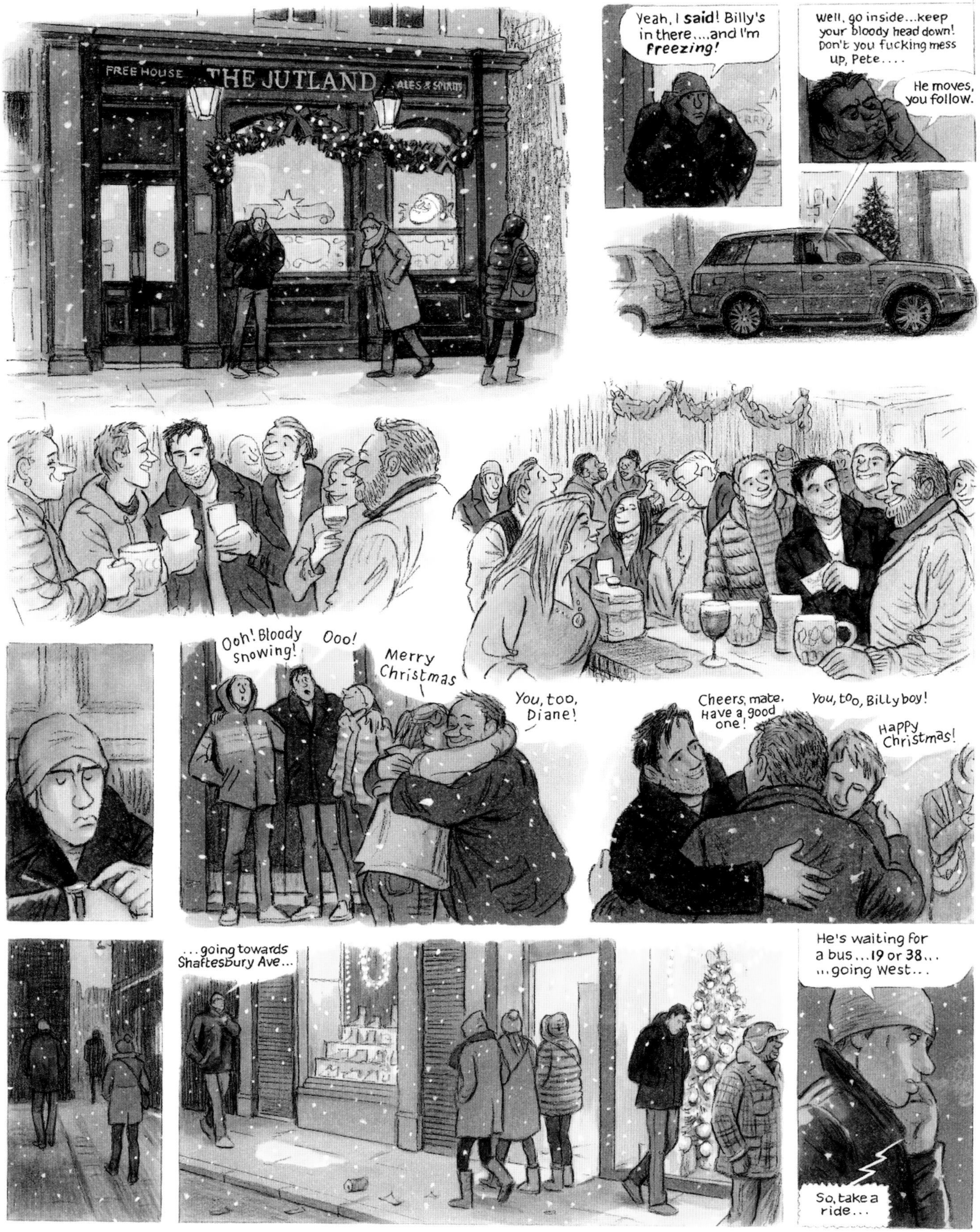
FREE HOUSE
THE JUTLAND
ALES & SPIRITS
Yeah, I **said**! Billy's in there....and I'm ***freezing***!
Well, go inside...keep your bloody head down! Don't you fucking mess up, Pete....
He moves, you follow.
Ooh! Bloody snowing!
Ooo!
Merry Christmas
You, too, Diane!
Cheers, mate. Have a good one!
You, too, Billy boy!
Happy Christmas!
...going towards Shaftesbury Ave...
He's waiting for a bus...**19** or **38**... ...going West...
So, take a ride...

December 21st 22.00

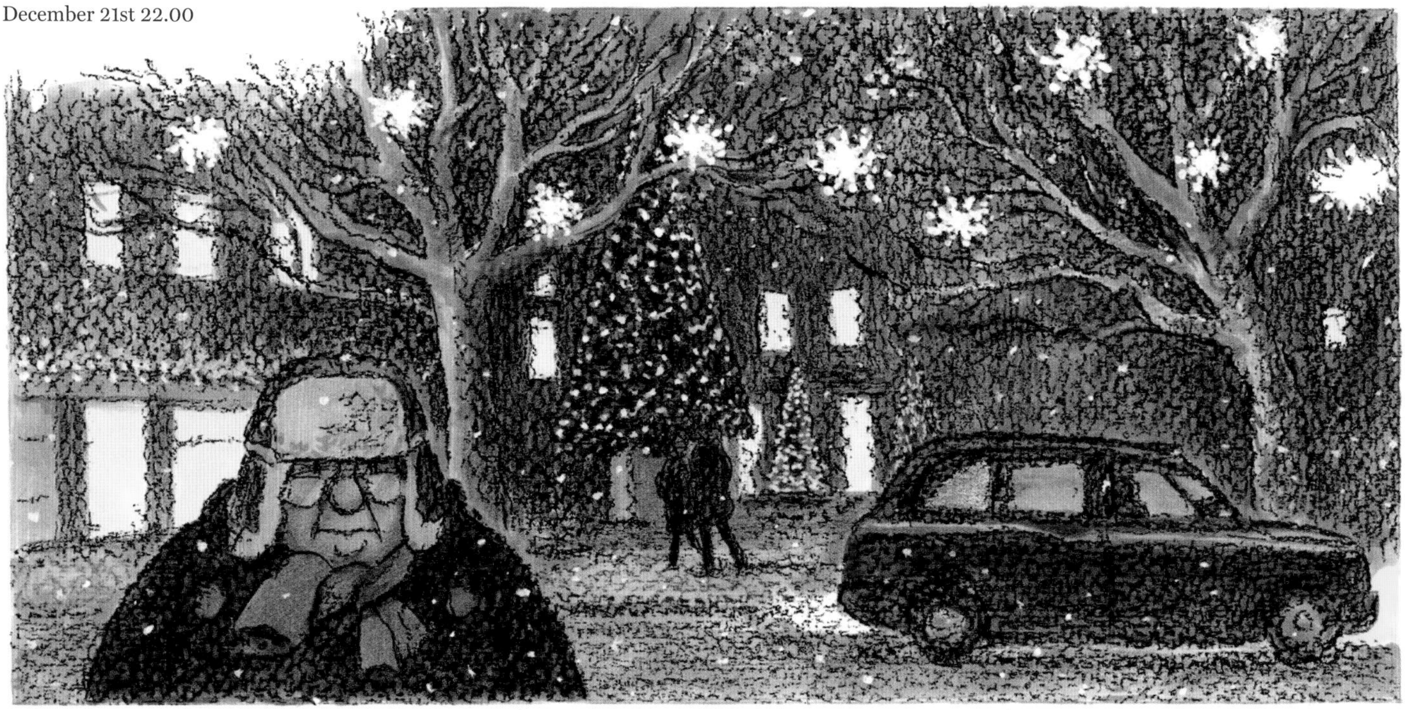

December 21st of last year is of course seared into my memory. The day I opened Jane McMullen's letter and knew I was undone, the day that confirmed Freddie's warning – or rather that of my unconscious: I had indeed landed in the chutney.
I remember clutching Jane's letter and pacing the gallery for hours, and that it was late when Corker and I arrived home. Nicki was still taking down the junk having left things to the last minute. She was leaving in the morning with her mother, how early I didn't know. I barely had the energy to speak to her …

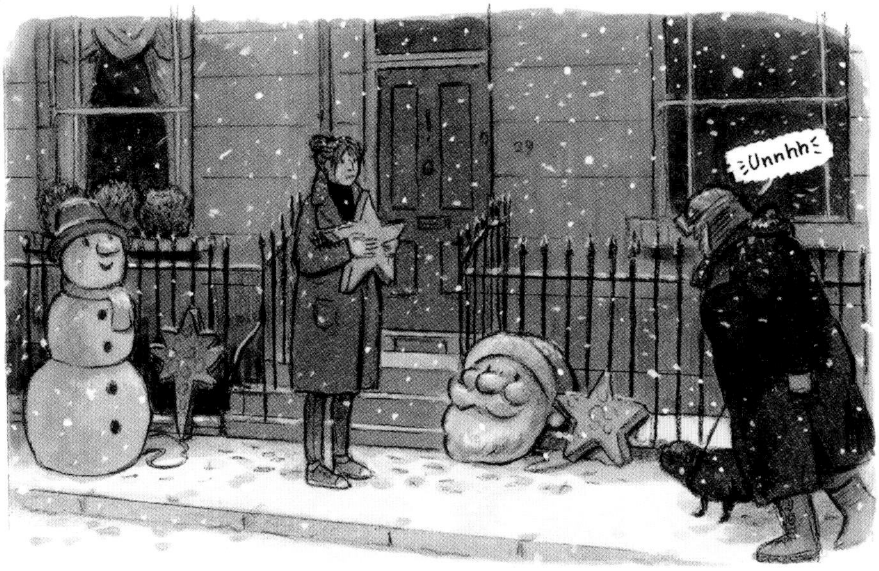
Unnhh

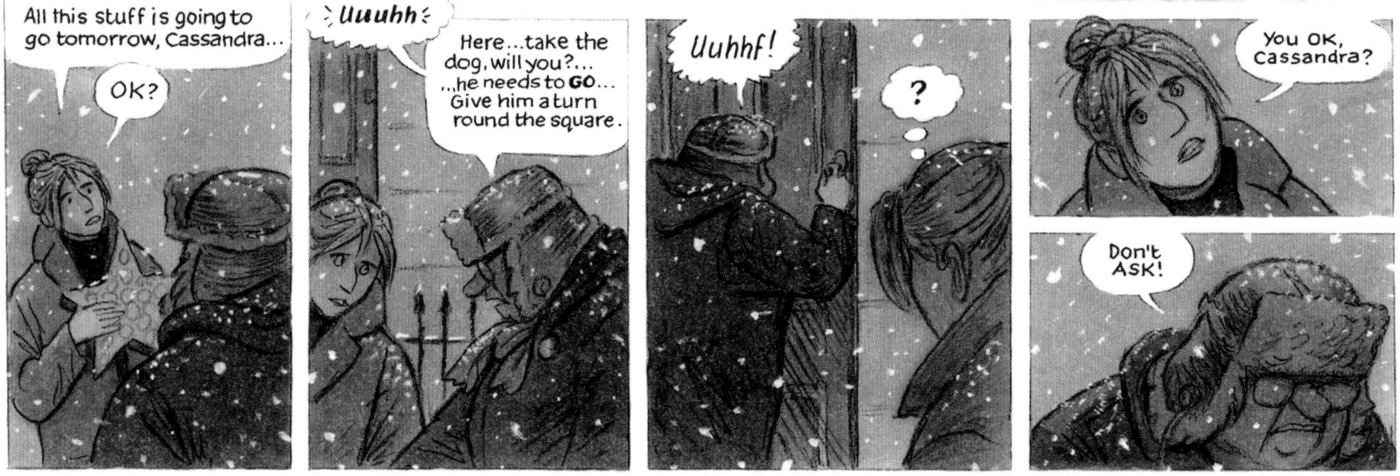
All this stuff is going to go tomorrow, Cassandra...
OK?
Uuuhh
Here...take the dog, will you?... ...he needs to GO... Give him a turn round the square.
Uuhhf!
?
You OK, Cassandra?
Don't ASK!

Bling-blinga Blong

Billy! How're you doing?

On the bus!... traffic's terrible. But I should be with you in five minutes.

Bling-blinga Blong

Hi, Mum.

Nicki! Have you seen Cassandra?

Apparently, no one's seen her all day!

She doesn't answer her phone...she...

Yeah, I just did.

She just got home.

Looking knackered.

Well, she's done something truly **DISGUSTING!**

What?

What's she done?!?

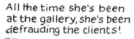
All the time she's been at the gallery, she's been defrauding the clients!

What!? Shi-it!

So, all the time Dad's been ill, she's been...?

Yes!

Jane McMullen — you remember her? — she's just told me...

It's **really** serious, Nicki....FRAUD...... I don't know **what** got into Cassandra...

What did she **DO**??

How did she rip people off? God! I mean...

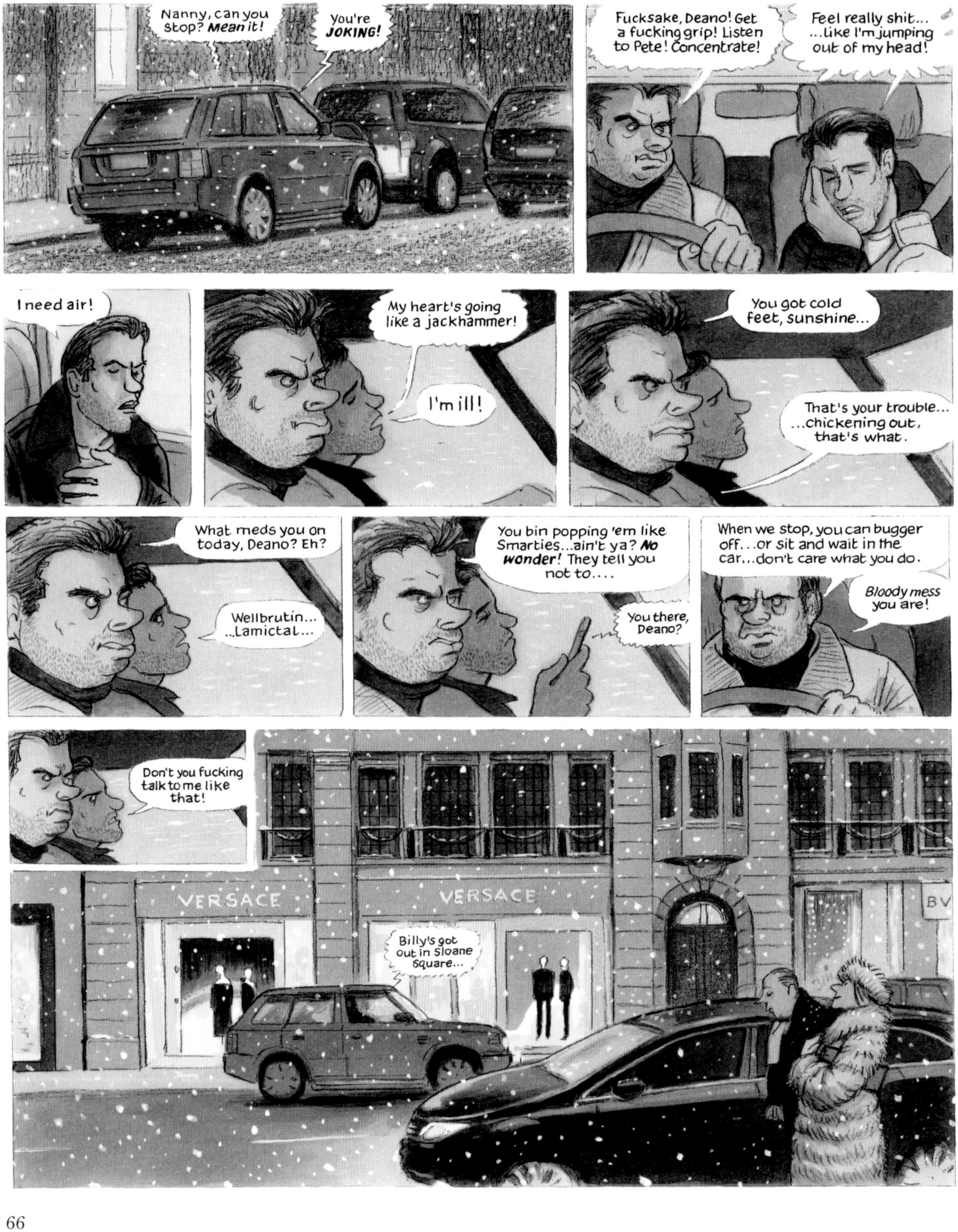
Nanny, can you stop? Mean it!
You're JOKING!
Fucksake, Deano! Get a fucking grip! Listen to Pete! Concentrate!
Feel really shit... ...like I'm jumping out of my head!
I need air!
My heart's going like a jackhammer!
I'm ill!
You got cold feet, sunshine...
That's your trouble... ...chickening out, that's what.
What meds you on today, Deano? Eh?
Wellbrutin... ...Lamictal...
You bin popping 'em like Smarties...ain't ya? No wonder! They tell you not to....
You there, Deano?
When we stop, you can bugger off...or sit and wait in the car...don't care what you do.
Bloody mess you are!
Don't you fucking talk to me like that!
VERSACE
VERSACE
Billy's got out in Sloane Square...
BV

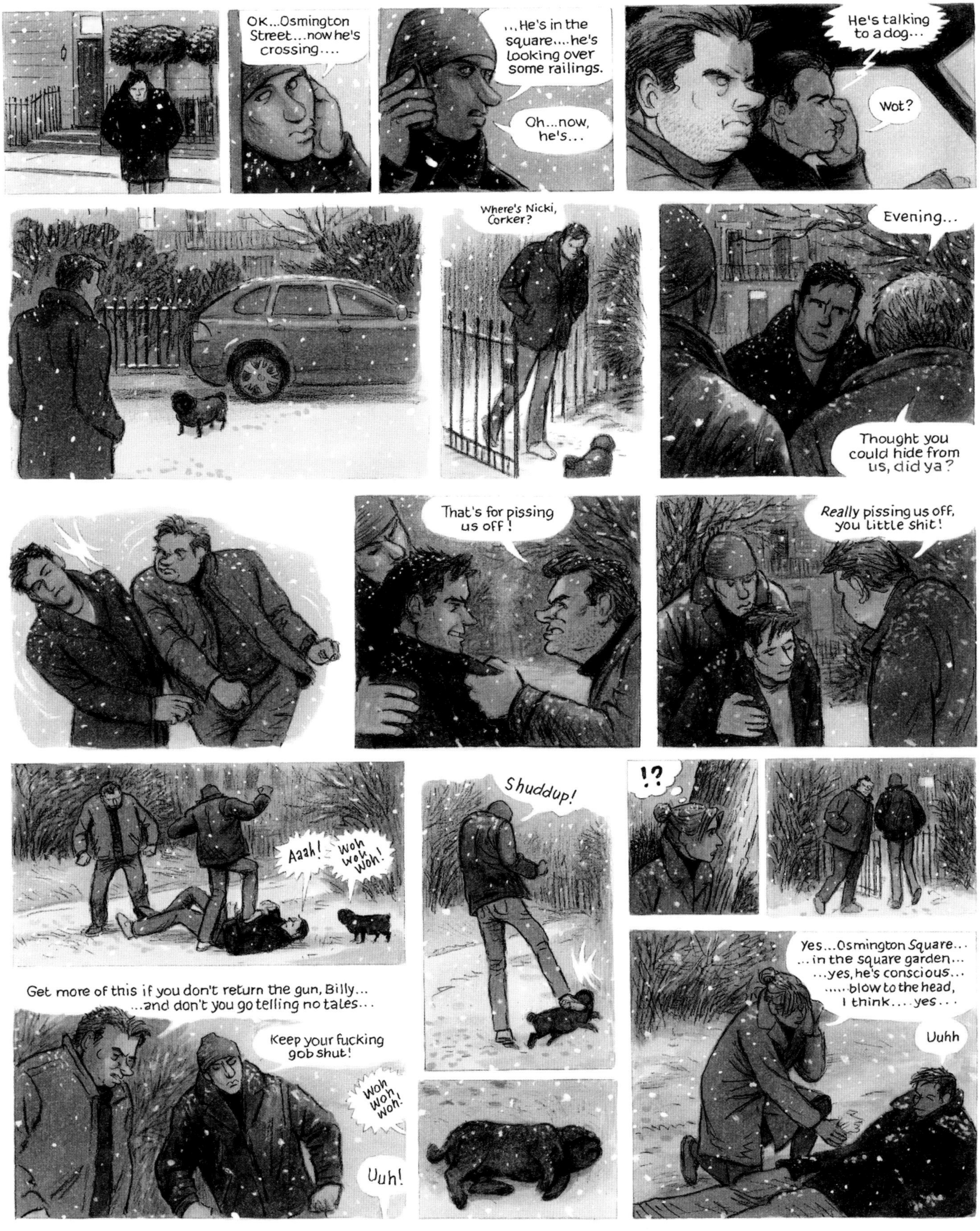
OK...Osmington Street...now he's crossing....
...He's in the square....he's looking over some railings.
Oh...now, he's...
He's talking to a dog...
Wot?
Where's Nicki, Corker?
Evening...
Thought you could hide from us, did ya?
That's for pissing us off!
Really pissing us off, you little shit!
Aaah!
Woh woh woh!
Get more of this if you don't return the gun, Billy...
...and don't you go telling no tales...
Keep your fucking gob shut!
Woh woh woh!
Uuh!
Shuddup!
!?
Yes...Osmington Square...
...in the square garden...
...yes, he's conscious...
.....blow to the head, I think....yes...
Uuhh

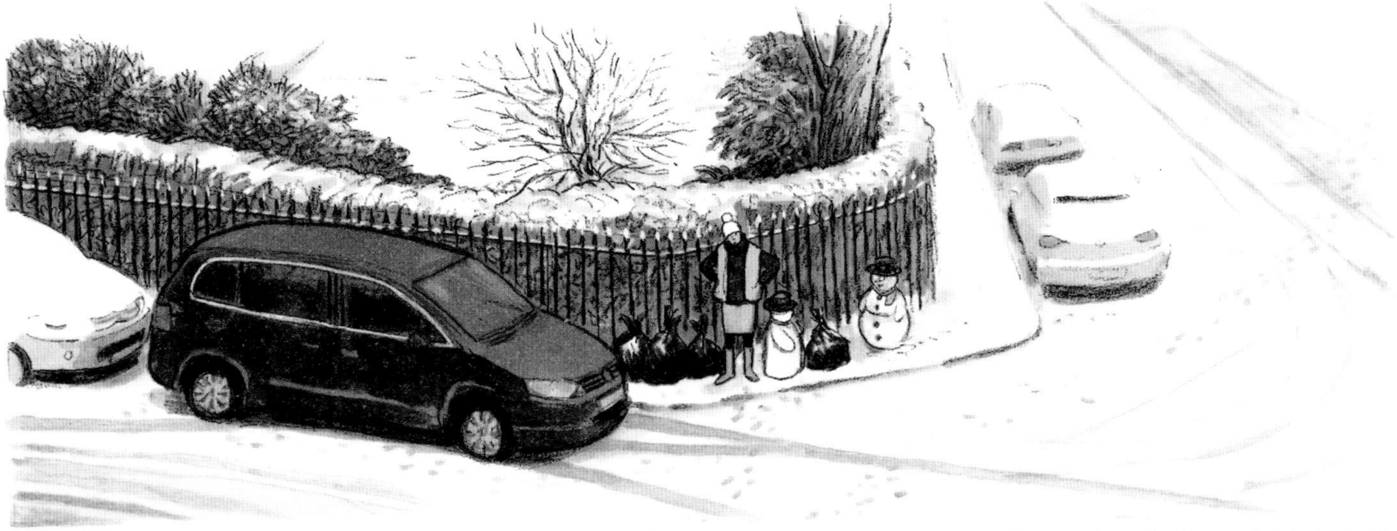

Often on her visits to London Margot would go out of her way to see me, but that morning, evidently aware of my crimes, she stayed by the car while Nicki cleared her stuff from the basement. I didn't waste much time watching them, having urgent things to do – talking to my solicitor and arranging for the Pet Crematorium to come and collect poor Corker's body.

The night before when Nicki broke the news about Corker, I had rather lost track of time, having downed several whiskies. From her account it was clear that she was partly to blame – Corker would not have wandered off if he'd been on the lead. Nicki said she'd been distracted by a phone call and when she found Corker, he was at the far end of the square, lying near an injured man. A mugging victim. She called an ambulance and waited for it to arrive, before picking up the poor dog and ringing my doorbell. Someone had kicked him in the head, she thought, possibly the mugger. She laid Corker down in the hall and and left saying that she would be gone by twelve the next day.

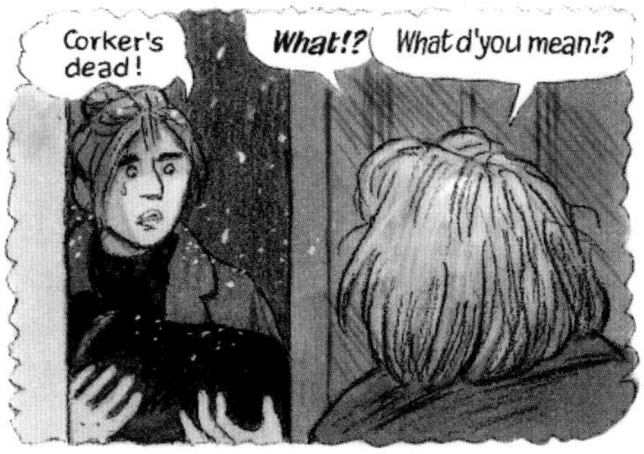
Corker's dead!
What!?
What d'you mean!?

Just before noon I heard Nicki post the basement keys through my letterbox. I watched her hugging her mother on the pavement. Nicki seemed to be in tears. For all her talk of independence and disaffection for her family, there she was returning to its bosom. No doubt to be press-ganged into all those Yuletide rituals which Margot liked to capture and feature on her Christmas cards. (I had just received the most recent, obviously sent before Margot knew of my misdeeds.) Idyllic snaps like these posted on social media must bring great comfort to the poor and lonely.

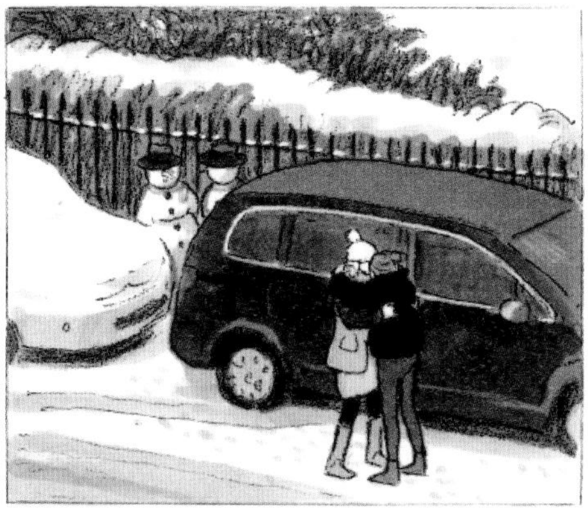

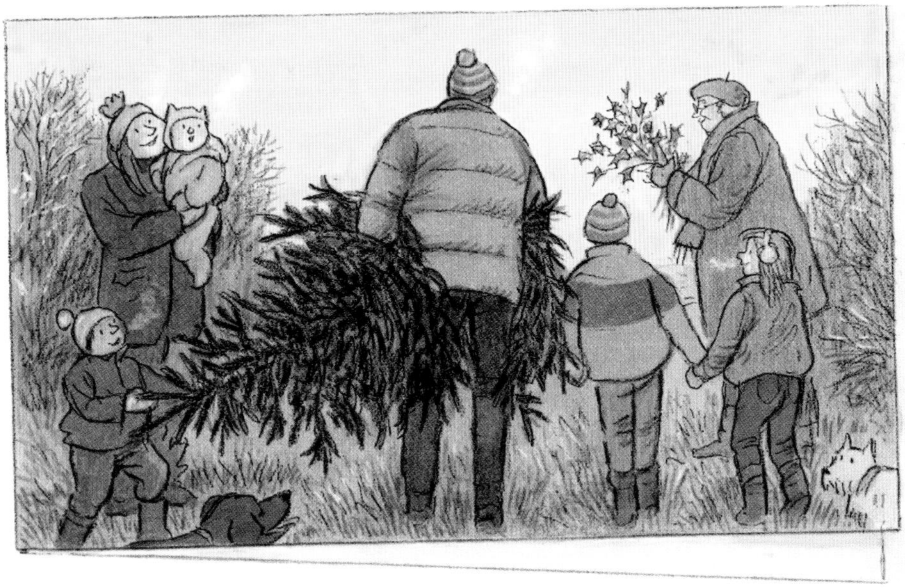

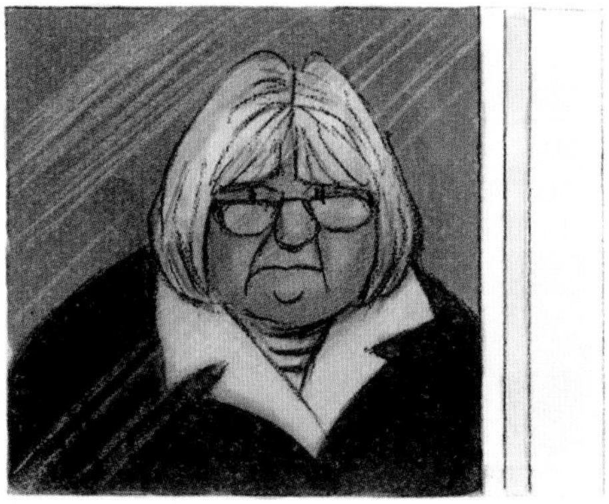

That afternoon Corker's body was driven away in a van. The snowmen Nicki left on the pavement disappeared during the night.

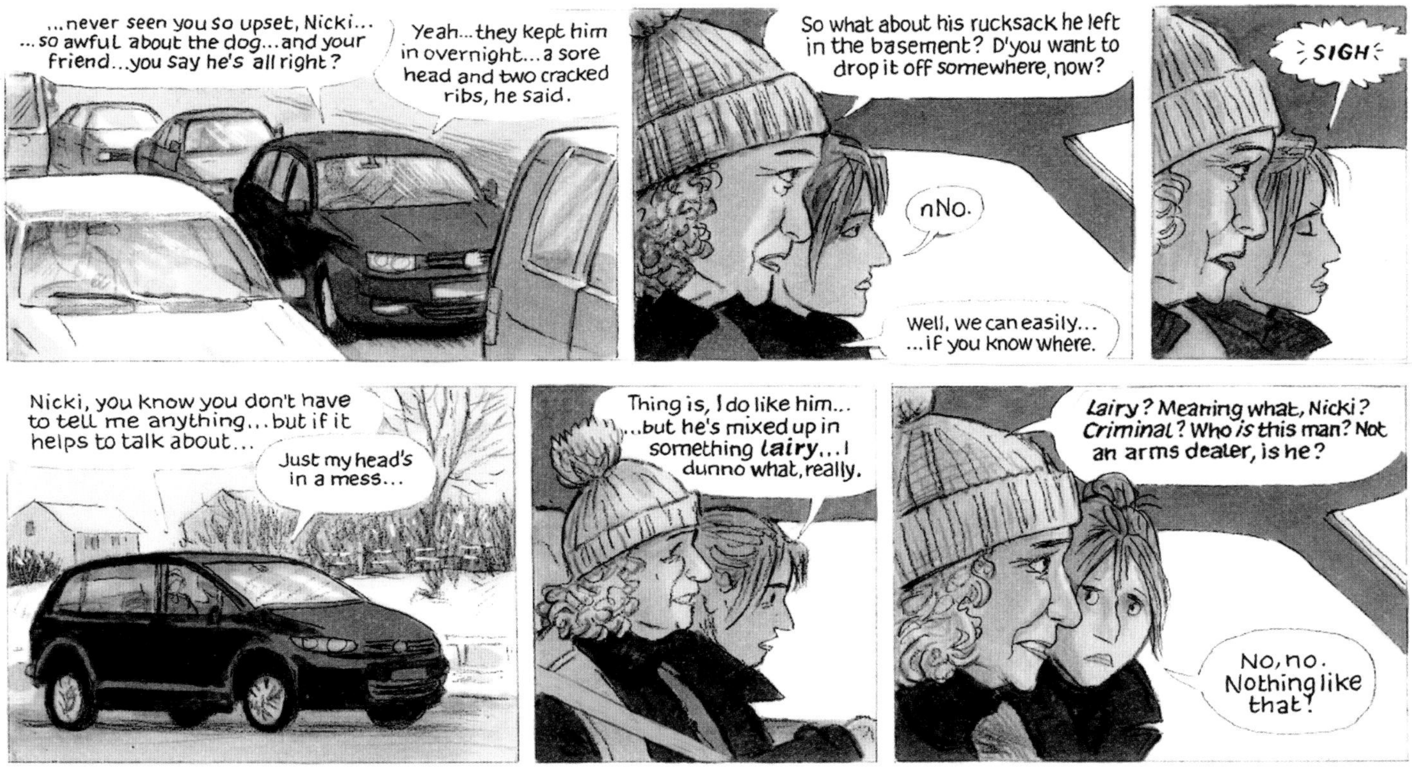
...never seen you so upset, Nicki... ...so awful about the dog...and your friend...you say he's all right?
Yeah...they kept him in overnight...a sore head and two cracked ribs, he said.
So what about his rucksack he left in the basement? D'you want to drop it off somewhere, now?
nNo.
Well, we can easily... ...if you know where.
SIGH
Nicki, you know you don't have to tell me anything...but if it helps to talk about...
Just my head's in a mess...
Thing is, I do like him... ...but he's mixed up in something lairy...I dunno what, really.
Lairy? Meaning what, Nicki? Criminal? Who is this man? Not an arms dealer, is he?
No, no. Nothing like that!

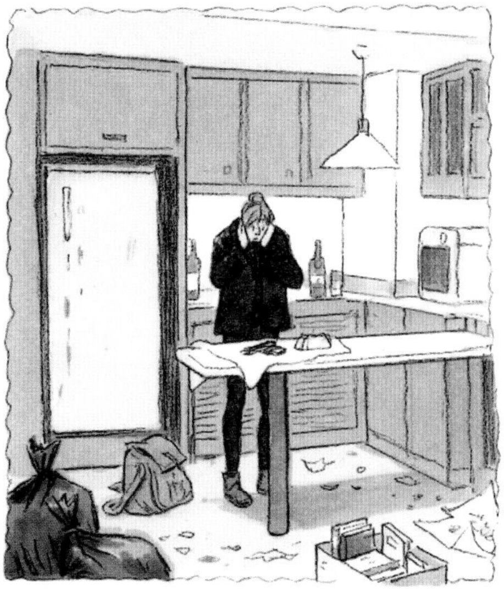

What a mistake, Nicki thought, telling her mum anything. But then car rides with her mum were always a mistake, like being trapped in a mobile confessional. It was as if she was still a teenager, being picked up, taken home, and grilled on the way. Luckily, there was the diverting subject of Cassandra (her fraud, meanness, total lack of humanity), which kept her mum theorising for miles and miles of motorway.

Nicki thought about Billy. He might as well be an arms dealer for all she knew. Difficult to know what to believe about him. Earlier, on the phone, he hadn't wanted to talk about being beaten up, or anything else much. He told her to "take care".

After the call, as she was clearing the basement, Nicki picked up Billy's rucksack. Serve her right for looking inside, she thought. Underneath a sweater and stuff there was a dirty towel wrapped around something heavy: Deano's gun. And some other things, bullets, a glove and a little bag. Billy really messed her mind. He had bloody lied, when he said he'd given the gun back. Her mum was flapping to get on the road. Nicki thought, fuck it, and shoved the gun, everything, in the bathroom bin. The rucksack went in the car although Nicki thought it unlikely that she and Billy would see each other again.

...poor Toby's got flu...did I tell you, Nicki? So we'll be 17 on Christmas Day...all the grandchildren will be there...I've ordered a colossal turkey from Bennet's...

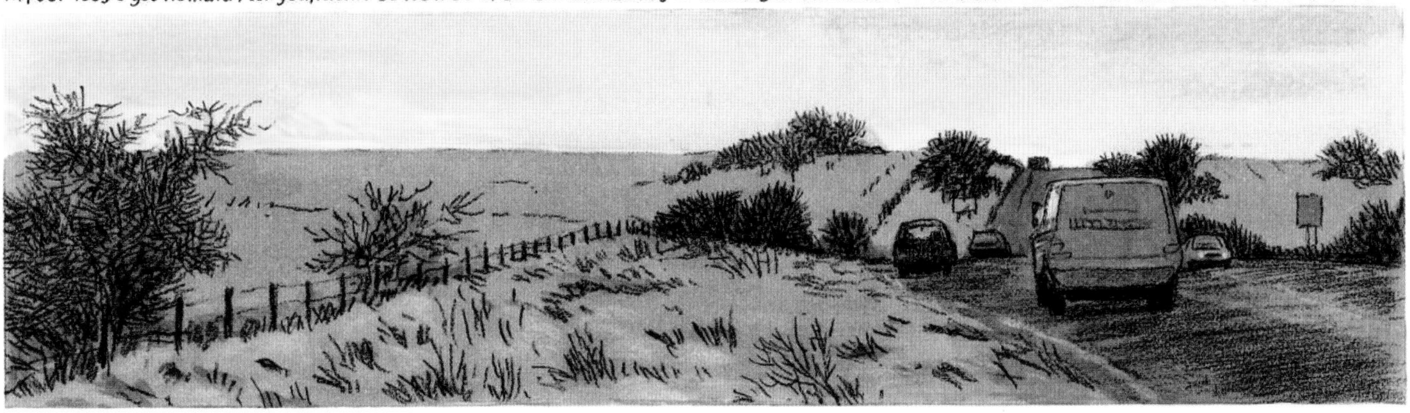

December 2017

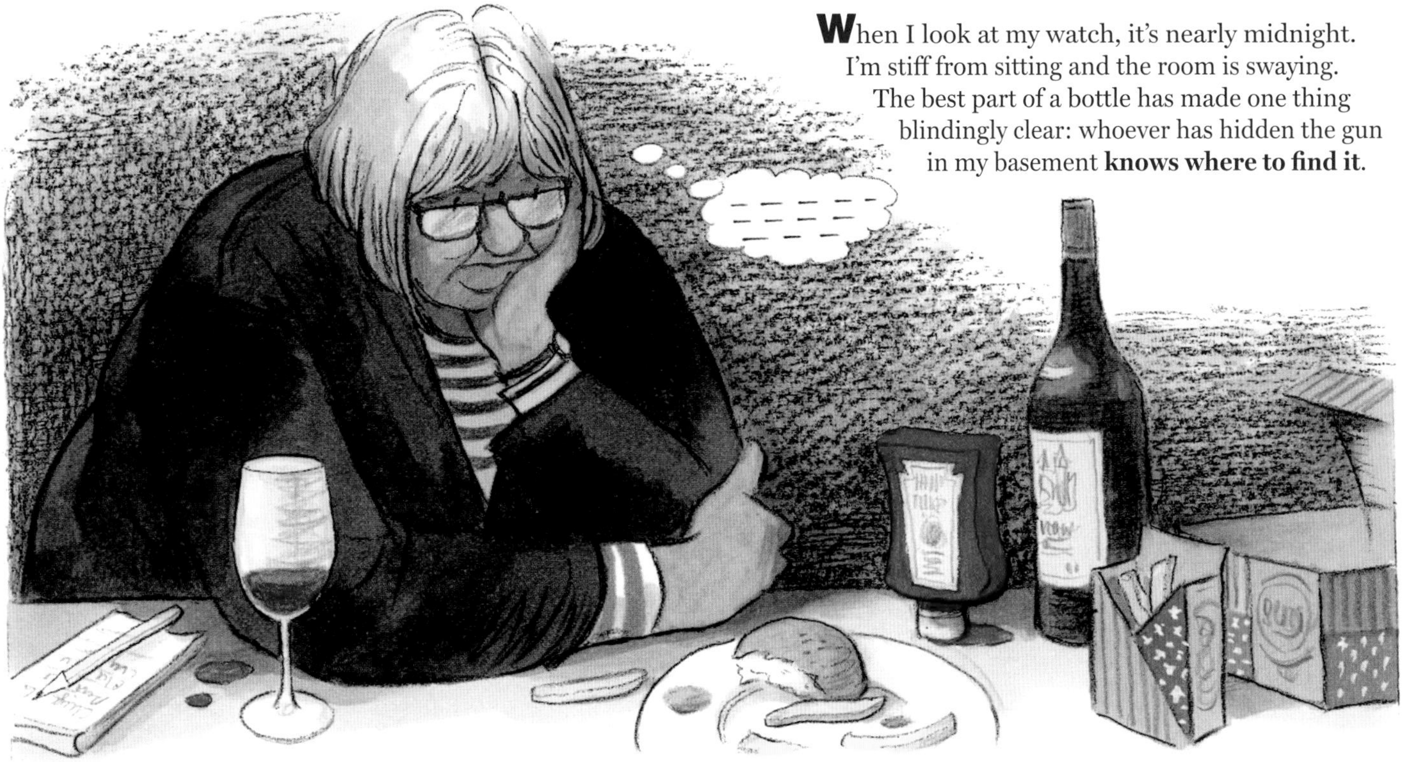

When I look at my watch, it's nearly midnight. I'm stiff from sitting and the room is swaying. The best part of a bottle has made one thing blindingly clear: whoever has hidden the gun in my basement **knows where to find it**.

Moments later, I have another thought: someone will come and find the gun and **use** it. To prevent this, someone (me) must remove the bloody thing, an imposition which makes me charge about the kitchen, finding a basket, torch and rubber gloves (no fingerprints). Impressive to have thought of this. Anger fuels my rush outside and down to the basement, and the swift removal of the things from the bin. My ascent and re-entry to the house is more wary, although there's no one about in Osmington Square. There rarely is.

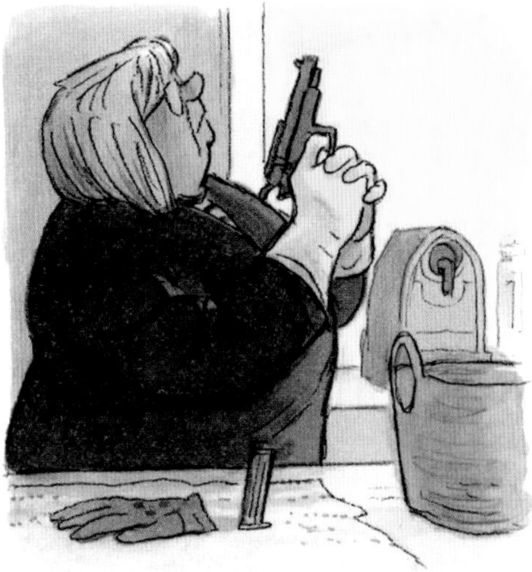

Before deciding on a hiding place I unpack the basket and examine the contents. A thoroughly depressing collection of items – the glove and cheap make-up suggesting a female assassin. The pistol is particularly disturbing. I have sometimes imagined ending things with a gun, but the reality! I've never held one before … the awful way it fits the hand. And as for the bullets, you'd have to handle the evil little slug bound for your brain.

By now I realise how drunk I am. I roll everything up in the dirty towel the gun was wrapped in and shove it in my washing machine. Tomorrow I will think of a better hiding place.

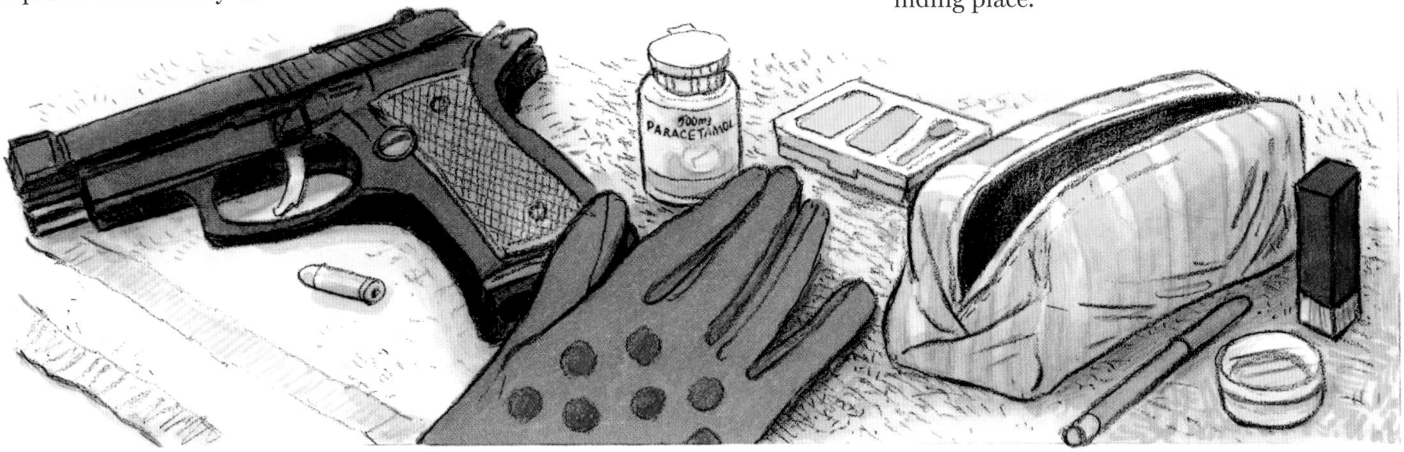
500mg
PARACETAMOL

The next day I ring Margot on the pretext of asking how Freddie's memorial service went. (Margot is touched I was there. Nicki has obviously let on that she saw me.) In the course of a lengthy chat, I discover Nicki's current whereabouts. She has a house share in Tooting and is now working for a smart gallery off Dover Street.

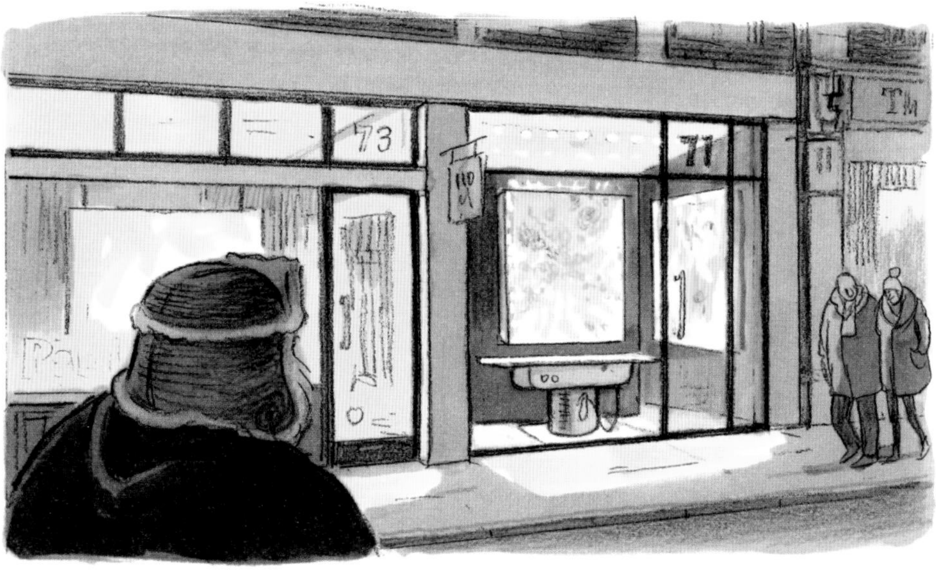

73
71

A couple of hours later I'm loitering near Gallery 71/73. I've been told to wait as Nicki has apparently been sent to the Post Office with some bulky parcels. And so there is time to examine the list of artists who show at 71/73, most of them very young. While I have nothing against youth I generally prefer to look on the harvest rather than the green corn. And there is time, rather too much time, to study the exhibition: a pristine postmortem extraction table in the window and huge lightboxes with transparencies of ... probably bodily fluids. Rather beautiful, in fact.

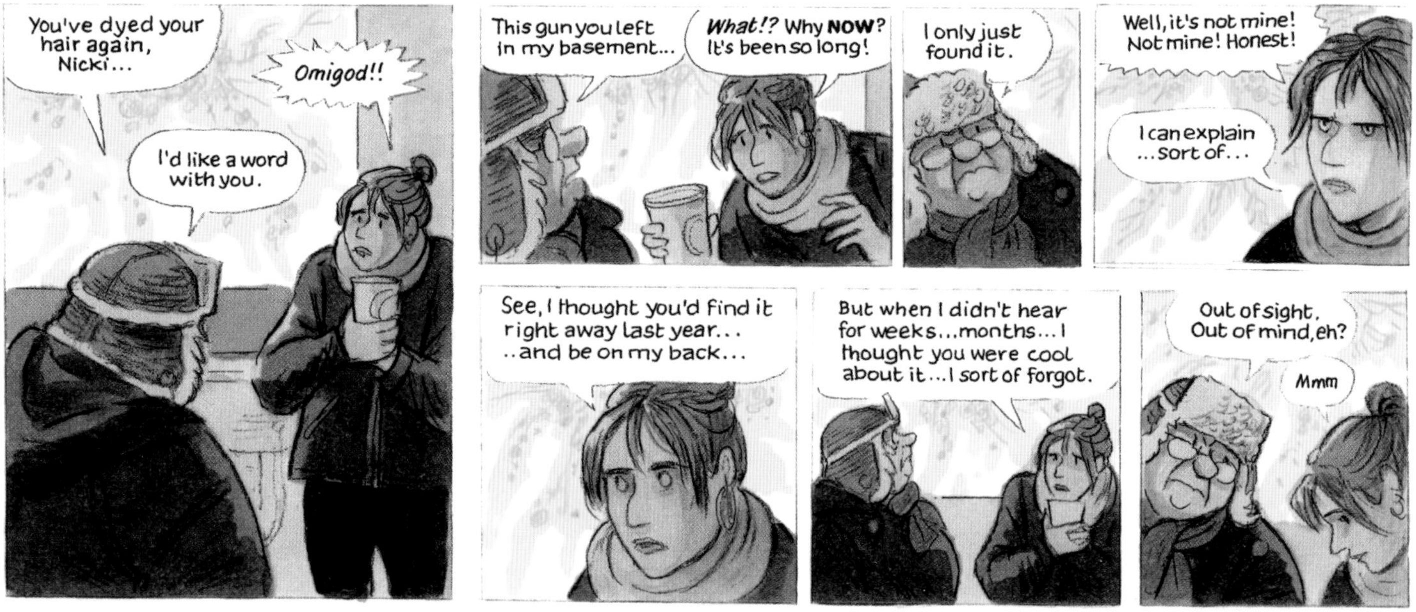

You've dyed your hair again, Nicki...
Omigod!!
I'd like a word with you.
This gun you left in my basement...
What!? Why NOW? It's been so long!
I only just found it.
Well, it's not mine! Not mine! Honest!
I can explain ...sort of...
See, I thought you'd find it right away last year... ..and be on my back...
But when I didn't hear for weeks...months... I thought you were cool about it...I sort of forgot.
Out of sight, Out of mind, eh?
Mmm

When Nicki stops talking my head is literally buzzing – so many "isn'ts", "wasn'ts", "doesn'ts": the dumper of the gun was her boyfriend last year but isn't now; the gun doesn't belong to him but to someone else who has, or perhaps hasn't, done something awful ... which her ex-boyfriend doesn't know about, or maybe does.
The last Nicki heard from him was soon after she left Osmington Square, when he said it was safer for her if they didn't see each other.

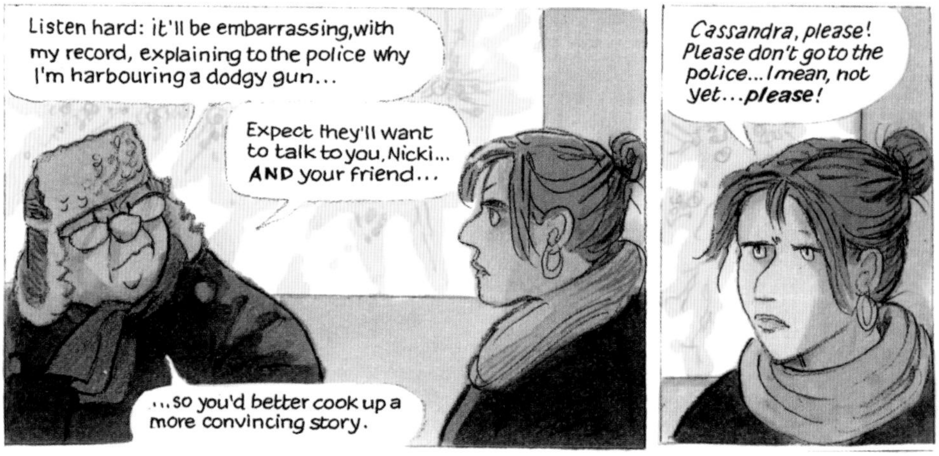

Listen hard: it'll be embarrassing, with my record, explaining to the police why I'm harbouring a dodgy gun...
Expect they'll want to talk to you, Nicki... AND your friend...
...so you'd better cook up a more convincing story.
Cassandra, please! Please don't go to the police... I mean, not yet... please!

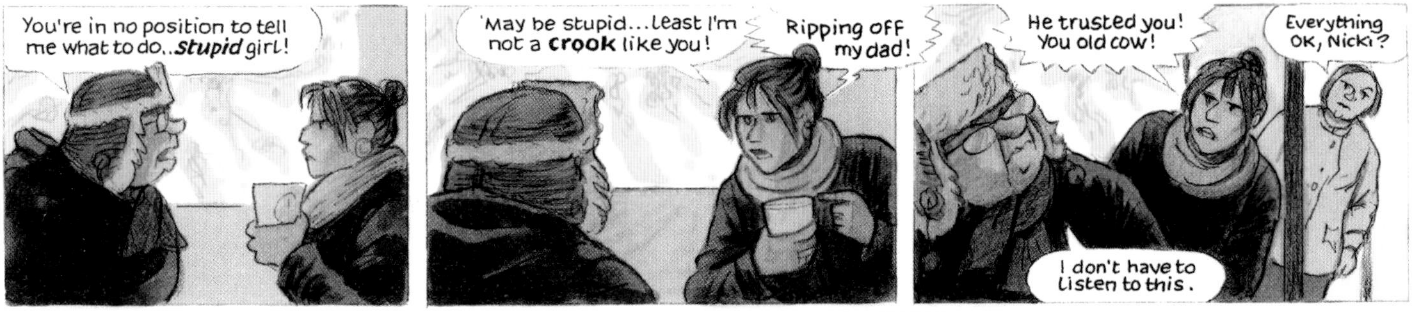
You're in no position to tell me what to do.. ***stupid*** girl!
'May be stupid... Least I'm not a **crook** like you!
Ripping off my dad!
He trusted you! You old cow!
Everything OK, Nicki?
I don't have to listen to this.

I am now too agitated to go and sit on a bus. I need to keep moving. Walking steadies me. (The reason I gave up a car, apart from a driving ban, was my inability to keep calm in traffic.)
I pad past Christmas windows, their sterile perfection contrasting with the scrum of shoppers inside, racking up debt, sharing their seasonal bugs – norovirus, coughs, colds, flu.
I pad past office buildings, each with a Christmas tableau, the components as fixed as those of a crib scene: tree, reception desk, giant vase, someone keeping watch by night.

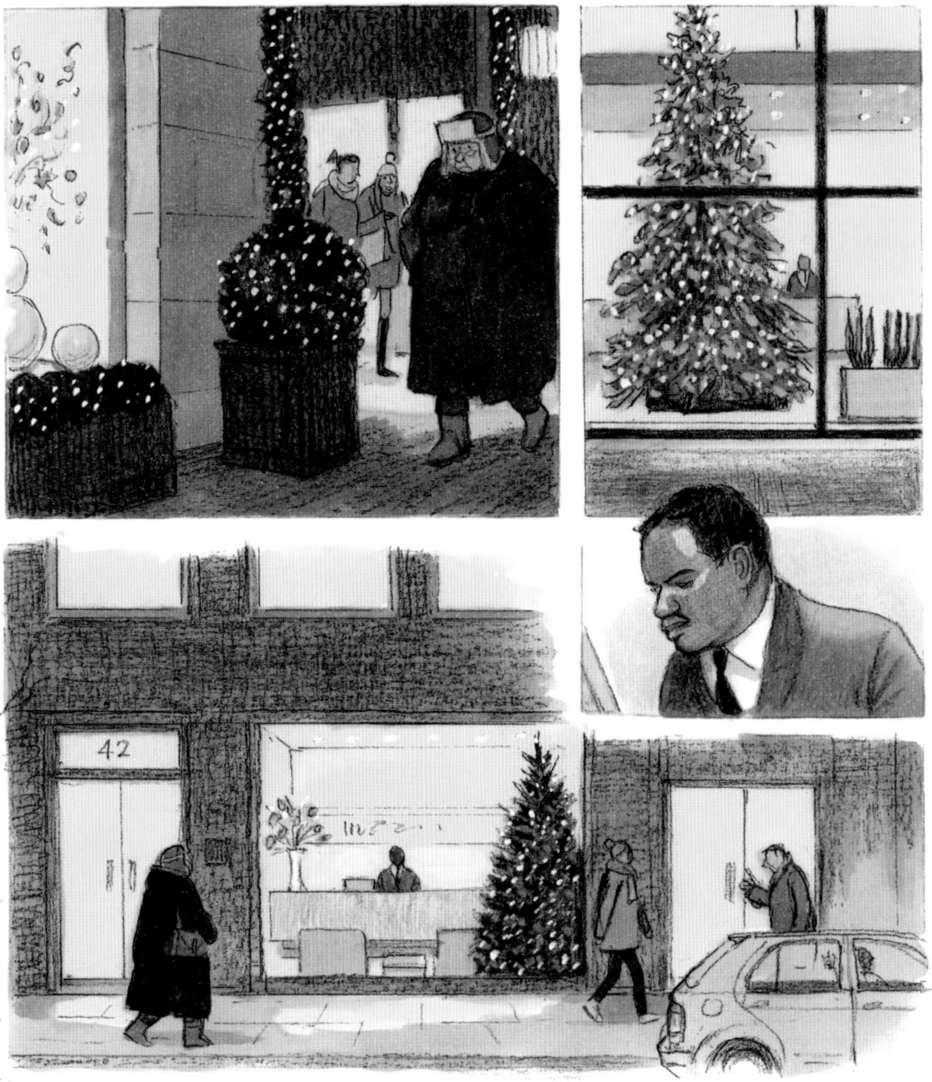
42

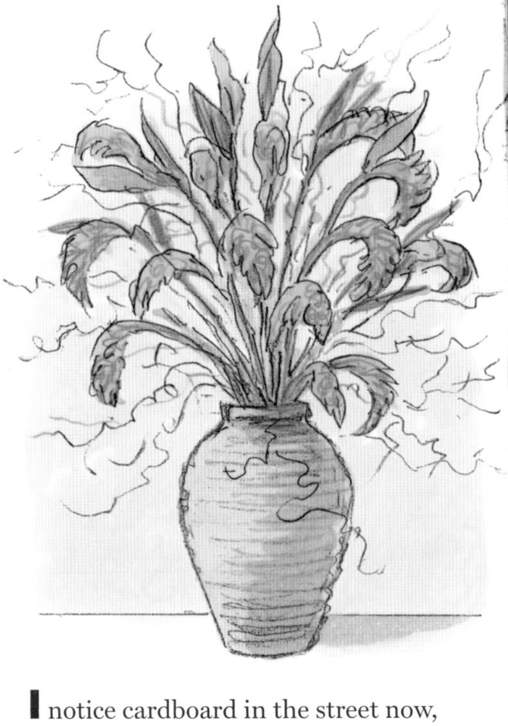

I notice cardboard in the street now, thanks to Nicki, but I ignore the beggars – my small change won't do anything to help their drink and drug problems.

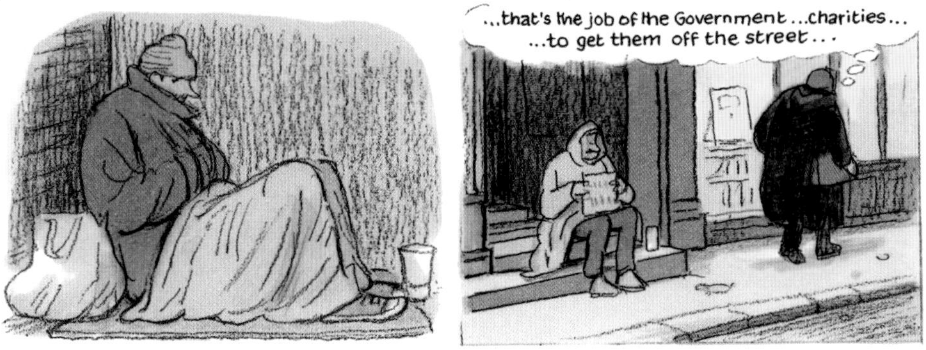
...that's the job of the Government ...charities... ...to get them off the street...

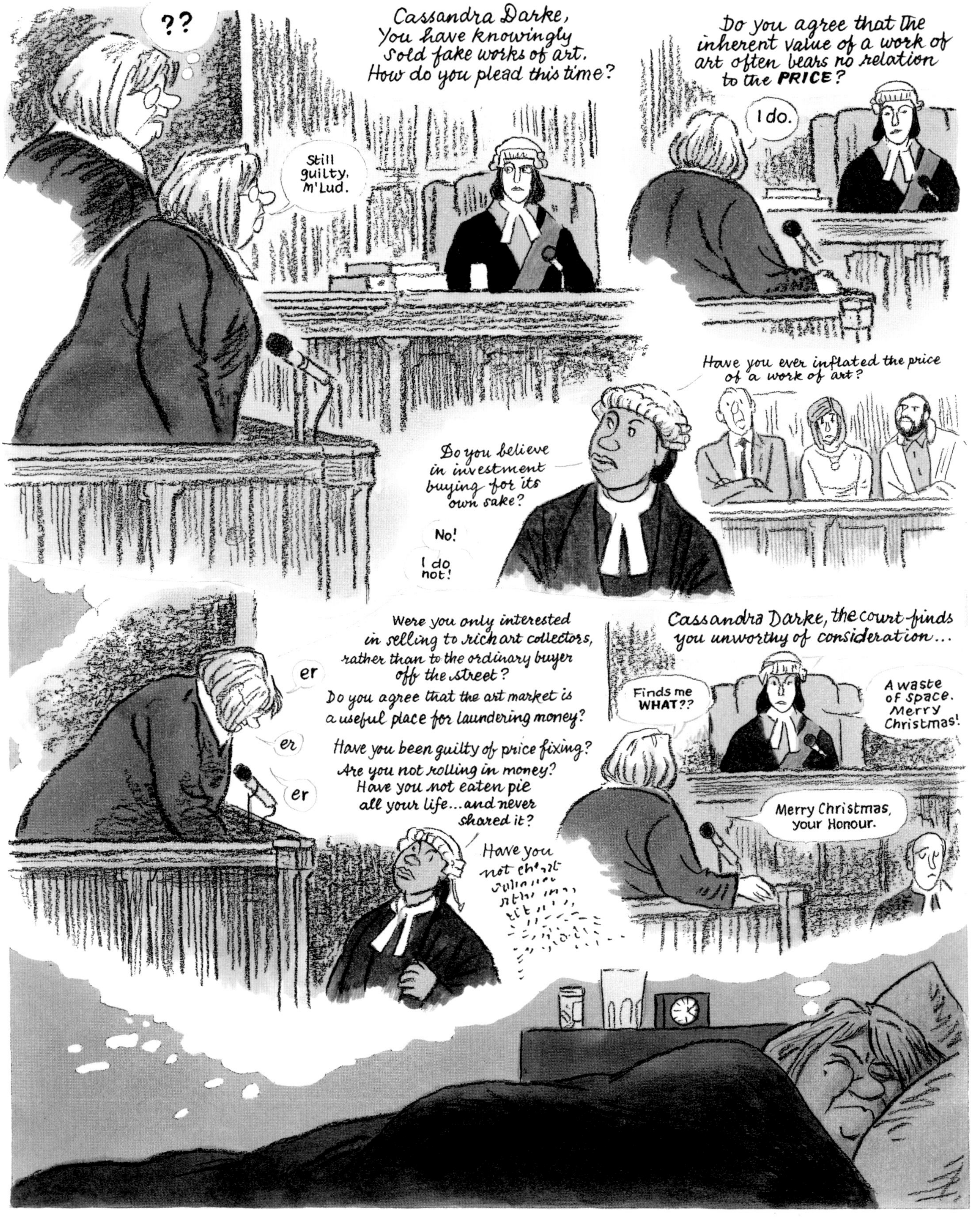
??
Cassandra Darke, You have knowingly sold fake works of art. How do you plead this time?
Still guilty, M'Lud.
Do you agree that the inherent value of a work of art often bears no relation to the PRICE?
I do.
Have you ever inflated the price of a work of art?
Do you believe in investment buying for its own sake?
No!
I do not!
Were you only interested in selling to rich art collectors, rather than to the ordinary buyer off the street?
er
Do you agree that the art market is a useful place for laundering money?
er
Have you been guilty of price fixing?
er
Are you not rolling in money? Have you not eaten pie all your life... and never shared it?
Have you
Cassandra Darke, the court finds you unworthy of consideration...
Finds me WHAT??
A waste of space. Merry Christmas!
Merry Christmas, your Honour.

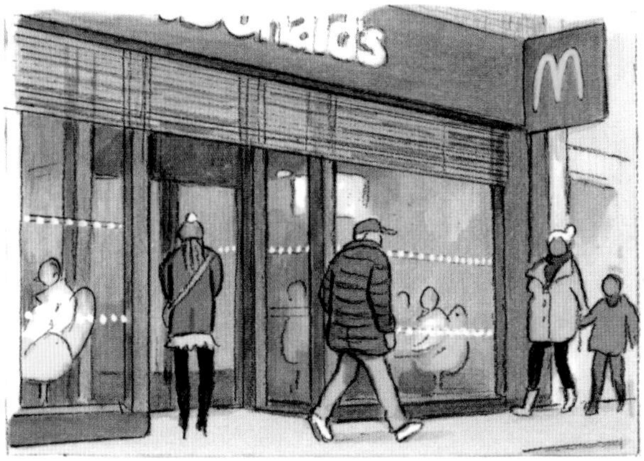

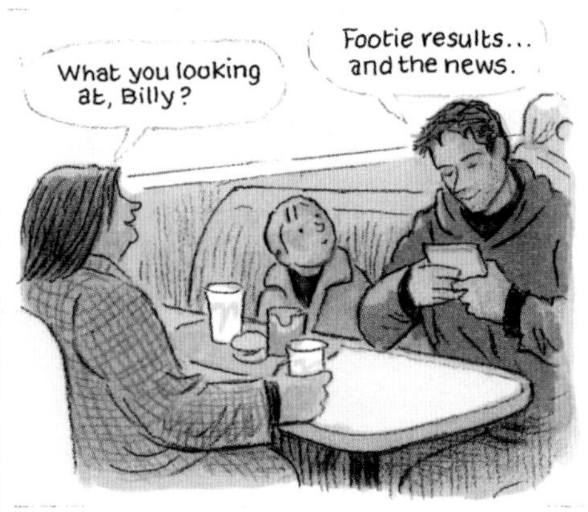
What you looking at, Billy?
Footie results... and the news.

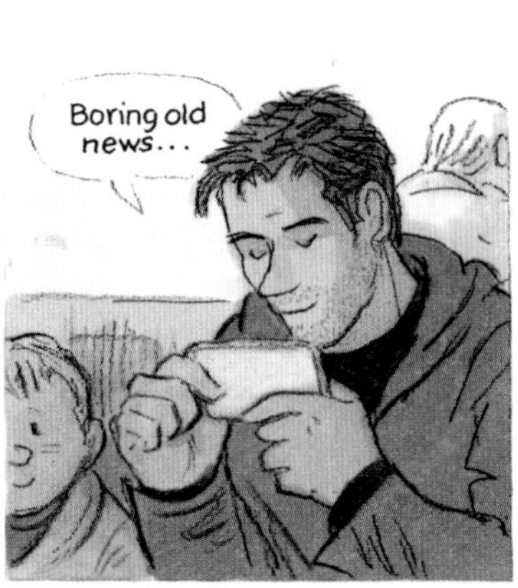
Boring old news...

for Manchester United next season.

3 minutes ago

Two injured in M5 pile-up.
11 vehicles collide in dense fog.

1 hour ago

Surrey police reveal clues to identity of female remains found in woods.

45 minutes ago

Features

Food moths: The silent enemy in your kitchen.

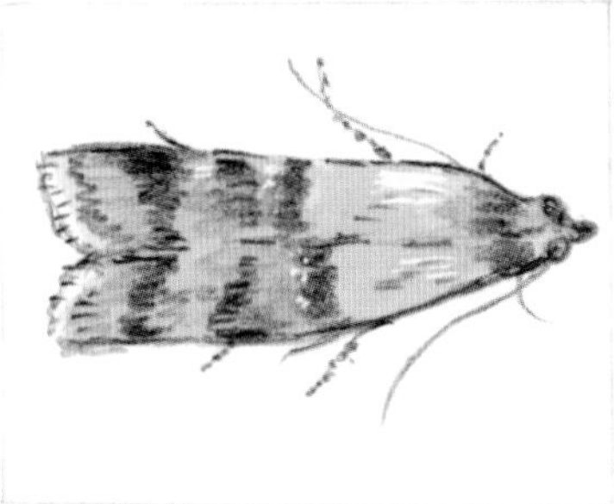

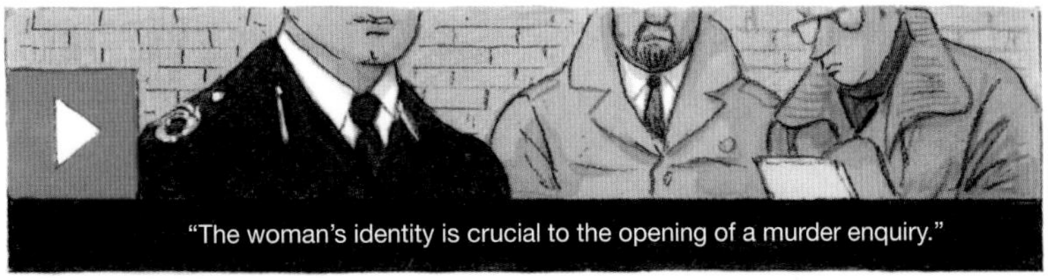
"The woman's identity is crucial to the opening of a murder enquiry."

The remains were found by a couple looking for their dog in woods near Wrysley. Detectives uncovered an entire female skeleton. Police believe the death was the result of homicide.

A full DNA profile has been obtained which does not match anyone on the database of the UK Missing Persons Bureau.

The remains were wrapped in a quilted nylon hooded jacket. Size 12. The distinctive glove (left hand) was inside a pocket.

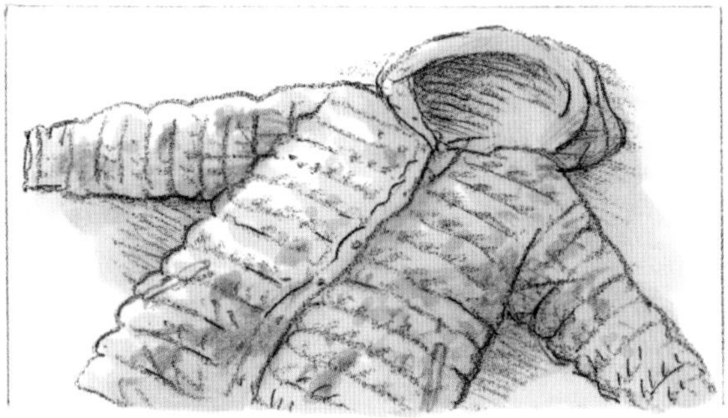

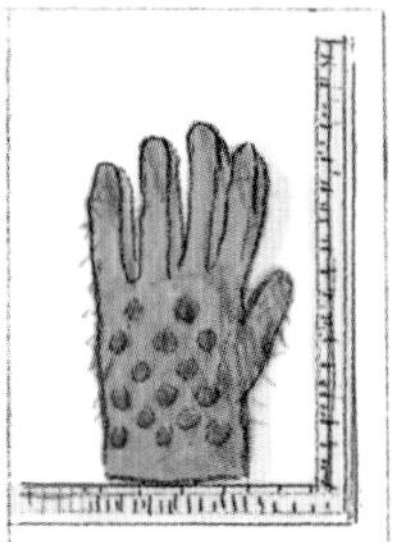

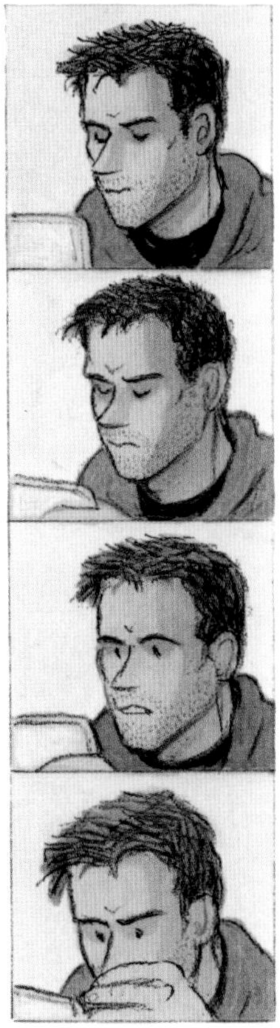

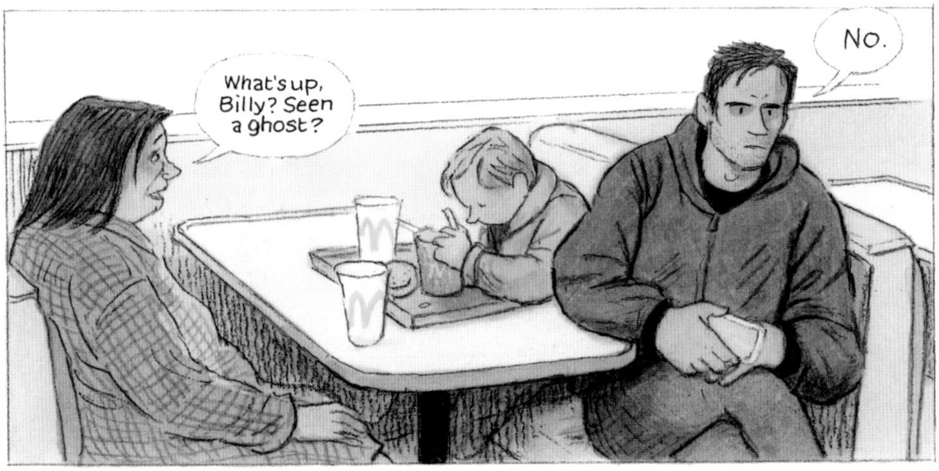
What's up, Billy? Seen a ghost?
No.

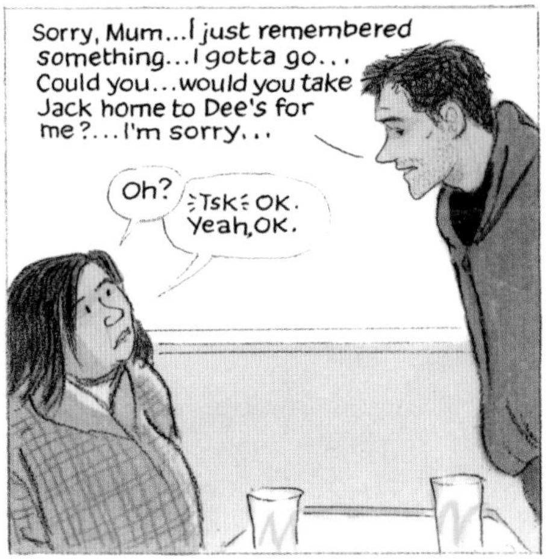
Sorry, Mum... I just remembered something... I gotta go... Could you... would you take Jack home to Dee's for me?... I'm sorry...
Oh?
Tsk OK. Yeah, OK.

Billy, thought you should know: saw Cassandra. She's taking D's property to cop shop. x Nicki

Thx. Can we meet? Something else come up. Advice needed asap. Will call. x B

Billy called Nicki from a phonebox, sounding paranoid, and told her just enough about the police report, the body, the coat and glove to make her think "Fuck, I don't need this!" Her heart went thud, thud, and she nearly hung up.
Billy sounded dead embarrassed, just like he did a year ago when they split up and he said, "It's not you, Nicki, it's me," then apologised for being bad news, for inflicting a gun, thugs, violence and a dead pug on her. Sometimes Nicki wondered if all that stuff hadn't happened, would she and Billy still be an item? They'd never examined their relationship at the time, had left their feelings for each other unspoken. It wasn't just sex, there were feelings, Nicki knew. Quite strong feelings. "Better for you if we don't see each other," Billy had said. Did he mean it was better for him? She never asked.

Now there was a body. And possibly murder to add to Billy's list of bad news.
In spite of this Nicki agreed to meet him. After all he said he only wanted advice.

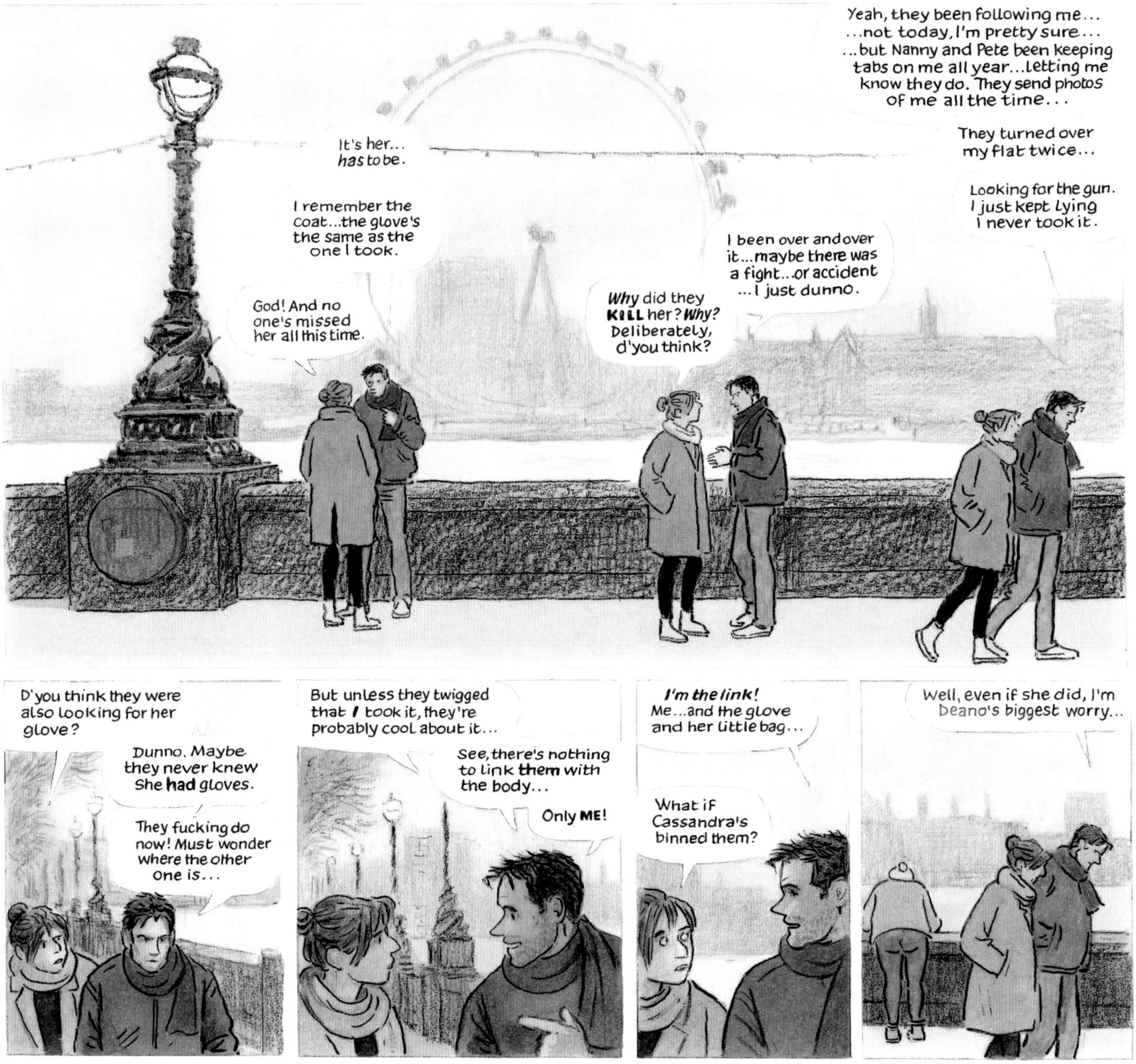
It's her... has to be.
I remember the coat...the glove's the same as the one I took.
God! And no one's missed her all this time.
Why did they KILL her? Why? Deliberately, d'you think?
I been over and over it...maybe there was a fight...or accident ...I just dunno.
Yeah, they been following me... ...not today, I'm pretty sure... ...but Nanny and Pete been keeping tabs on me all year...letting me know they do. They send photos of me all the time...
They turned over my flat twice...
Looking for the gun. I just kept lying I never took it.
D'you think they were also looking for her glove?
Dunno. Maybe they never knew she had gloves.
They fucking do now! Must wonder where the other one is...
But unless they twigged that I took it, they're probably cool about it...
See, there's nothing to link them with the body...
Only ME!
I'm the link! Me...and the glove and her little bag...
What if Cassandra's binned them?
Well, even if she did, I'm Deano's biggest worry...

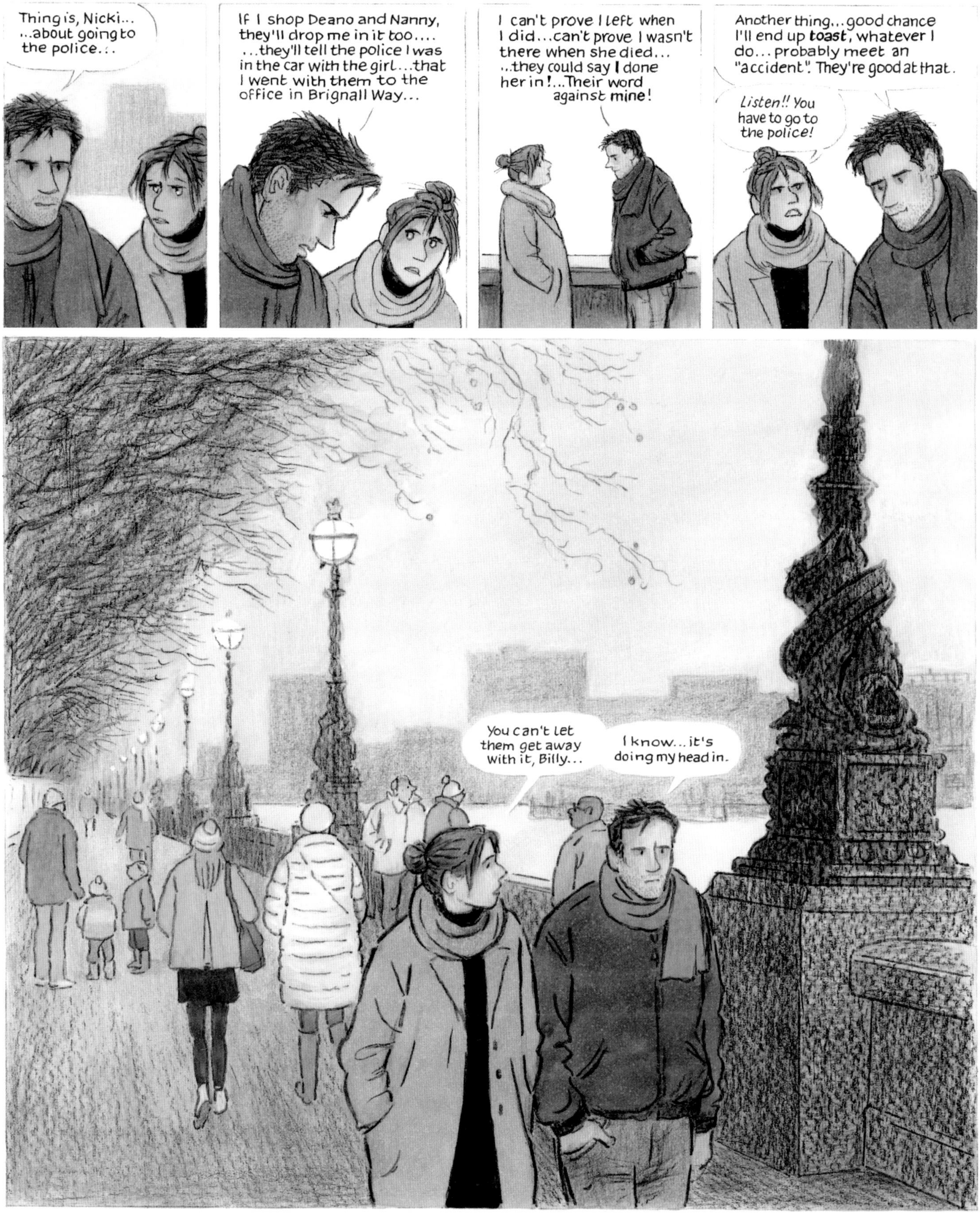
Thing is, Nicki... ...about going to the police...
If I shop Deano and Nanny, they'll drop me in it too.... ...they'll tell the police I was in the car with the girl...that I went with them to the office in Brignall Way...
I can't prove I left when I did...can't prove I wasn't there when she died... ...they could say I done her in!...Their word against mine!
Another thing...good chance I'll end up toast, whatever I do...probably meet an "accident". They're good at that.
Listen!! You have to go to the police!
You can't let them get away with it, Billy...
I know...it's doing my head in.

I've been sleeping badly, waking from nightmares, full of guilt and pointing fingers. But in the small hours, apart from selling fakes, I find my conscience largely clear. Of course the world has always found me deviant, a "failure" as a woman – and I admit to this. I haven't lived as a woman is supposed to live – even these days. Yes, I once obeyed convention and married. A terrible mistake, but a useful lesson (know thyself) : I am bad at living with people. I have no interest in domesticity or children. I am solitary, a natural spinster, answerable to no one, a burden to no one.

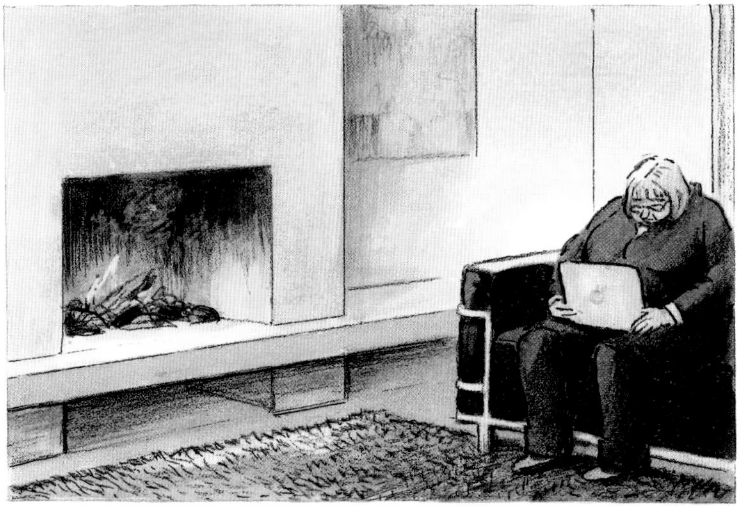

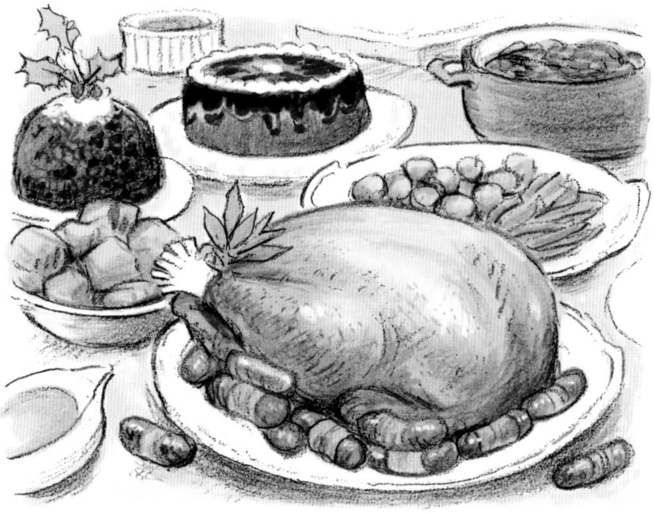

I've felt knackered all day and am now barely watching *Coronation Street*, being roused every so often by ads for monstrous turkey dinners. Usually I look forward to my own Christmas supplies – caviar, Stilton, a large Vacherin, Dundee cake, port, champagne. This year I haven't bothered.
I've had enough. All my life I've had enough – enough money, education, choice, freedom, travel, comfort. I've seen enough art, opera, theatre, films, listened to enough music, read enough books, drunk enough wine. I've just had quite enough.

It's cold. This morning my garden was full of frost. Perfect weather for hypothermia.

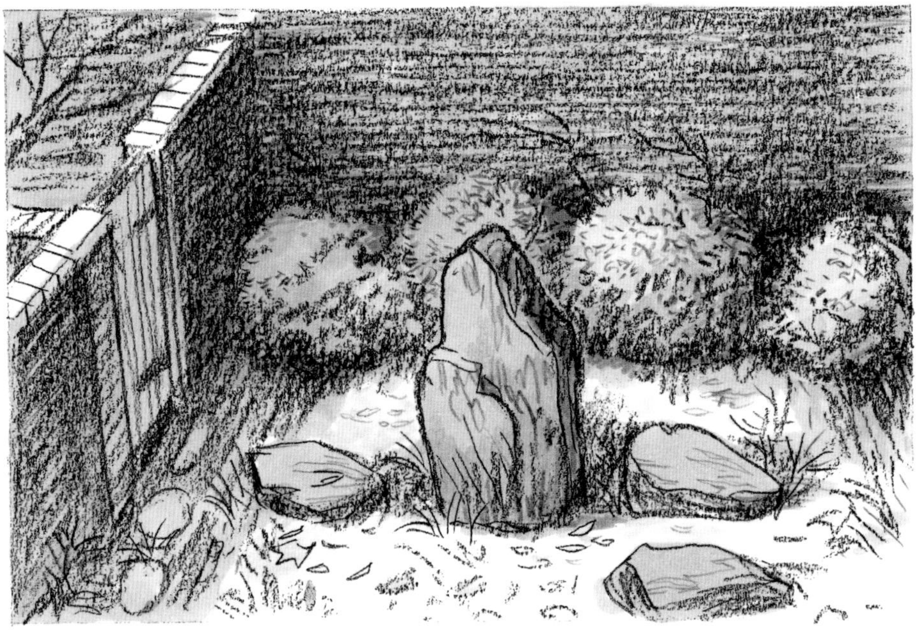

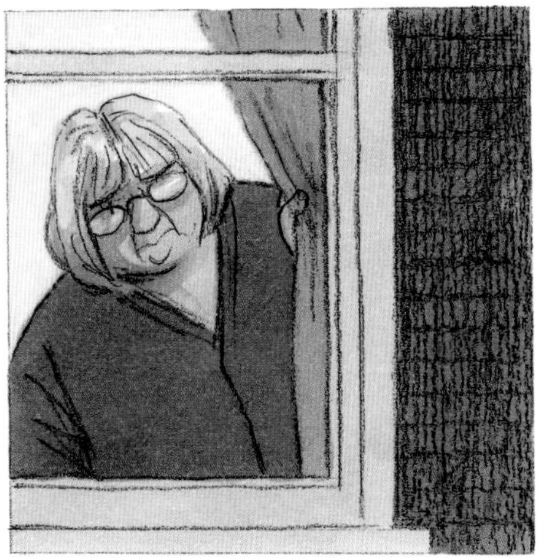

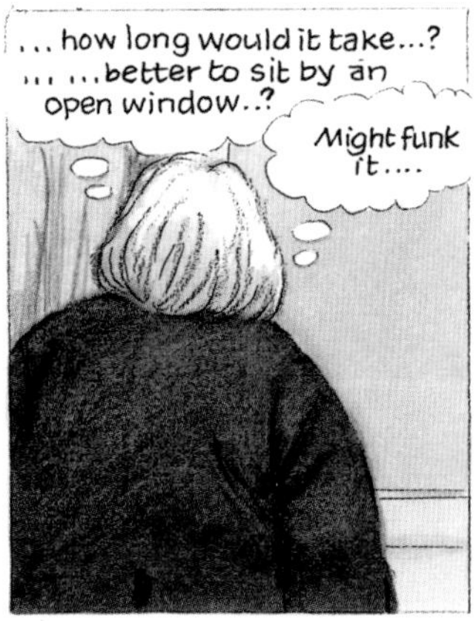
... how long would it take...?
... ...better to sit by an open window..?
Might funk it....

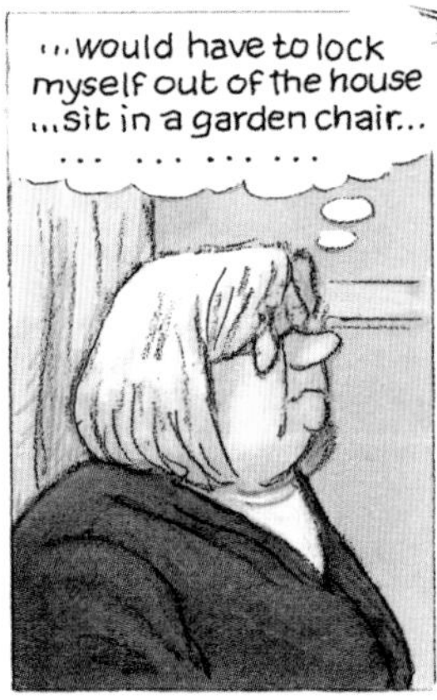
...would have to lock myself out of the house ...sit in a garden chair...
... ...

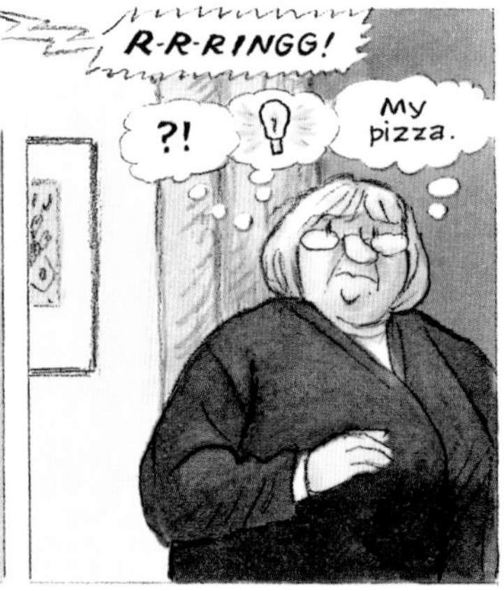
R-R-RINGG!
?!
My pizza.

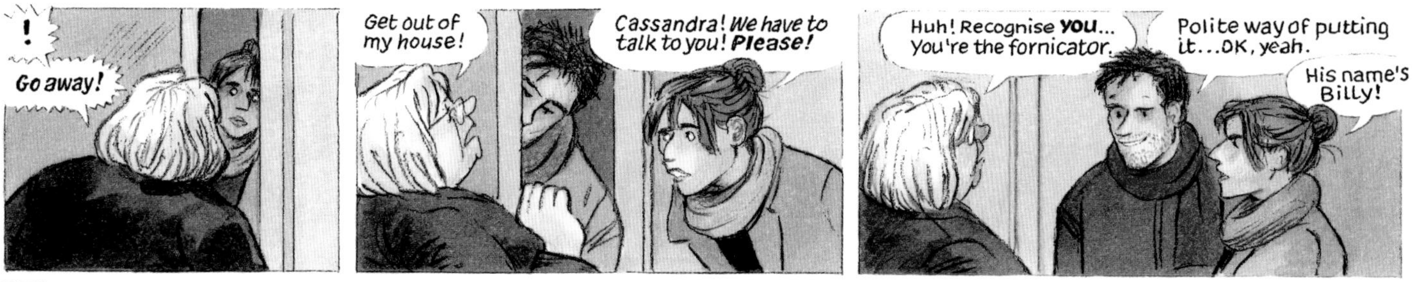
!
Go away!
Get out of my house!
Cassandra! We have to talk to you! Please!
Huh! Recognise you... You're the fornicator.
Polite way of putting it...OK, yeah.
His name's Billy!

Weird. The first time I saw this Billy, he was all la-di-dah, but now he's got a London accent. He asks if I would give him the gun, the glove, and the make-up bag. Evidence, he says, in a murder or manslaughter which has been in the news. I could look it up online. Billy the Fornicator plans to grass on the thugs involved.

Nicky makes a confession. They did some other things which affected me. I might have an interest in getting the thugs banged up, she says, seeing as one them killed Corker. It all came out.

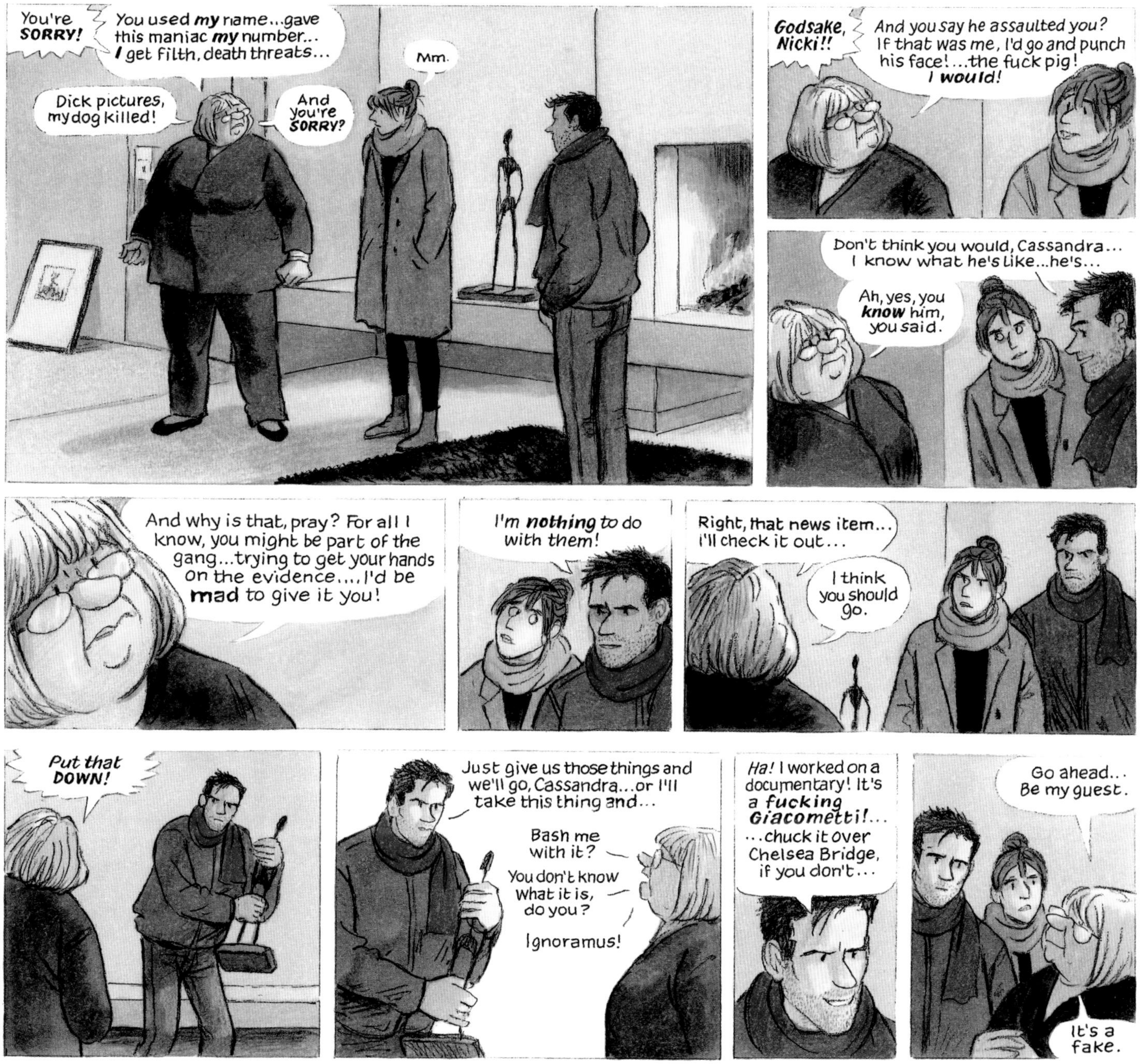
You're SORRY!
You used my name...gave this maniac my number... I get filth, death threats...
Mm.
Dick pictures, my dog killed!
And you're SORRY?
Godsake, Nicki!!
And you say he assaulted you? If that was me, I'd go and punch his face!...the fuck pig! I would!
Don't think you would, Cassandra... I know what he's like...he's...
Ah, yes, you know him, you said.
And why is that, pray? For all I know, you might be part of the gang...trying to get your hands on the evidence...I'd be mad to give it you!
I'm nothing to do with them!
Right, that news item... I'll check it out...
I think you should go.
Put that DOWN!
Just give us those things and we'll go, Cassandra...or I'll take this thing and...
Bash me with it?
You don't know what it is, do you?
Ignoramus!
Ha! I worked on a documentary! It's a fucking Giacometti!...
...chuck it over Chelsea Bridge, if you don't...
Go ahead... Be my guest.
It's a fake.

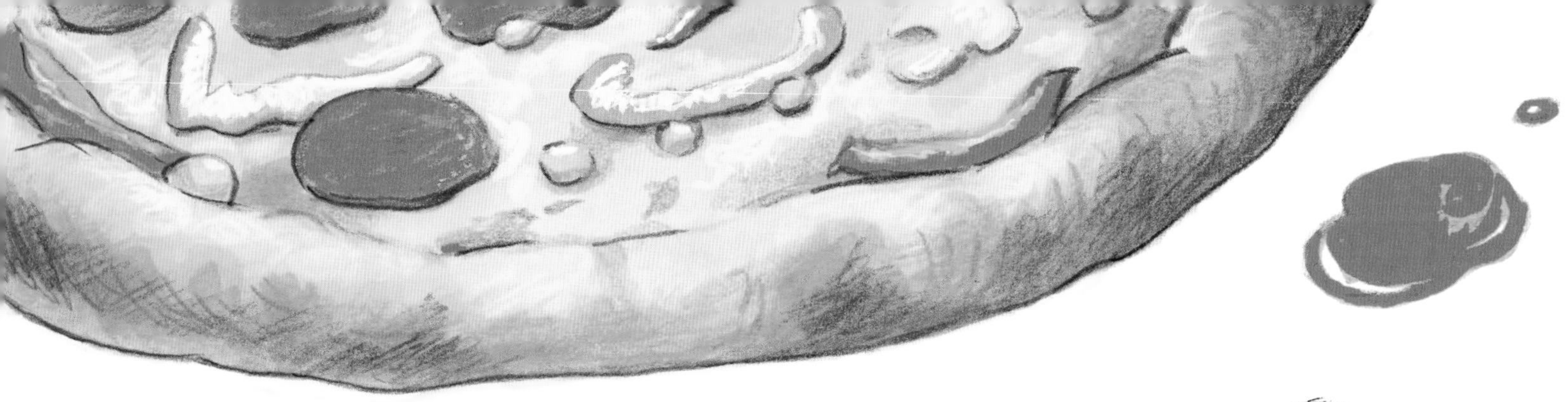

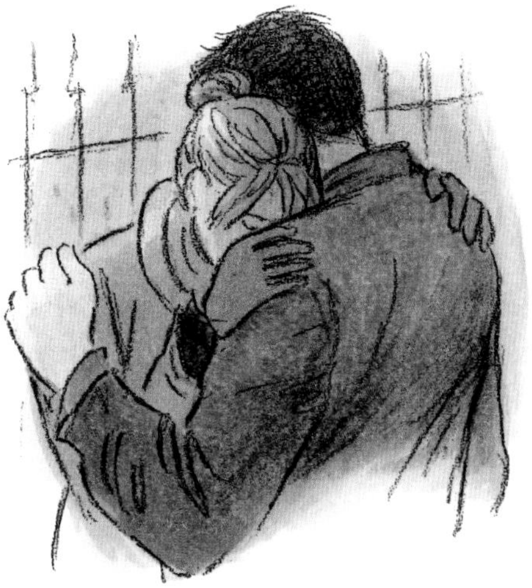

I am so outraged that I pretty well push the pair down my steps, Nicki still squeaking apologies and Billy still hoping for my help. My help? When he's threatened me? When she's used my name and linked me with a gang of violent arseholes? I have promised, however, and perhaps rashly, to check their story and get back to them. On the pavement, Nicki and Billy clutch each other until my pizza delivery disturbs their tender moment.

Online, I tap in "Wrysley skeleton" and find several newspaper reports and a reference to the most recent *Crimefile* – a programme available on ReplayIt. Wrysley is the second item and follows the usual formula: a detective's report showing the glove! The left-hand one, identical to the one I've hidden in my washing machine! This is followed by an appeal to the public for information and an interview with a couple, near where they discovered the remains last month. I play the whole item backwards and forwards ...

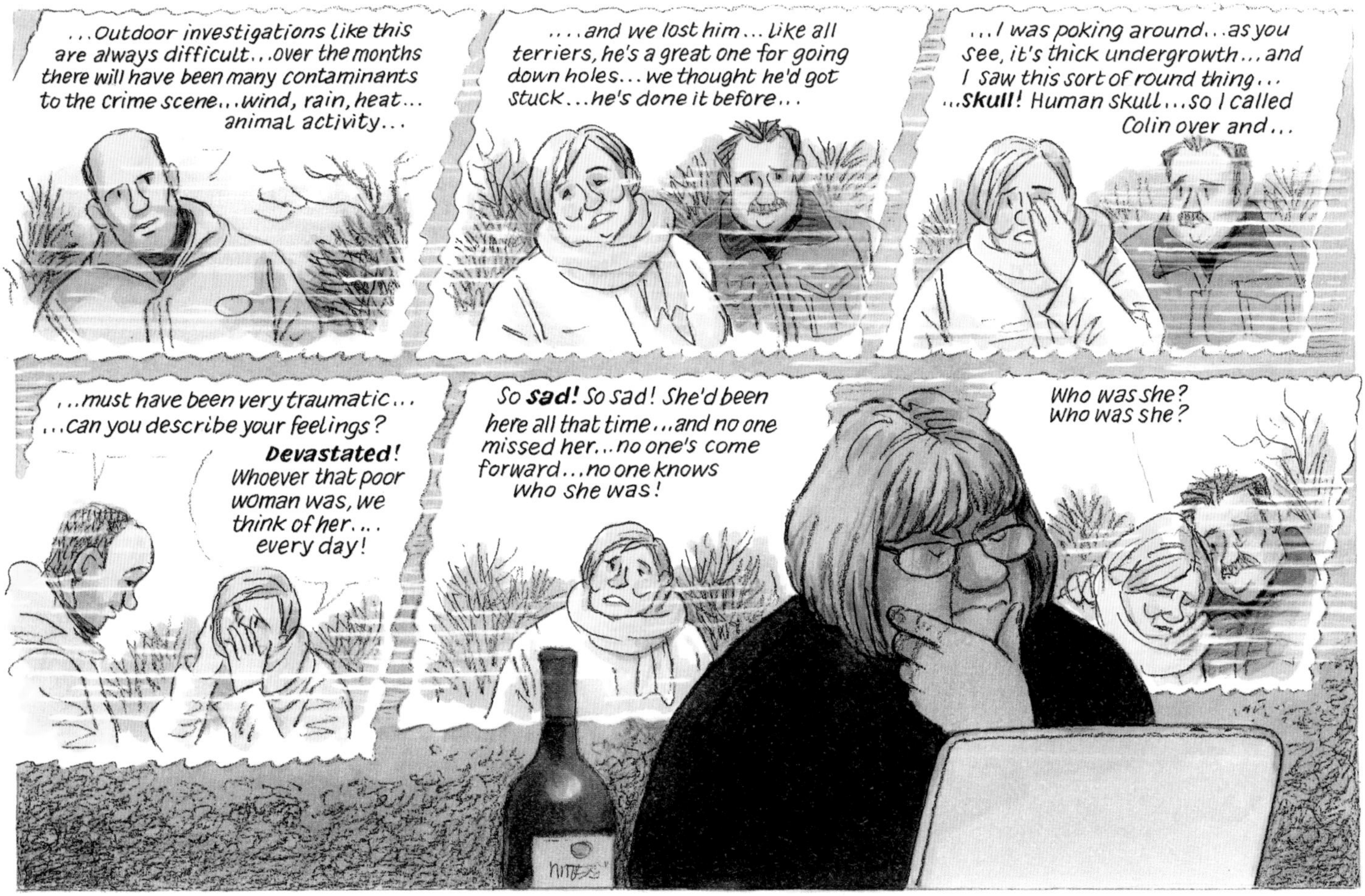
...Outdoor investigations like this are always difficult...over the months there will have been many contaminants to the crime scene...wind, rain, heat... animal activity...
....and we lost him... like all terriers, he's a great one for going down holes... we thought he'd got stuck...he's done it before...
...I was poking around...as you see, it's thick undergrowth...and I saw this sort of round thing... ...**Skull!** Human skull...so I called Colin over and...
...must have been very traumatic... ...can you describe your feelings?
Devastated! Whoever that poor woman was, we think of her.... every day!
So **sad!** So sad! She'd been here all that time...and no one missed her...no one's come forward...no one knows who she was!
Who was she? Who was she?

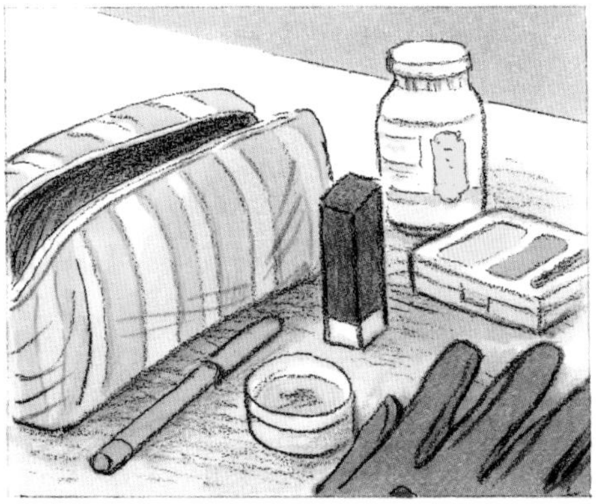

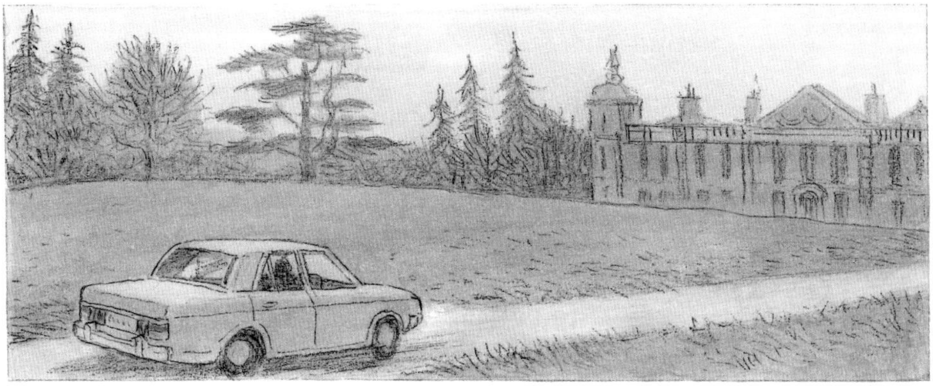

Who was she? According to Billy, if one can believe him, she was in her twenties, white, slim, an unremarkable face and a strong foreign accent. What sort of foreign he couldn't tell. She'd been hitching rides to London and was evidently up for slap and tickle with one of the gang. Billy never heard her name.

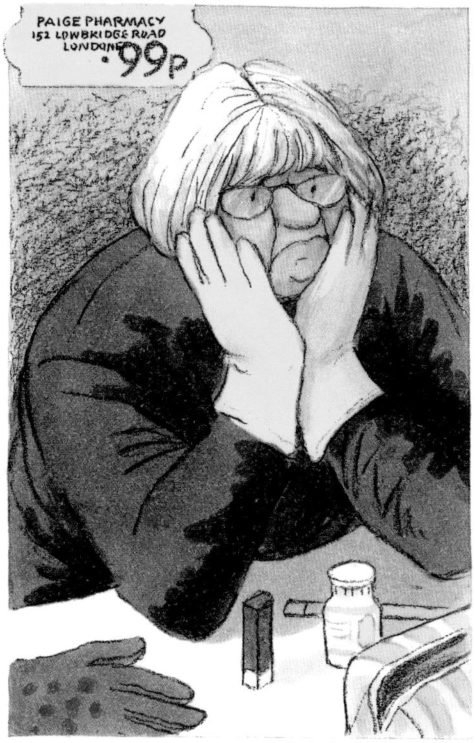
PAIGE PHARMACY
152 LOWBRIDGE ROAD
LONDON
·99p

I have a tingle, a familiar feeling from my early days in the art market. I had a good memory then and a knack for identifying works catalogued as "unknown artist", simply by following clues in the brushwork, pigment, subject, date, weave of the canvas and so on. When we were first together, Freddie considered us the best team ever. "My gob, your eye," he used to say. (He could sell anyone anything.) We would go off in his Cortina to auctions in the grand country houses that were selling up at the time. My God, the things I spotted – Dutch porcelain in butlers' pantries, any number of Ferneleys and Herrings among the gilt-framed paintings.

Who was she? In front of me the glove and make-up bag must be fizzing with her DNA. Her lips have worn "Pink Magic" to a stub; her index finger went in the lip gloss; she stroked the brown pencil on her lids, preferred the peach shadow to the beige. The paracetamol container has the address of a London pharmacy on a price label. Three tablets left. Perhaps the day she died she had a headache ... period pain ...

A few pathetic remains, of a short perhaps dismal life that was snuffed out. Somehow. Dumped in undergrowth, unnamed, unknown, unmissed.

The next morning I find myself on the tube going east, far east, to a stop I've never heard of.

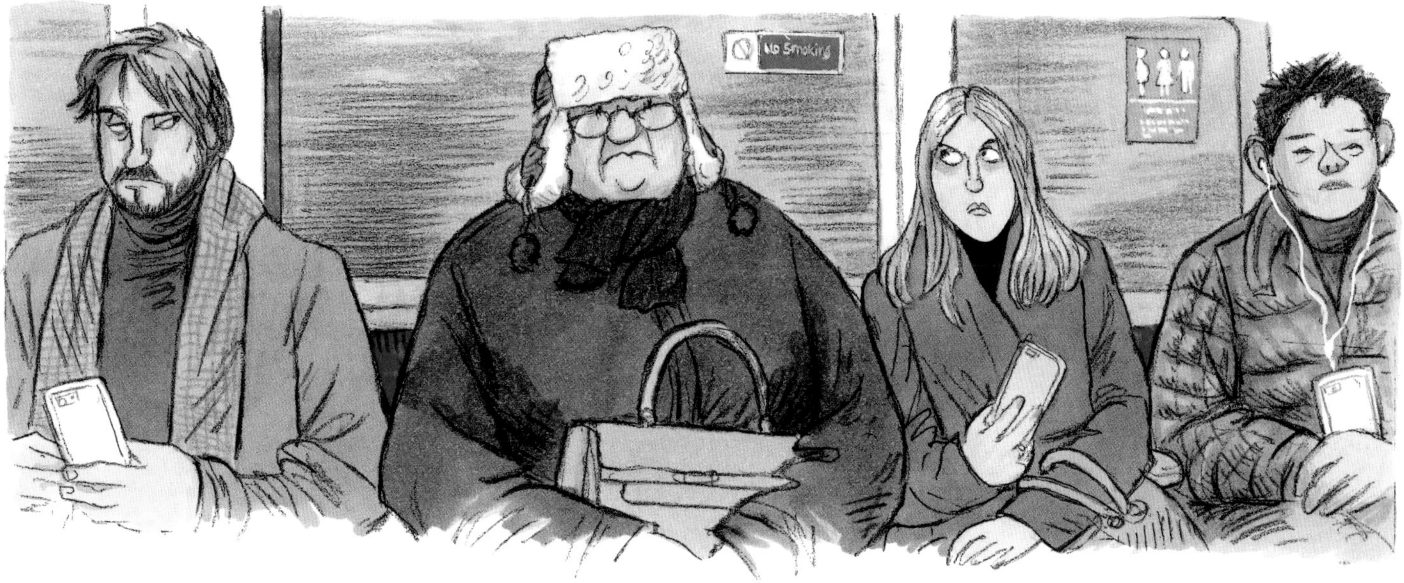
No Smoking

Lowbridge Road has little to recommend it – a long noxious thoroughfare surrounded by streets of decaying semis.

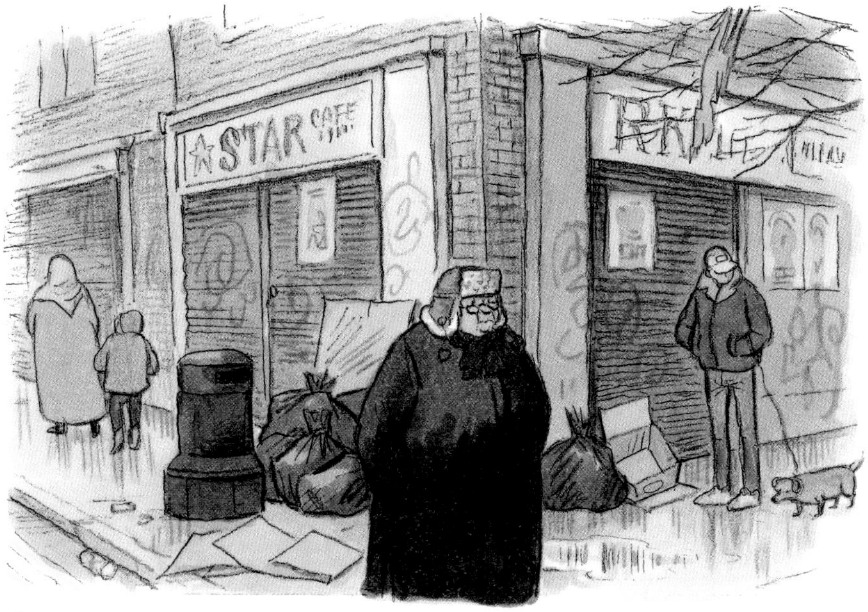
STAR CAFE

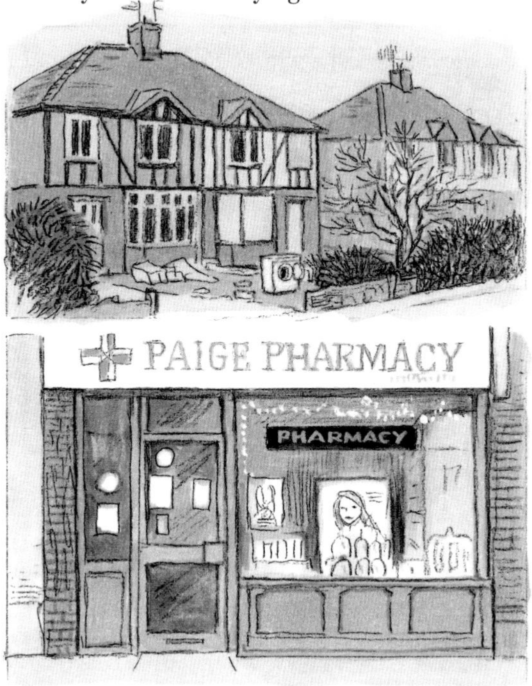
PAIGE PHARMACY
PHARMACY

I have no real plan, except to patronise a few shops and ask questions about the area, starting with the chemist where the paracetamol came from.

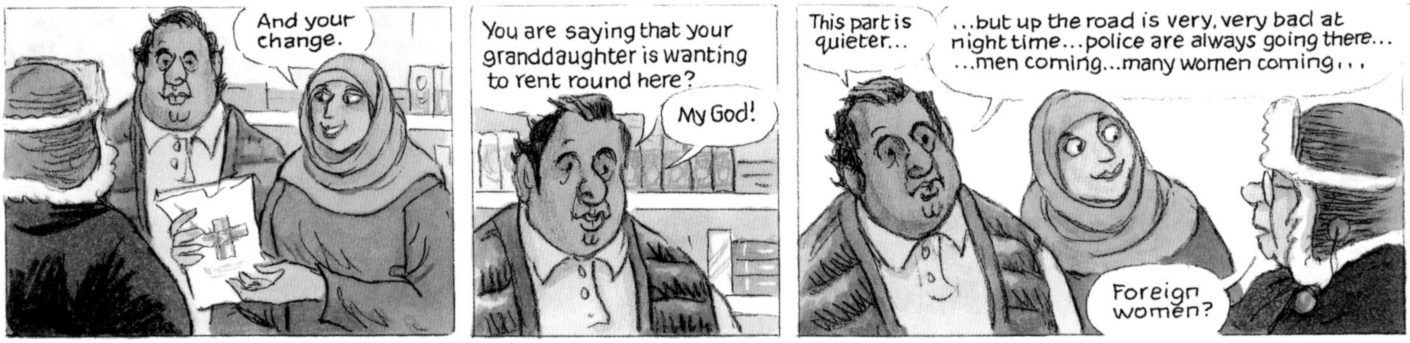
And your change.
You are saying that your granddaughter is wanting to rent round here?
My God!
This part is quieter...
...but up the road is very, very bad at night time...police are always going there... ...men coming...many women coming...
Foreign women?

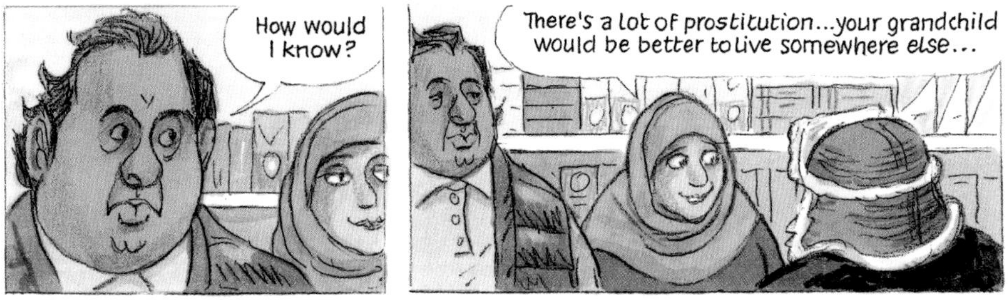
How would I know?
There's a lot of prostitution...your grandchild would be better to live somewhere else...

In the chippy the woman shrugs and says she is new to the area, but the next shop, where I buy half a bottle of scotch, is more rewarding.

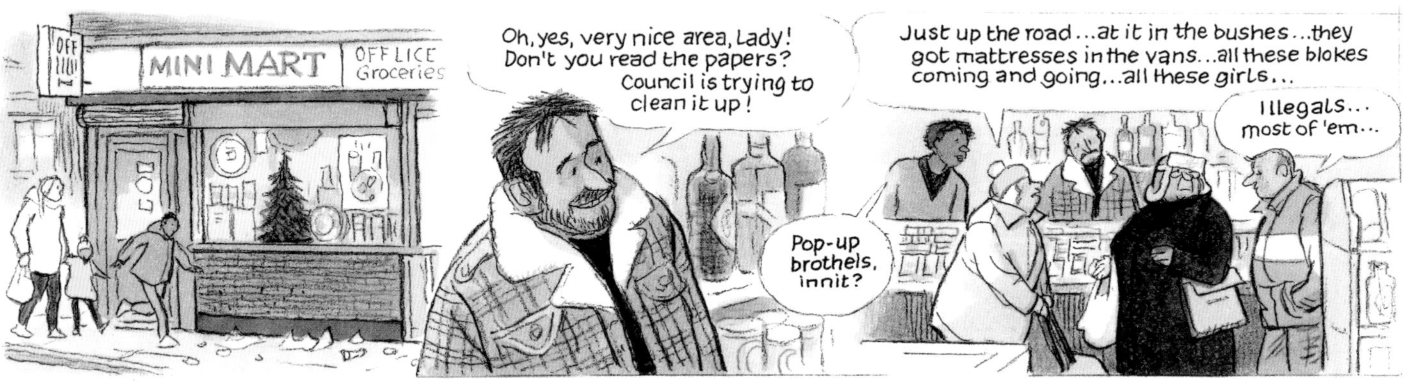
OFF LICENCE
MINI MART
OFF LICE Groceries
Oh, yes, very nice area, Lady! Don't you read the papers? Council is trying to clean it up!
Pop-up brothels, innit?
Just up the road...at it in the bushes...they got mattresses in the vans...all these blokes coming and going...all these girls...
Illegals... most of 'em...

I'm certainly not putting two and two together. Just because the dead girl was foreign and bought something locally, doesn't make her a sex worker. Someone else may have bought her the tablets and she may never have set foot in this horrible road – which, I note, in spite of its decay, has Christmas lights and bursts of laughter coming from pub doors.

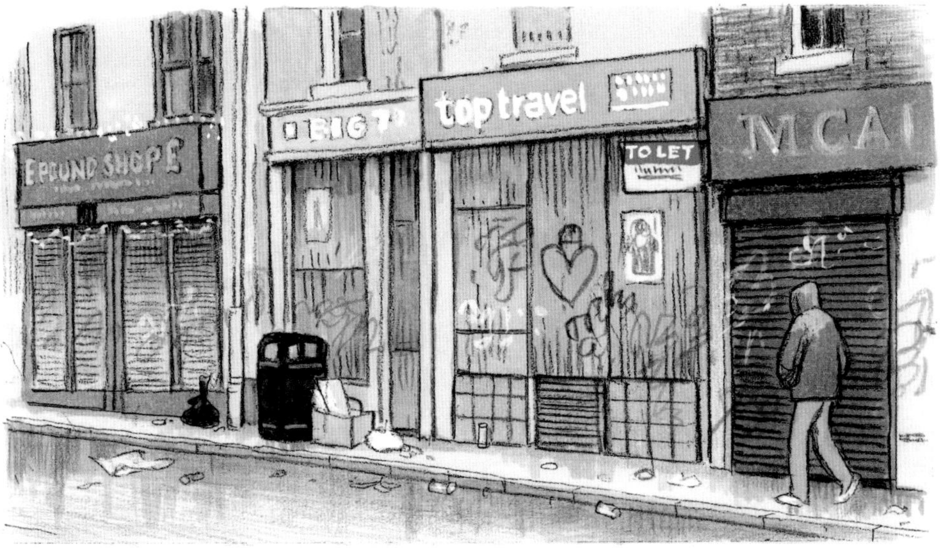
top travel
TO LET

Down the road in a shop which sells the local paper I discover my wallet has gone, and with it my bank cards, cash and travel pass. Difficult to know whether it was dropped or stolen. Either is possible. My phone is no use – I seldom need it these days and forget to charge it. All I have is 90p, nowhere near enough for the tube home.

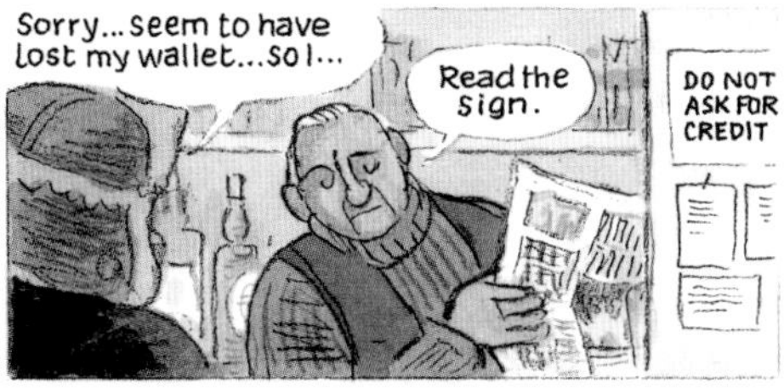
Sorry...seem to have lost my wallet...so I...
Read the sign.
DO NOT ASK FOR CREDIT

The irony of becoming a beggar isn't lost on me. I simply haven't the gall to ask any of these deprived people for spare change, nor can I face being ignored or told to fuck off. My best hope is a cab driver trusting enough to take me back to Chelsea and my petty cash drawer. Only there are no taxis. I tramp down the main road looking in vain. And too late I think of taking the whisky back to the shop and getting a refund. Too late, because I've had a couple of nips to keep out the cold.

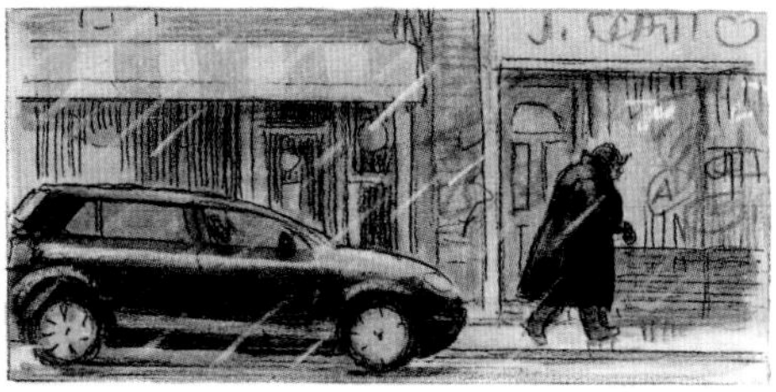

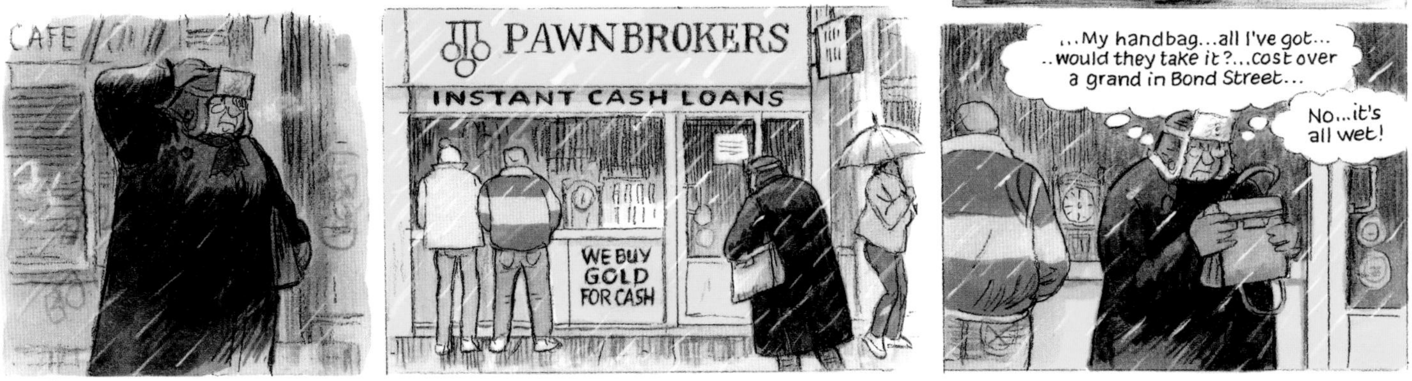
CAFE
PAWNBROKERS
INSTANT CASH LOANS
WE BUY GOLD FOR CASH
...My handbag...all I've got...
..would they take it?...cost over a grand in Bond Street...
No...it's all wet!

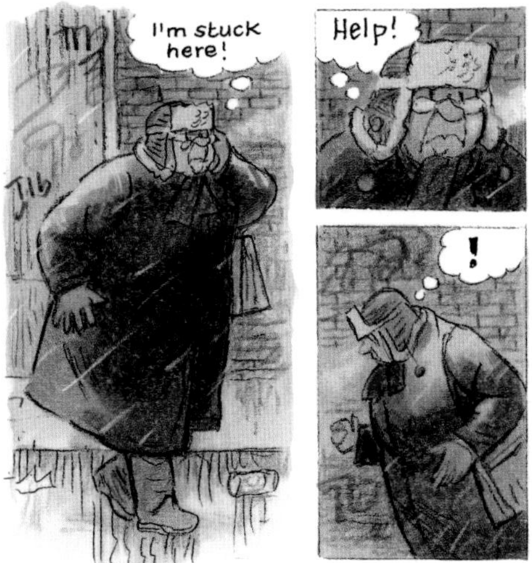
I'm stuck here!
Help!
!

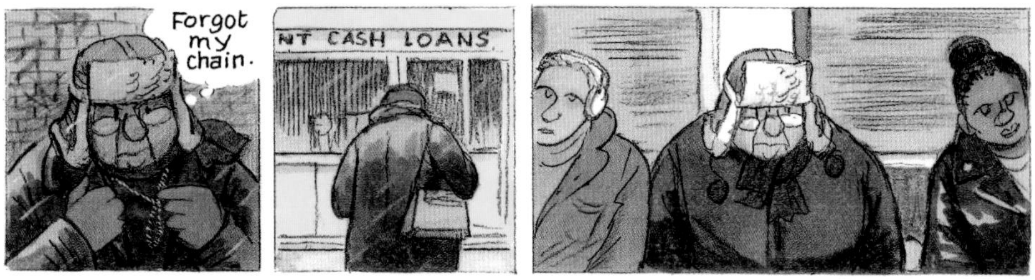
Forgot my chain.
NT CASH LOANS

I've rarely felt more disgusted with myself – snivelling because I was cold, wet and penniless for about 90 minutes max. There's also something shabby about the ease of my deliverance. All it took was a trifling bit of gold jewellery, which I won't bother to redeem. The price of an Oyster card and I'm out of here.
Did the dead woman live in the area of Lowbridge Road? I'm no wiser but in my bones I feel she did.

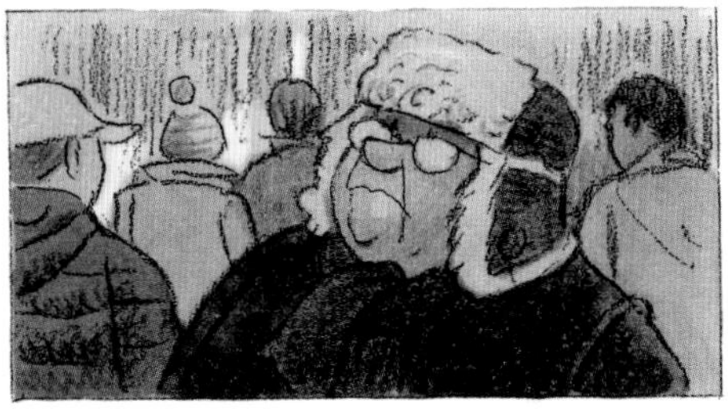

I emerge from the tube at Knightsbridge, where the contrast with Lowbridge Road couldn't be more stark. The billionaires' blocks are across the road, utterly banal on the outside, grand luxe inside and largely unlived-in – like very many places round here, according to Nicki. She hated the area, thought it blighted, called it "the empty quarter".
I remember protesting to her that at least I *lived* in my house and considered my rich absentee neighbours rather a blessing ...

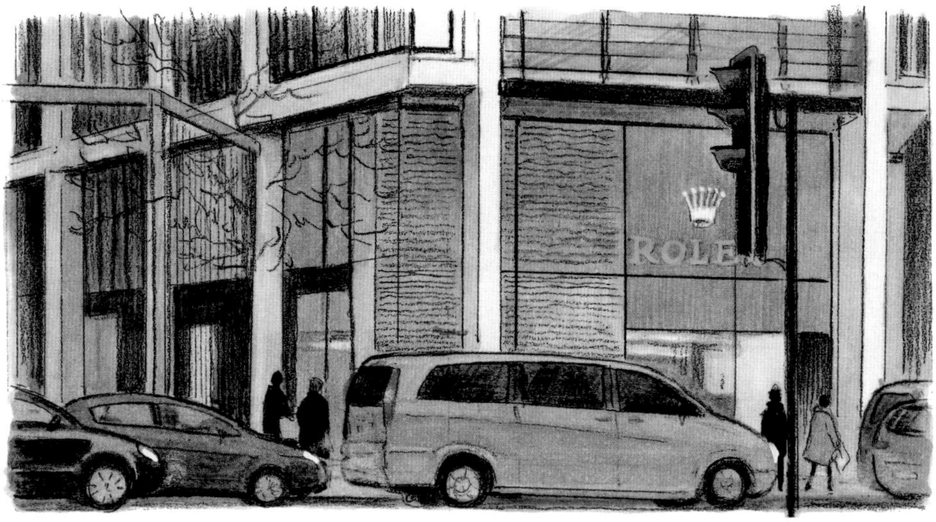
ROLE

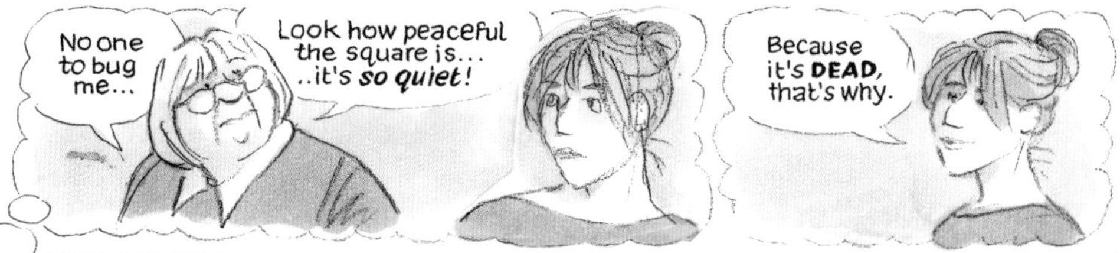
No one to bug me...
Look how peaceful the square is... ..it's so quiet!
Because it's DEAD, that's why.

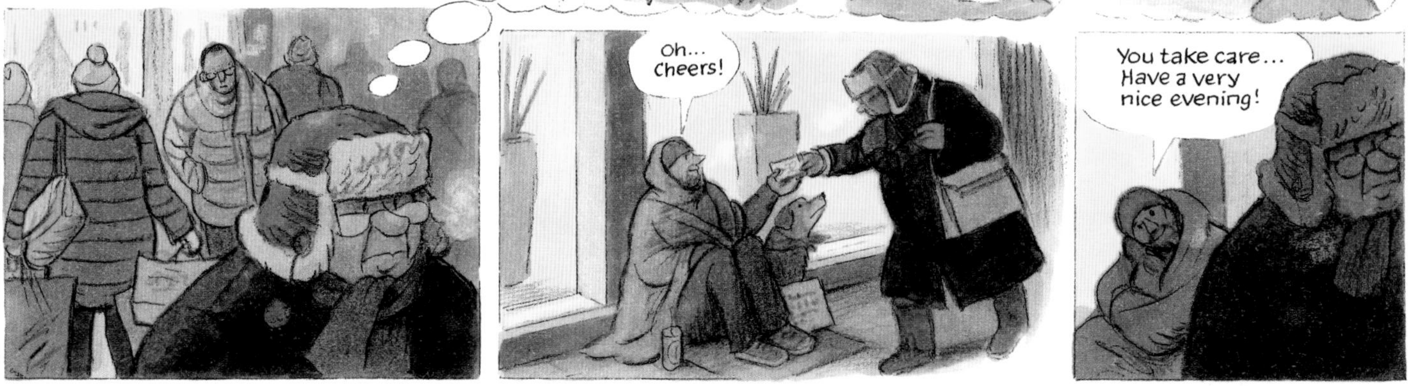
Oh... Cheers!
You take care... Have a very nice evening!

My evening is spent watching armed police on *Crimefile* – which reminds me of the gun, still in the washing machine. I worry about damp affecting it and wonder about the owner, perhaps a murderer, perhaps the sender of those filthy texts, whose arse I'd like to kick.

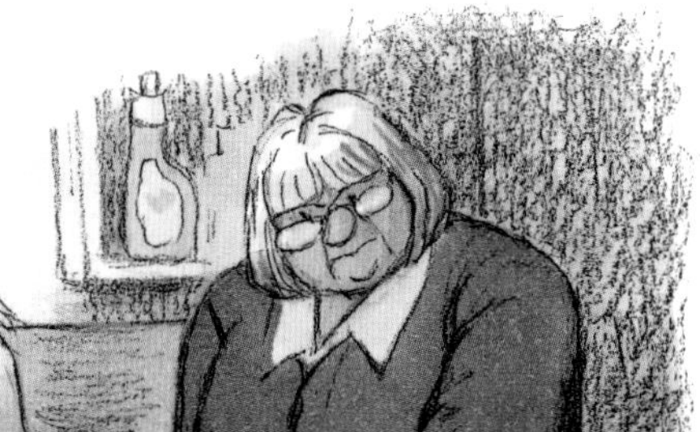
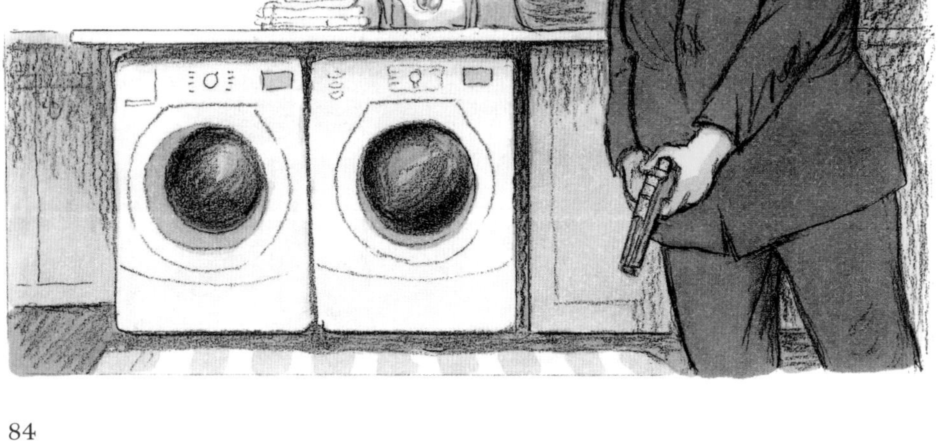
Persil

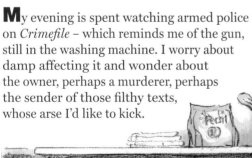

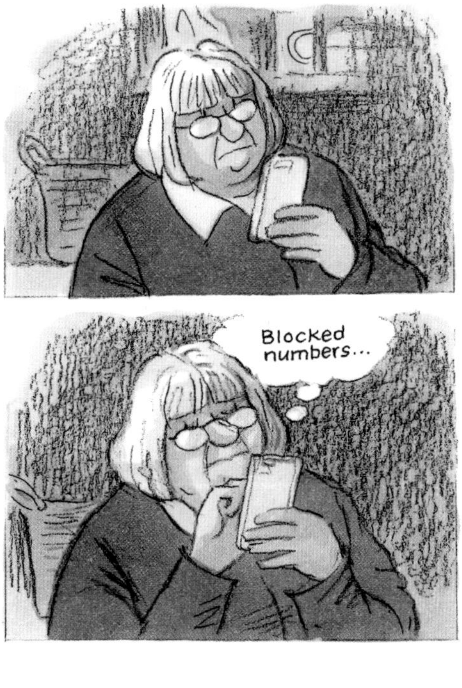
Blocked numbers...

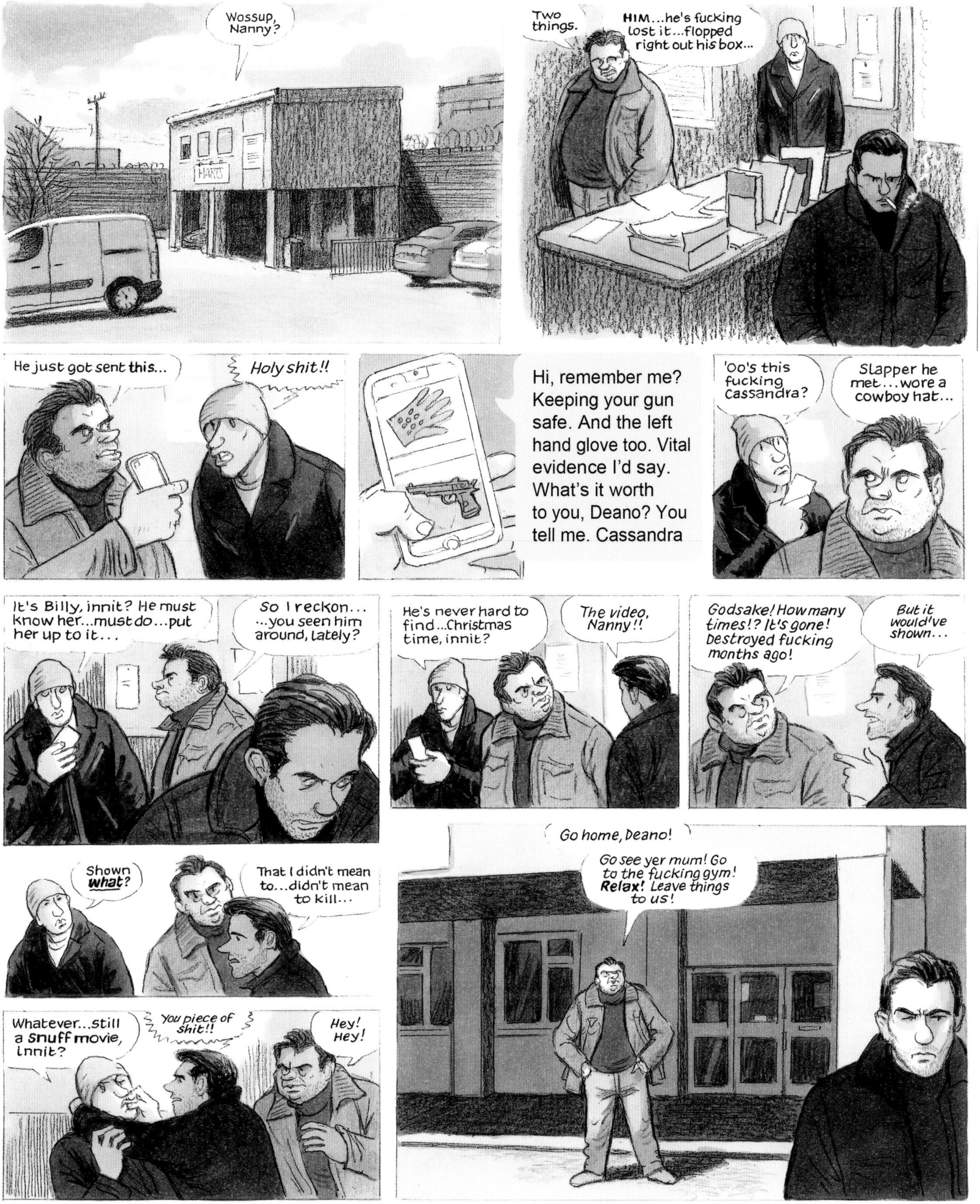
Wossup, Nanny?
Two things.
HIM...he's fucking lost it...flopped right out his box...
He just got sent this...
Holy shit!!
Hi, remember me? Keeping your gun safe. And the left hand glove too. Vital evidence I'd say. What's it worth to you, Deano? You tell me. Cassandra
'Oo's this fucking Cassandra?
Slapper he met...wore a cowboy hat...
It's Billy, innit? He must know her...must do...put her up to it...
So I reckon... ...you seen him around, lately?
He's never hard to find...Christmas time, innit?
The video, Nanny!!
Godsake! How many times!? It's gone! Destroyed fucking months ago!
But it would've shown...
Shown what?
That I didn't mean to...didn't mean to kill...
Whatever...still a snuff movie, innit?
You piece of shit!!
Hey! Hey!
Go home, Deano!
Go see yer mum! Go to the fucking gym! Relax! Leave things to us!

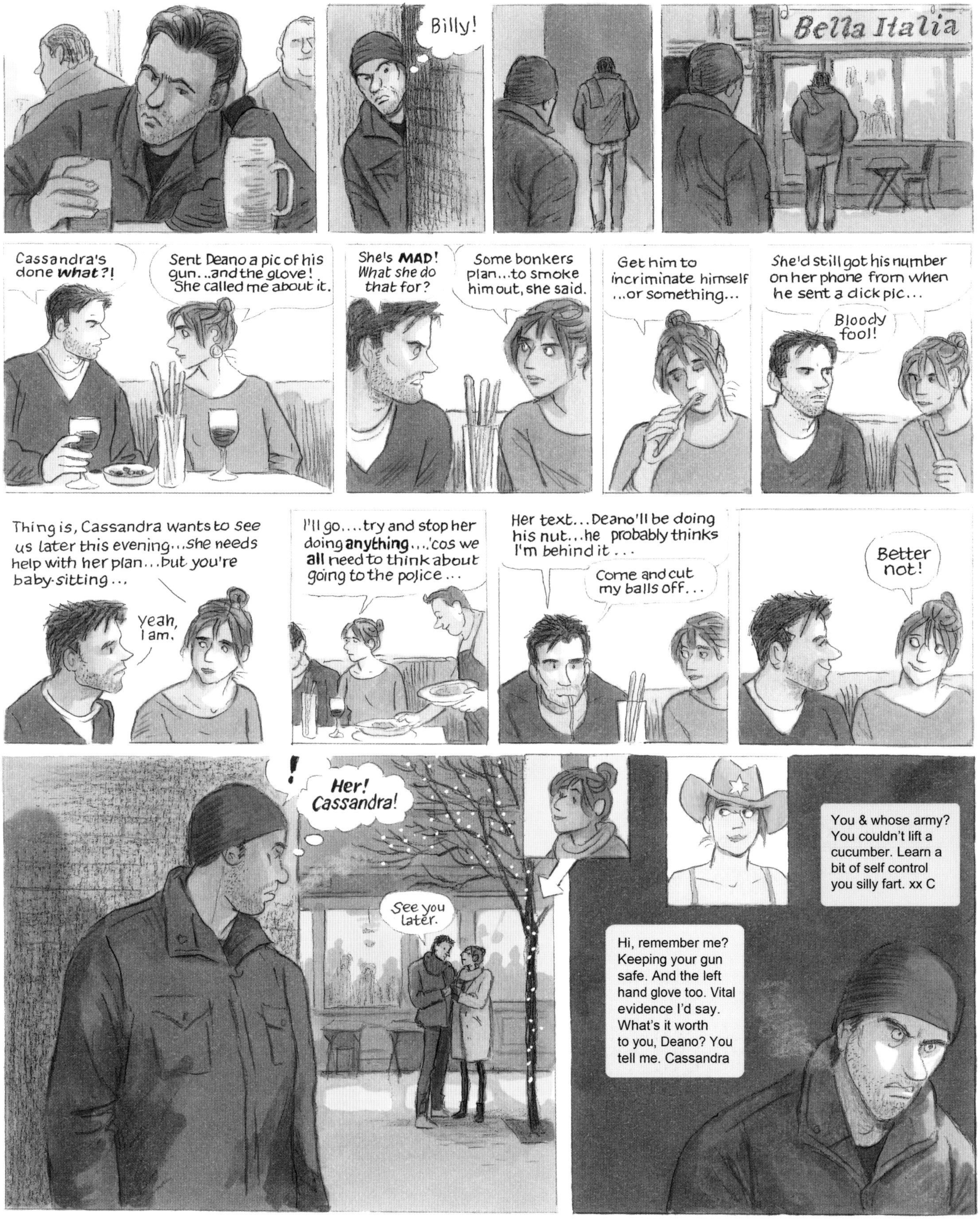

Bella Italia
Billy!
Cassandra's done what?!
Sent Deano a pic of his gun...and the glove! She called me about it.
She's MAD! What she do that for?
Some bonkers plan...to smoke him out, she said.
Get him to incriminate himself ...or something...
She'd still got his number on her phone from when he sent a dick pic...
Bloody fool!
Thing is, Cassandra wants to see us later this evening...she needs help with her plan...but you're baby-sitting...
Yeah, I am.
I'll go....try and stop her doing anything...'cos we all need to think about going to the police...
Her text...Deano'll be doing his nut...he probably thinks I'm behind it...
Come and cut my balls off...
Better not!
!
Her! Cassandra!
See you later.
You & whose army? You couldn't lift a cucumber. Learn a bit of self control you silly fart. xx C
Hi, remember me? Keeping your gun safe. And the left hand glove too. Vital evidence I'd say. What's it worth to you, Deano? You tell me. Cassandra

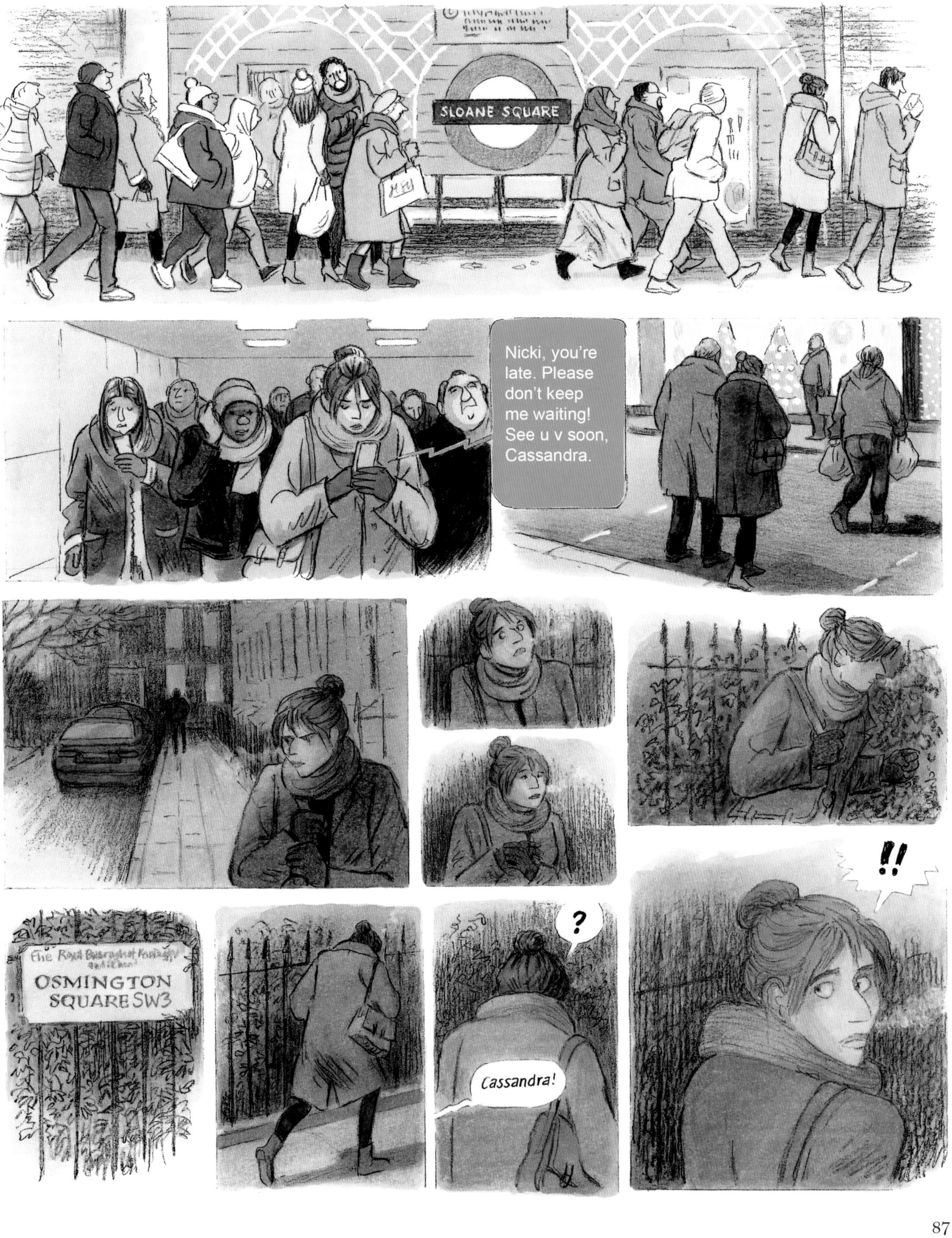
SLOANE SQUARE
Nicki, you're late. Please don't keep me waiting! See u v soon, Cassandra.
OSMINGTON SQUARE SW3
?
Cassandra!
!!

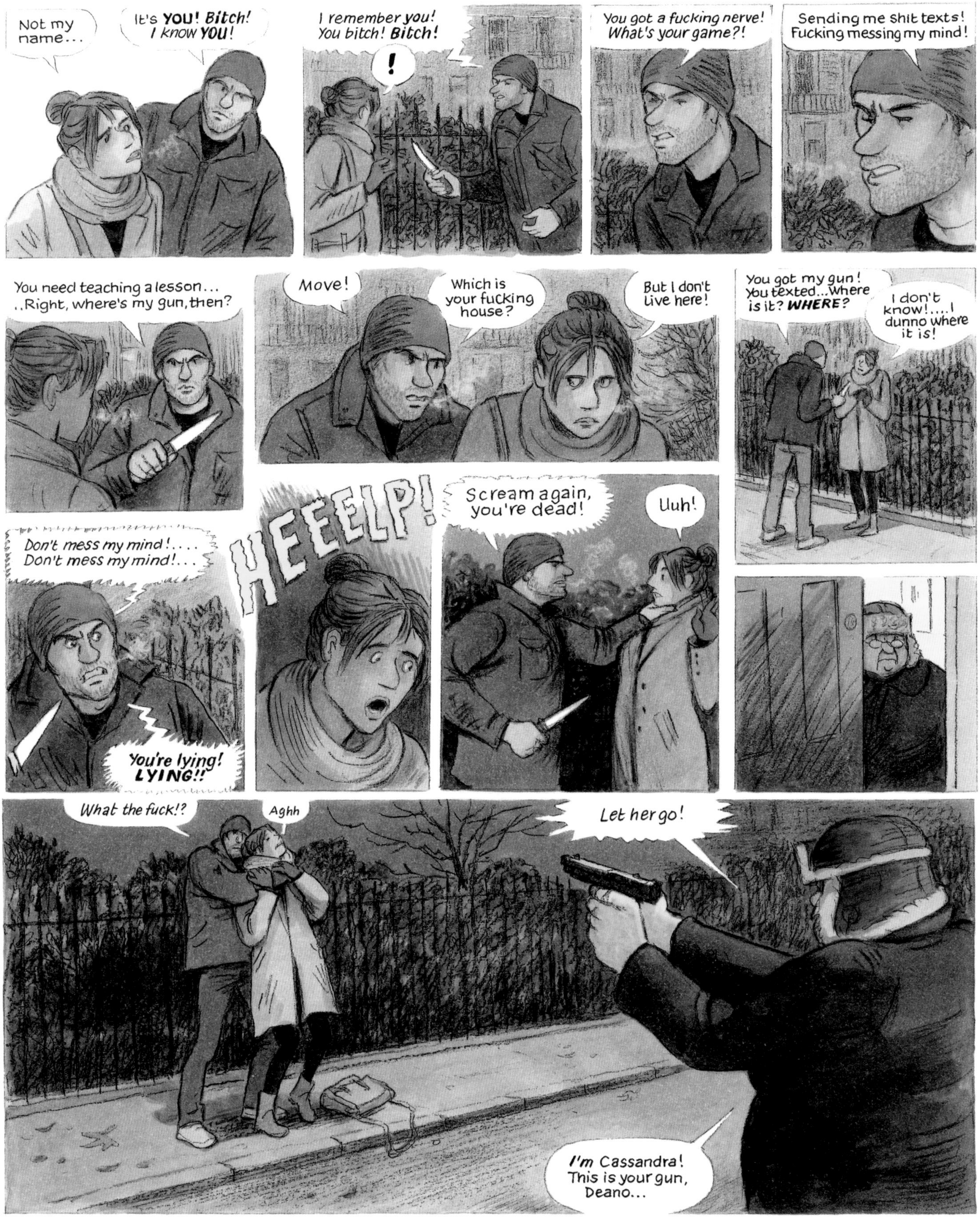

Not my name...
It's YOU! Bitch! I know YOU!
I remember you! You bitch! Bitch!
!
You got a fucking nerve! What's your game?!
Sending me shit texts! Fucking messing my mind!
You need teaching a lesson... ..Right, where's my gun, then?
Move!
Which is your fucking house?
But I don't live here!
You got my gun! You texted...Where is it? WHERE?
I don't know!....I dunno where it is!
Don't mess my mind!.... Don't mess my mind!...
You're lying! LYING!!
HEEELP!
Scream again, you're dead!
Uuh!
What the fuck!?
Aghh
Let her go!
I'm Cassandra! This is your gun, Deano...

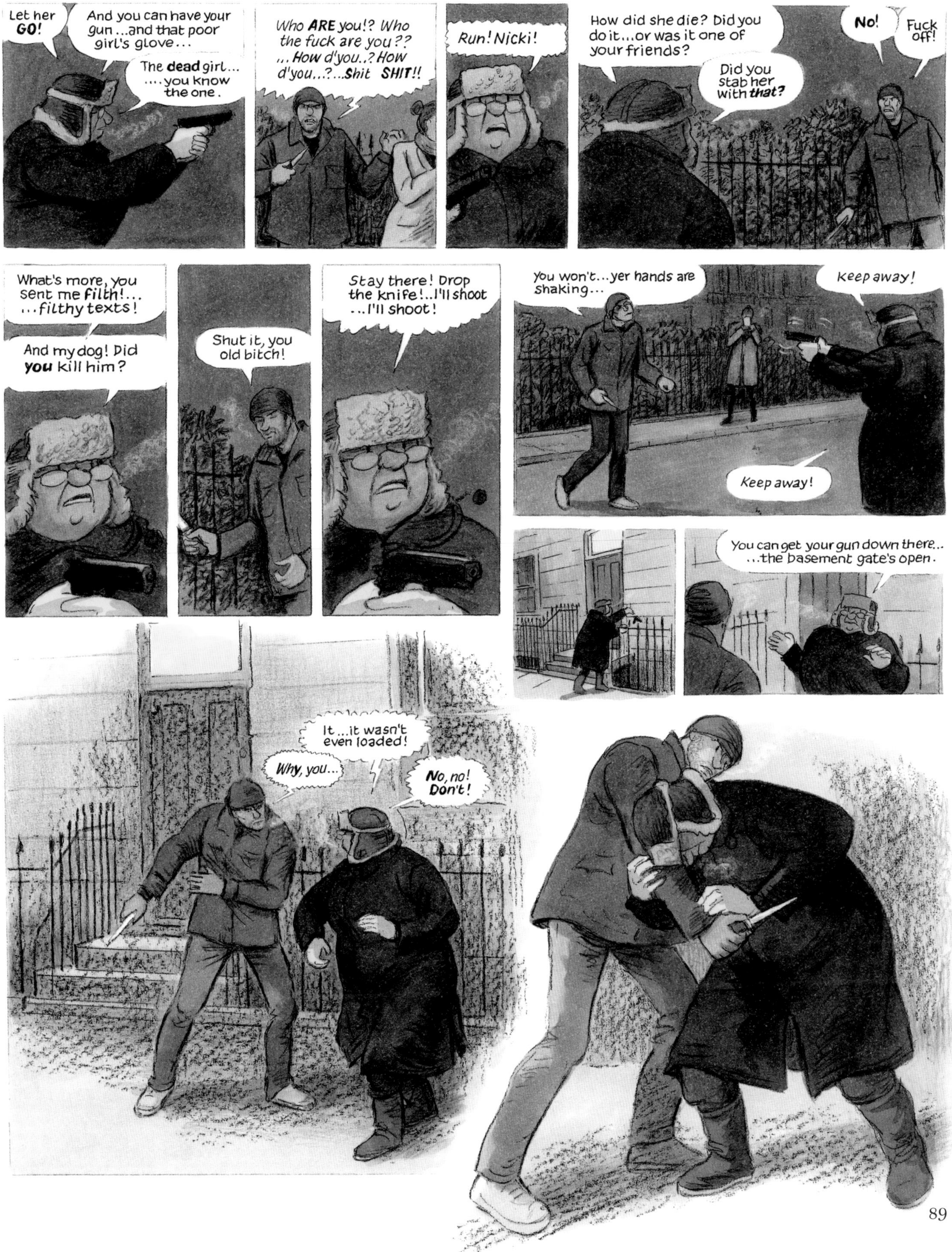

Let her GO!
And you can have your gun ...and that poor girl's glove...
The dead girl... ....you know the one.
Who ARE you!? Who the fuck are you?? ...How d'you..? How d'you..?...Shit SHIT!!
Run! Nicki!
How did she die? Did you do it...or was it one of your friends?
Did you stab her with that?
No!
Fuck off!
What's more, you sent me filth!... ...filthy texts!
And my dog! Did you kill him?
Shut it, you old bitch!
Stay there! Drop the knife!...I'll shoot ...I'll shoot!
You won't...yer hands are shaking...
Keep away!
Keep away!
You can get your gun down there... ...the basement gate's open.
It...it wasn't even loaded!
Why, you...
No, no! Don't!

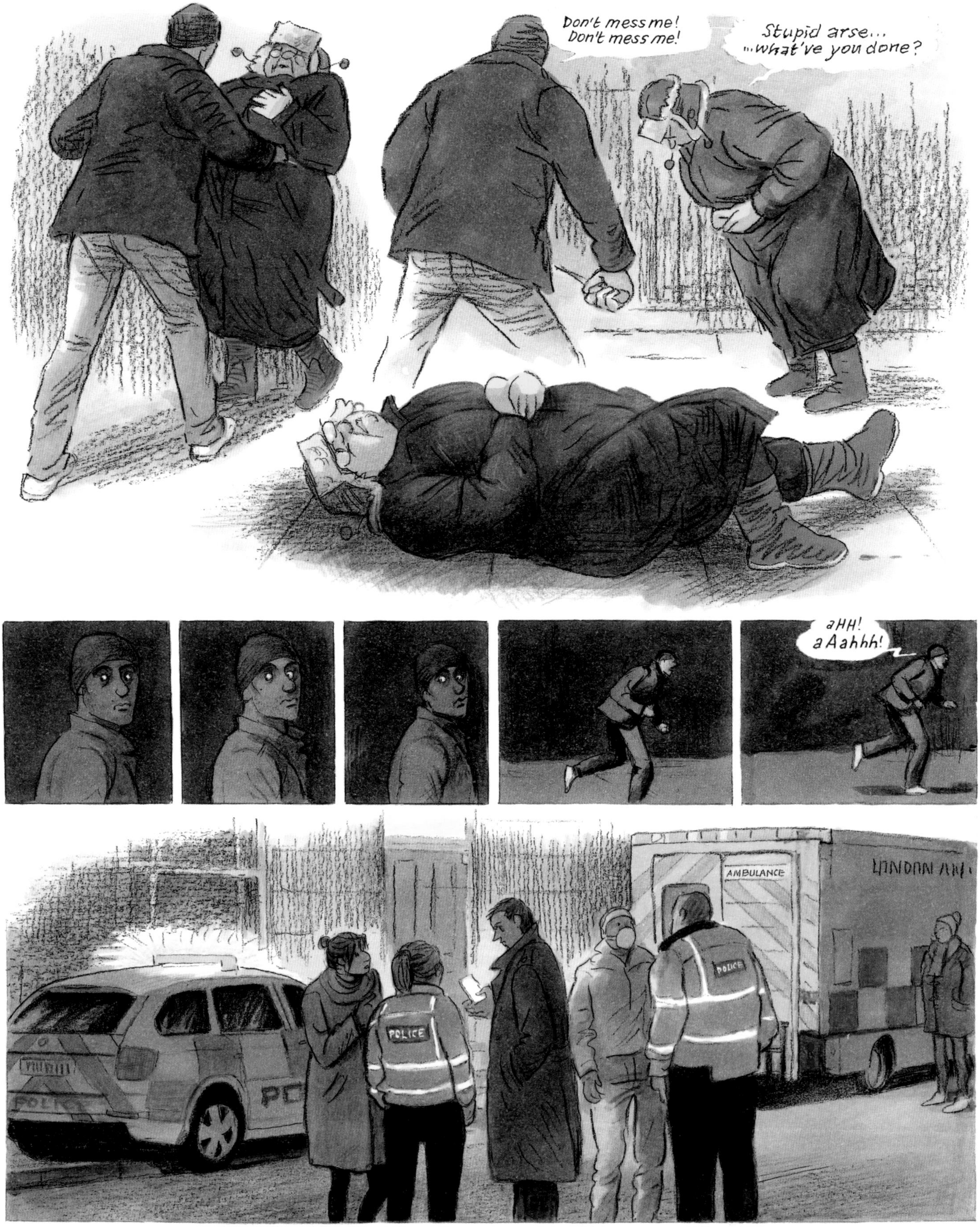
Don't mess me!
Don't mess me!
Stupid arse...
...what've you done?
aHH!
a Aahhh!
AMBULANCE
POLICE
POLICE
POLICE

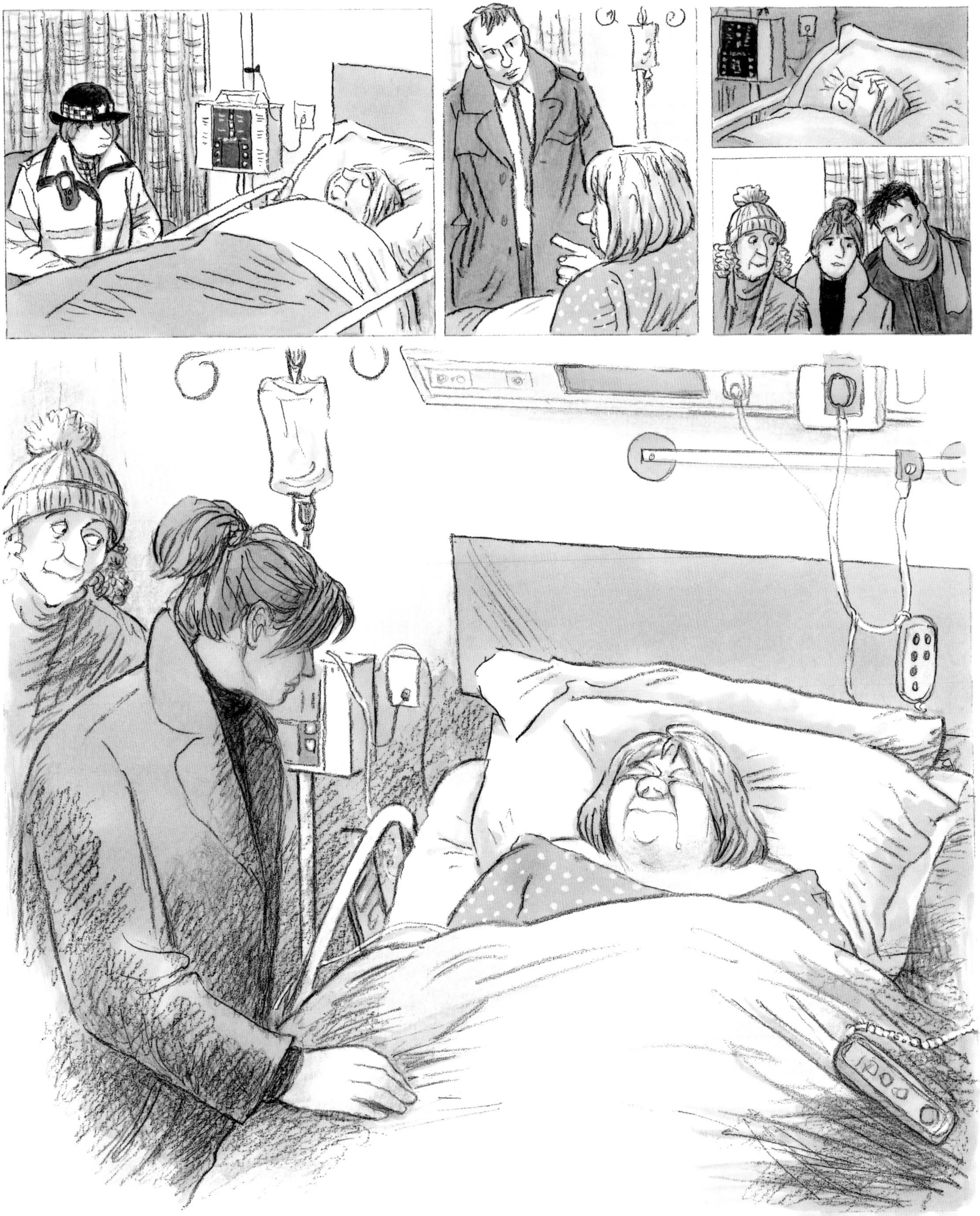

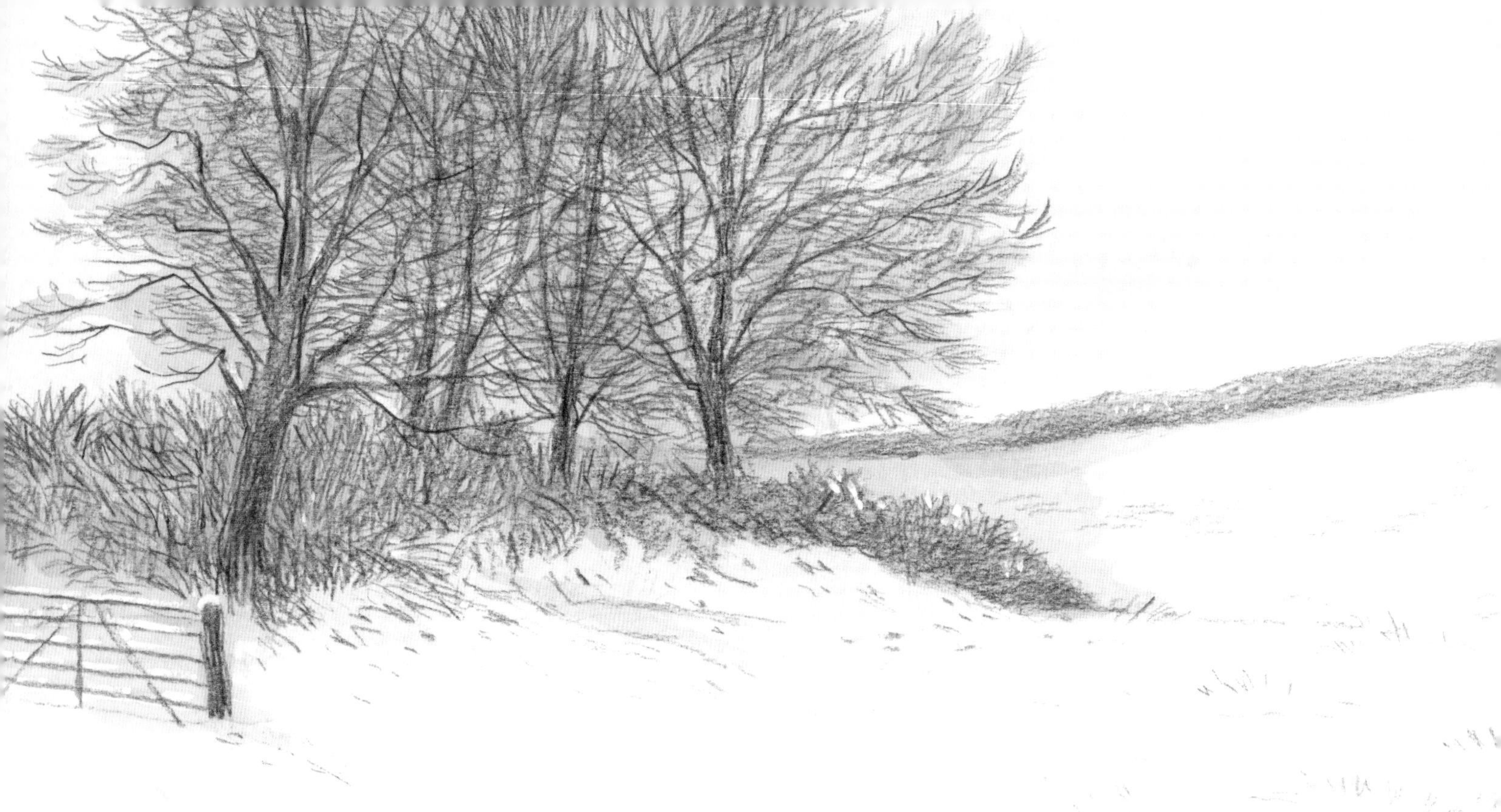

January

Since leaving hospital I've been looked after by Margot in Oxfordshire. She's used to caring for invalids and seems more than happy to do so. Of course she has her own motives of "re-bonding" and "closure", processes that previously I would have found toe-curling, but which I'm quite enjoying. It's been a long time since we talked about our childhood. Each of us had a parent who died, my father in the war, her mother from peritonitis. Each of us had a step-parent. We both married Freddie. All this stops me from going over what happened in December and from re-reading the papers. (The press hailed me as a heroine and also someone with a criminal record, which seems entirely fair.)

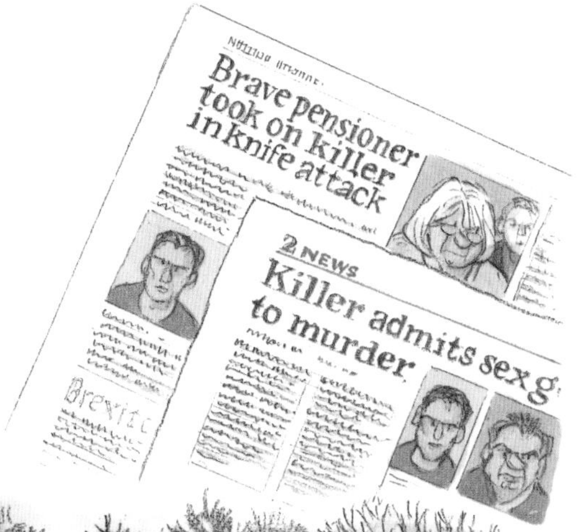
Brave pensioner took on killer in knife attack
NEWS
Killer admits
to murder

Dean Hart went straight home, where he was arrested later that night. He confessed immediately. My blood was on his knife and Nicki had evidence of the struggle on her phone. He also confessed to strangling the girl a year ago, apparently while having sex with her. Deano's uncle and cousin, unaware of his visit to Osmington Square, were also arrested. All three are on remand charged with various offences – murder, GBH with intent. I would like to add a charge of dogslaughter but perhaps I'll never know who bumped off Corker.

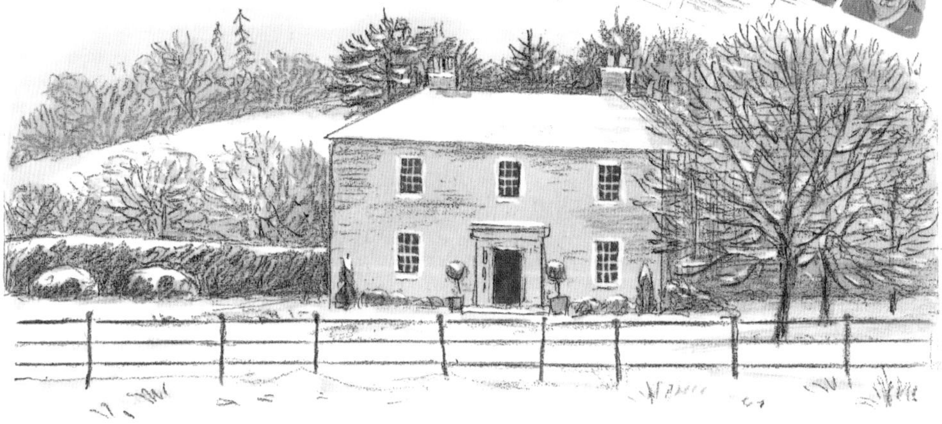

By far the best news is that the dead girl now has a name, a face and a story. My hunch about her connection to Lowbridge Road led detectives to the area and subsequently to the squalid flat where she lived with five other girls. Analysis of a toothbrush provided matching DNA to the sample from her remains. Police found her passport at the home of one of the criminal gang who controlled the girls.

Her name is Anca Radu. She was 23, grew up in a Romanian orphanage, was groomed and trafficked to the UK and forced to work as a prostitute. According to one of the girls, Anca had managed to escape the flat with the help of a sympathetic client. She was very trusting, the girl said, and believed she would find a new life. No one was surprised when they didn't hear from her. Somewhere there's somebody who dumped her on a foggy road near Newbury … where she hitched a fatal lift. No one missed her. I think of Anca Radu every day.

When I was in hospital they discovered pancreatic cancer. I've refused treatment and haven't long to live the doctors say. The house in Osmington Square is on the market and I plan to leave the proceeds to various charities, including women's refuges. There are legacies for Margot and Nicki and for my cleaner Milena and even for Elsa, whose cooking was so sublime. I've got used to Margot's house, have come to terms with the chintz and the fitful central heating. (Margot believes one only needs an extra dog on the bed in cold weather.) And I'm strangely happy, looking out on the winter landscape, counting the pregnant sheep.

5 7 9 10 8 6

Jonathan Cape, an imprint of Vintage
20 Vauxhall Bridge Road
London SW1V 2SA

Jonathan Cape is part of the Penguin Random
House group of companies whose addresses can
be found at global.penguinrandomhouse.com.

First published by Jonathan Cape in 2018

penguin.co.uk/vintage

A CIP catalogue record for this book is available
from the British Library

ISBN 9780224089098

Colour reproduction by Altaimage Ltd, London
Printed and bound in Italy by LEGO S.p.A., Vicenza

Penguin Random House is committed to a
sustainable future for our business, our readers
and our planet. This book is made from Forest
Stewardship Council® certified paper.